Praise for *With O...*

"Dorothy Marcic uses her incredible talent as a playwright to impart mystery, suspense, and sheer investigative guts on every page of this rapid-fire real-life thriller. Meticulous research brings the narrative to life, while extraordinarily, at the same time, it solves a cold case. Exciting, beautifully written, a sure bet for any serious true-crime fan."
—**M. William Phelps**, *New York Times* bestselling author of *Dangerous Ground*

"When Dorothy Marcic starts probing through her family's closet she discovers skeletons that are very real. Someone did commit murder and it was someone intimately close to the author. Dr. Marcic skillfully tells the story of her own journey of discovery. As she discovers the web of relations that led to murder, she is at the same time rediscovering her own childhood. It is a gripping tale, well worth reading."
—**Lawrence M. Miller,** author of *Barbarians to Bureaucrats*

"In my twelve years writing 'The Ethicist' for *The New York Times*, I got a good look at human treachery and—as impressive—our ability to rationalize our own horrible conduct. But lest I think I'd seen it all, Dorothy Marcic excavates new depths of perfidy, cruelty, and lies. And delightfully so. If by 'delightfully' we mean 'disturbingly.' And I do."
—**Randy Cohen,** former ethicist for *The New York Times*, host of NPR's *Person Place Thing*

"Dorothy Marcic has written a riveting, true-crime, personal story of her beloved uncle and the mystery of who brutally murdered him, and how the American justice system is often flawed and corrupt. We take the journey with Dorothy as she carefully reconstructs the past and leaves no stone unturned in her search for the truth. A personal odyssey through family—and on a larger scale, American—dysfunction."
—**Kaylie Jones,** author of *Lies My Mother Never Told Me* and *A Soldier's Daughter Never Cries*

WITH
ONE SHOT

Family Murder and a
Search for Justice

DOROTHY MARCIC

CITADEL PRESS
Kensington Publishing Corp.
www.kensingtonbooks.com

CITADEL PRESS BOOKS are published by

Kensington Publishing Corp.
119 West 40th Street
New York, NY 10018

All Kensington titles, imprints, and distributed lines are available at special quantity discounts for bulk purchases for sales promotions, premiums, fund-raising, educational, or institutional use.

Special book excerpts or customized printings can also be created to fit specific needs. For details, write or phone the office of the Kensington sales manager: Kensington Publishing Corp., 119 West 40th Street, New York, NY 10018, attn: Sales Department; phone 1-800-221-2647.

CITADEL PRESS and the Citadel logo are Reg. U.S. Pat. & TM Off.

ISBN-13: 978-0-8065-3855-6
ISBN-10: 0-8065-3855-4

First Citadel printing: April 2018

10 9 8 7 6 5 4 3 2 1

Printed in the United States of America

First electronic edition: April 2018

ISBN-13: 978-0-8065-3856-3
ISBN-10: 0-8065-3856-2

To Vernie, Jenylle, and Shannon: the three who lost the most.

CONTENTS

AUTHOR'S NOTE

The following account is based on true events. What I wrote is to the best of my memory on the murder of my uncle, LaVerne Stordock, and its aftermath. I also read the voluminous court transcripts and police/forensic reports, as well as the reams of newspaper articles about Vernie and Suzanne. I interviewed more than sixty people: every member of my family, as well as anyone else tangentially related to the case, such as people in Oregon, Wisconsin (a village fourteen miles south of Madison surrounded by miles of farmland), friends of the family, associates of one of Suzanne's former boyfriends, and relatives of Suzanne's previous husbands. I talked with District Attorney James C. Boll, who had originally prosecuted the case, and the one officer still alive who was first on the crime scene. Finally, I visited Suzanne and her children four times and spent a total of fourteen hours interviewing Suzanne herself. To protect privacy, I have changed a number of the names in this book.

Well, I think I'm the one who ended his life, if I remember correctly. . . . With that one shot I took out both Vernie and my mother. —Suzanne, March 2015

Both our fingerprints were on the gun and the police almost arrested me. . . . Dorothy, you have no idea how traumatic it was for my mom and me that night.
—David, Suzanne's son, December 2014

I am quite sure David pulled the trigger. . . . When I heard Suzanne got off on an insanity plea, I knew she had conned the system. —Franklin, Suzanne's brother, May 2015

Prologue—Why I Still Cry

The house was Queen Anne style, built in 1906, with steeply pitched roofs, front-facing gable, and asymmetrical layout. As the largest and most elegant home in Oregon, Wisconsin, it was known for its graceful beauty, wraparound porches, and leaded-glass windows.

It was unusually quiet that March 1, 1970, at 2:06 A.M. An occasional car could be heard out the front windows, perhaps someone who'd been partying too late in nearby Madison, rushing home before anyone noticed. Down the neatly shoveled sidewalks you could see the reflection of streetlights on the white snow, which showed spots of brown near where the sidewalk ended and the street began. Only one light was on in the neighborhood of the mostly large Victorian houses, in the kitchen of the Queen Anne house.

The upstairs hallway light went on at 2:10 A.M., just about the same time as the kitchen light went off. Then the master bedroom light was on, the hallway light off. A few moments after the master bedroom light went on, a single gunshot sound echoed through the ten-below-zero air outside. Several lights immediately switched on in nearby houses.

Dressed in a pink robe, a short, frail woman, with loosely tied dyed-blond hair, stood in the bedroom with her back to the door.

She was clutching a rotary phone, her thin fingers sweeping the dial clockwise, again and again. She moved her plait of hair from back to left front in a gesture that seemed more habitual than nervous; then she lifted her right hand to the top of her head, perhaps where a beehive hairdo had sat earlier in the day.

"This is Mrs. Stordock," she said calmly. "My husband's been shot."

"Is he alive?" asked the male voice on the other end.

"I don't know," she replied, not even glancing at the lifeless body lying on the floor next to the bed. The right side of its head was blown off; blood, brains, and tissue had sprayed across the sheets and beige chenille bedspread, the blue plaster wall, and even in the laundry basket of freshly washed underwear and towels.

"Is the perpetrator still there?" he asked.

"I don't know," she said quietly and hung up.

CHAPTER ONE
Metamorphosis

When the call came February 11, 2014, I was sitting in my New York City apartment and there was no way I could have known this conversation would change the course of my life for the next three years, nor that I would have an opportunity to use all the research skills I had honed over many years as a university professor and the writer of over fifteen books.

"I found them," my cousin Shannon said breathlessly from Eugene, Oregon. She and her husband had moved out there some years after Shannon's father was killed, and I could almost see her with her graying hair and showing a few more pounds than when we were younger.

I immediately knew who she was talking about. For the past decade every conversation Shannon and I had included our failed attempts at finding out anything about Suzanne, "that tramp," as my grandmother used to call her. The woman who broke up the marriage of Shannon's parents. Suzanne, who'd already had three marriages and three children (one from each of those husbands) when she met my uncle, Vernie Stordock. They began an adulterous affair, which resulted in his murder seven years later. Suzanne confessed, but my family always had doubts.

After he took up with Suzanne, I felt I was on one of those old *Twilight Zone* episodes where you wake up one day and the person you're in bed with isn't your spouse, but says he is. Uncle Vernie had been tall and handsome, with a neat crew cut, but had become pudgy and wan after being with Suzanne; this man had always been the jokester, always teasing and trying to get a rise out of someone; the husband who loved his wife and doted on his daughter suddenly became obsessed with this woman he called "Sue." He left his wife as if in a drugged stupor. Maybe the aliens had come with a pod and replaced the real Uncle Vernie.

I was only fourteen when I first met Suzanne in 1963 and didn't really understand what was going on with their affair. Nor could have I predicted Vern's obsession would end in his murder one dark, cold night seven years later.

After his death we lost contact with Suzanne and her three kids, the youngest of whom Vernie had adopted. Though Suzanne had confessed to the murder, there were rumors for years that her older son, David, had actually killed Vernie that night. The other two children were not in the house when it happened.

My uncle, LaVerne Gerald Stordock, had worked his whole life in law enforcement—twenty years as a police officer, then as a sergeant and later captain in Beloit, Wisconsin, where he retired as Captain in 1962.

He was the youngest of five children in a dirt-poor family with an alcoholic father and a mother who was forced to raise their kids alone during the Depression, bringing home scraps of food from her job as a cook at Beloit College. None of them went to college.

As soon as he was able, on his seventeenth birthday in 1943, Vernie enlisted in the navy and served during World War II, and probably quickly understood his skills lay in keeping order in society. After the war he joined the Beloit Police Department in 1948. Shannon told me, "He was recalled in September 1950 for the Korean Conflict. He was sent to Japan and served in the Okinawa Shore Patrol, because of his police experience. I remember him leaving on the train from Beloit and remember him coming home to the Great Lakes Naval Station in July 1952."

In the police department he was promoted to sergeant and later captain. After his work with the Beloit Police ended in 1962, he sat for a very demanding test and was one of only five who passed it. He was hired as a chief investigator for the Wisconsin Attorney General's Office, and later as an investigator for the Wisconsin State Medical Examiner's Board. According to newspapers, Vernie "played a prominent role" in one of his final cases, which involved a Dr. Milton Margoles, a Milwaukee physician who had been convicted in 1963 of tax evasion and obstruction of justice when he tried to bribe a judge and spent two years in prison. Margoles was attempting to get his license back and felt so strongly that the state medical examiner agents caused "public humiliation, public ridicule, scorn and derision" that he filed a $50 million lawsuit, with Vernie as one of the people named. But by the time the lawsuit went to court, Vernie was dead.

Vernie had worked undercover during the Korean War, when he was a narcotics agent in Japan. Later with the attorney general (AG), he worked on some high-profile cases of racketeering in the mob, prostitution, and drug dealing. Because of the corruption and crime he uncovered, he received death threats.

He also had a creative side. During his last years in Beloit, he was host of a weekend radio program, *The Gerry Shannon Show*, a combination of his middle name and his only daughter's name, Shannon. Because of his media work and his later high-profile status in law enforcement, he was well known in the region. The day after his murder, twelve newspapers in Wisconsin, Michigan, and Minnesota carried twenty-six different articles about the crime. And many of them kept reporting on updates for over two years.

About ten years ago, Shannon and I both became obsessed to find out what happened to Sue and her family. Maybe it was our moving toward senior citizen status, or the fact that our children had grown up and we had time to focus on other family needs. And perhaps it was also the realization that Suzanne's family members were getting older, so time was passing us by.

Shannon and I proved to be good sleuths. We were motivated, adept at problem solving and conflict management. But in those early years of our investigation, Shannon and I unearthed nothing substantial in our search for Sue's family. Do you know how many people named David Briggs there are in the United States? We looked for Louisa (pseudonym), Suzanne's daughter from her first marriage, who was away at college the night of the murder, but that name yielded an overwhelming number of hits. Suzanne Stordock as an identity had evaporated, so we looked for her previous legal name, Suzanne Briggs. No person showed up whose age matched hers. During the searches Shannon learned that the youngest son, the one my uncle had adopted, had killed himself in 1992.

In 2006, after attending a friend's funeral in Madison, I drove my rental car out to Oregon and found "the Mansion." Luckily, the husband of the family was in the backyard and seemed willing to talk to me and remembered being in Oregon in 1970. He was tall and thin, with neatly combed brown hair, and was dressed in jeans and a T-shirt while he tended some flowers. He said no one in town had talked much about the murder. I found it strange that in a small village of five thousand, the high-profile killing of one of its residents had not been the subject of gossip. Or was he just reluctant to talk about that violent stain on the fabric of quiet, peaceful Oregon? He gave me the names of the people who had lived in the house previously, and Shannon called them later on, but they claimed ignorance, too.

On that bright summer day in 2006, I got in my car and drove the ten blocks to the Oregon Police Station, where I imagined they kept archival data. For about fifteen minutes I sat in my car, immobilized, as I stared at the dark redbrick building with the two large glass doors. Why couldn't I go inside? Was I afraid some man would tell me it wasn't my business? Finally I climbed out and walked toward the entrance. I felt the stainless-steel door handle under my hand. It was the kind with grooves, to help you grip it. Maybe I could find some answers here. Perhaps they had records I could look at.

But as I began to pull the door open, something inside me collapsed. How could any good come from my walking into that building? After all, who was I to question officers of the law, or at least those charged with safekeeping their reports?

This incident is indicative of my whole family's underwhelming reaction to what we always felt was a miscarriage of justice. My family members were poor but honorable folk, and if you look at the level of civic engagement of such people, it is shockingly low. And so on that sunny day I drove back to Madison. It would be another eight years before I found my own internal strength about the murder and understood the power I had to ask for legal documents.

By 2014, Shannon and I were getting desperate. Suzanne was getting older, eighty-five by now, and any chances of asking questions could disappear suddenly. We were grateful that the Internet was carrying more and more information each month. But time was running out!

The ticking clock really motivated Shannon. She started by locating the Find A Grave website, and she looked for the younger son's resting place. That's when she discovered Suzanne had gone back to her birth name, Suzanne Brandon, something that now seems so obvious, but we hadn't even thought of before. Shannon's pursuit also unearthed Suzanne's location and her daughter Louisa's current name.

"They all live northeast of Chattanooga in Tennessee," Shannon said on that February 2014 call, with triumph in her voice.

I asked what she meant by "all," and she told me that Suzanne, her daughter, Louisa, and Louisa's husband, all lived on a farm, with Suzanne's son David a couple of towns away. How could it be possible that I too had lived in Tennessee, for fifteen years before moving to New York, and didn't even know they were in the same state? Had they been there a long time?

Shannon didn't know. She gave me their phone number. I had spent many weekends at my uncle's house while I was a student at the University of Wisconsin, so I had more familiarity with Suzanne's family.

"Dorothy, call them. We have to find out what really happened," Shannon said with an urgency in her voice I had never heard before. Here was reality giving us its own selfie. After talking about Suzanne's family for decades, we finally had the opportunity to *see* them. Moving from theory to practice was daunting. My heart beat fast as my stomach churned around as if I had just jumped off a whirling carousel.

"Okay," I said with a mix of trepidation and exultation, "I'll fly to Tennessee and drive the four hours to go see them."

"I can't ask you to do that," Shannon said.

"Someone has to find out, in person, what happened."

"But it's dangerous."

"They haven't done anything in, what, forty years?"

"That we know of," she said again, soberly. "And don't forget, one of them murdered my father."

But which one? That was the mystery to solve. Shannon agreed. We both desperately wanted to know.

"I am the only person in the entire world who can go to that family and ask questions. There's nobody outside of our family who cares much about getting answers, and I'm the only one of us who spent endless weekends at the house in Oregon with your father and Suzanne and the kids, and I'm the only one who had contact with her after the shooting."

And by "the shooting," I meant what happened March 1, 1970, when Suzanne—or was it David?—murdered Vernie shortly after 2:00 A.M. Just like everyone old enough remembers where they were when President Kennedy was shot, I remember that day quite precisely.

That Sunday morning I was asleep at my grandmother's house in Beloit, Wisconsin, visiting from college in Madison. Around 5:30 A.M. there was a loud knocking on the front door. At first, I thought it was part of a dream. After all, it was a surreal time between the darkest night and the first light of dawn. I stumbled out of bed, hugging my arms tight to keep warm as I went to the door. Was that my mother and uncle standing outside? Or was I in that winter hallucination that can overcome even the hardiest soul in such arctic weather? If I had been more alert, I might have noticed the wad of tissue stuffed in my mother's hand and how she was biting her bottom lip.

When I think back to that day, I remember my tall and substantial mother being dressed in her church clothes and hat, but now I realize how memory can cloud reality. Because they had to drive the 62.7 miles over icy roads, she couldn't possibly have taken time for such elegance. She must have been wearing her brown slacks, worn at the knees, navy wool overcoat, which was two sizes too big from when she lost the weight, and her beige knit scarf, which was starting to pill. As a younger man, my uncle had been lanky, with blond hair, but now in his forties had more girth and gray hair. His eyes were narrow. My mother's were puffy and red, with her hair not combed, but sticking out in bunches in a short roller cut. They quietly marched across the linoleumed floor into the kitchen and sat down at the round maple table covered with red-gingham oilcloth. By this time my grandmother was up. It was clear looking at her and her children that my grandfather must have towered over her, as she was so much shorter than her offspring. She sat down on one of the four captain's chairs and looked expectantly at her children. This wasn't the first time she'd had bad news, so she was prepared.

"Vernie's gone," Mama blurted out as she let go with a gush of tears. My uncle was crying, too, a hankie to his eyes. I don't think I'd ever seen him cry before. Not this retired army sergeant who'd traveled the world working on important international assignments. Grandma just sat there in her robin-blue robe and slippers, staring out through the kitchen door to the covered porch, her white hair matted down from sleep.

My grandmother was seventy-seven years old. She had left Norway at age fifteen to make a new life in America and had never seen her own mother again. Her father had died before she was born. Now there was more loss. This was the third of five children dead, plus her husband and a grandson. I've had many years to wonder how she held up through all of that grief.

Her only remaining son took a break from his tears and continued. "Vernie and Suzanne were out drinking. Fighting in the bar. They got home and—the sheriff said—Suzanne shot him at two this morning." Because Uncle Vernie had been a police officer before the scandal, he kept guns around.

"His birthday was just last week. Forty-four," Grandma said quietly. She had found her voice. "Never shoulda married that tramp." Grandma got up and automatically walked toward the counter to make coffee for everyone. "I told Jenylle [his first wife], 'Don't give him a divorce. You've got Shannon to think about. He'll get tired of Suzanne and come back around.' Instead, he married that lowlife and started drinking himself to death." Such was the narrative I had heard many times in the past seven years, during which time Uncle Vernie had resigned in disgrace as Captain following his affair with Suzanne, who'd already had three husbands and three divorces.

I remembered the many weekends Uncle Vernie insisted I visit them, which were more frequent that first year of college, from 1966 to 1967. He'd pick me up in Madison and drive me the thirty minutes to Oregon to spend time with the family, which included Suzanne's three children. He and Suzanne drank like dehydrated desert inhabitants. My family had a lot of alcoholics, people who needed piped-in beer as accessible as city water, so I was accustomed to excessive alcohol consumption. But even I thought Vernie and Suzanne were extreme. Then they'd fight loudly with name-calling and arguments, but afterward make up with the same intensity with which they'd fought. I remember riding in the car with them in the days before seat belts, sitting on the front right side, with Suzanne in the middle. Suzanne would slide up so close to Vernie, you'd think they were soldered together. Her left hand would sit on his right leg, way too close to his crotch area for me to be able to even look at it. How can you even make small talk when this woman is fondling your uncle's genitals? I was embarrassed more than once when Suzanne would announce she was withholding sex from Vernie until he did what she wanted. It wasn't until I got deep into this research that I started to understand what behavioral changes she wanted from him.

It was such a contrast from the quiet and peaceful life he had shared in Beloit with the elegant and stately Jenylle and their daughter, Shannon, who was cute, with long, wavy brown hair and filled with enormous energy and smiles. Whereas Suzanne knew how to mix the perfect drink, Jenylle was known for her aromatic breads and tidy home. Vernie didn't drink much when he was with Jenylle.

My own family included a teetotaler father, which might sound positive compared to others in my tribe, but my father was a gambling addict, always sure the next bet would bring overflowing rewards and would spend our rent money on the next "sure thing," which, of course, was anything but sure.

When I was at Shannon's, it always felt so clean, so quiet, even when Jenylle would run the Hoover, which she did every day, as well as mopping the kitchen tiles. "Her floors were so clean, you could eat off of them," my grandma liked to say. Shannon and I would go outside and play croquet in the hot summer sun, then turn on the sprinkler and run through the cold water. Jenylle would call us in for lunch and serve perfect triangles of grilled cheese sandwiches, with sliced pickles on the side, on white china dishes, all placed in the center of blue square linen place mats.

Back then I didn't understand why Vernie would throw all that away. After years of my own therapy I can see that he must have wanted more drama in his life, so he took up with a woman who evidently kept his hormones raging. He left *Leave It to Beaver*'s June Cleaver for the Sharon Stone character in *Basic Instinct*. As each year went by, though, his words became increasingly slurred, his wrinkles that much deeper, and his sadness more intense.

Everyone in the family felt—I mean we just *knew*—he would come back crawling on his knees to his rejected wife. This possibility, or should I say "certainty," was evidently shared by Jenylle herself. Otherwise, why would an attractive and sociable woman never even date for seven years and then marry her high school sweetheart a year after the murder? Even at the funeral everyone treated Jenylle as Vernie's widow.

"Ma," said my uncle, his voice halting, "they're gonna have a closed casket."

"What?" Grandma shouted. Good Norwegians always had a "showing" before the funeral. When my own brother died eight years earlier, I remember my grandmother stroking his cold, hard hands as he lay in the casket. She told me how comforting that was. Helped her accept the loss a little easier, she said.

"It was a shotgun, Ma, and he's . . . he's—"

Grandma dropped the red Folgers coffee can and spilled grounds all over the counter as she bolted toward the tiny bathroom and locked the door with the tiny s-shaped hook. We heard her screaming and wailing and thrashing about, as much as you could in four by seven feet. This was not my grandmother, the stoic family leader, who is always the role model of calmly solving the worst of problems, of thoughtfully analyzing alternative solutions to a crisis. Now I look back and think her aberrant behavior was, for a few minutes, more like Suzanne's, who would always cause an emotional earthquake at every family gathering. The first I remember was another family funeral, not long after she and Vernie got together. We were all at the farmhouse afterward, sharing our collective mourning. Vernie was trying to console his siblings and spent some time in the kitchen with them, while the blond, frail Suzanne, who had eyes that were green with dots of brown (or was that violet?), was in the living room sitting like a queen holding court. After fifteen minutes of waiting for her subjects to appear, she started fidgeting and cursing under her breath. Then Suzanne jumped off the couch and burst into the kitchen like a tsunami hitting land. No one was spared. Her verbal attack wounded everyone.

"Oh, LaVerne! You can't leave me alone like this. I saw the way your sister [the author's mother] looked at me. And look at you [to his brother], supposed to be Vernie's loyal brother, you think I didn't catch that smile just now to your sweet little wife? Oh, I see it in all of your eyes. You're all just scheming with Vernie so he'll go back to that supposed saint, Jenylle. None of you fool me. This morning it was your mother and now the rest of you are plotting to get rid of me. Vernie!" she screamed at the top of her lungs with a shrillness that could have shattered a crystal goblet. "We are leaving right now. I mean, this minute." And out the door she marched, her breathing heavy, her face tight and drawn. A little later we heard the sound of her opening and then slamming the car door.

Vernie looked at all of us with that sheepish grin he had when he was trying to use his personality to cover up some uncomfortable truth. Then he was gone, but the smile remained.

All of this swirled in my mind as we sat there staring at Grandma's bathroom door. The wailing and thrashing had not stopped. No one said aloud what we were all thinking. Is she going to hurt herself? Is this death one too many for her? Can she not take it that her youngest child has been brutally murdered?

Did she wonder what Uncle Vernie had been thinking, pinned to his bedroom wall with the gun pointed at his head? Was he thinking that Jenylle had been his one true love and now he was paying the ultimate price for leaving her? Did he wish he could have willed himself back to his first marriage, in the quiet Beloit home? Did he wonder what in the hell he was doing in Oregon, Wisconsin? Did he know his brains were about to be splattered all over the plastered blue wall, with its stucco shaped in oval swirls?

My other living uncle became the interim leader of the family. That day at Grandma's, he took charge of the situation and pushed hard against the door and broke the fragile lock. Grandma was crying and throwing wads of Charmin against the wall. She came out and sat at the table, her face as still as the wood carvings another uncle had loved to make.

"We'll have the funeral in Beloit," she said.[1]

---

1. As a decorated World War II and Korean Conflict vet, my uncle is buried in the veterans' section of Eastlawn Cemetery in Beloit, Wisconsin.

CHAPTER TWO
The Visit

I was about to embark on interaction with unknown persons, or at least unknown for more than forty years. There was no way to know how much they'd changed, so I had to assume I was going into "foreign" territory and reminded myself to be as polite and inquisitive as I had been when my three daughters and I moved to Prague back in the 1990s, when I'd been selected as a Fulbright Scholar and was teaching Leadership at the University of Economics, Prague, and to MBA students at the Czech Management Center. By this time, I had also been teaching and writing a great deal about cross-cultural management (including one of my then ten published books), so I felt I had some background to help me in this unknown land.

My job was to be sensitive to this family's needs and their ways of interaction, so that I might be able to ask some difficult questions and they would trust me enough to give me straight answers.

I nervously considered my travel options, wrote them down on an Excel spreadsheet document as I sat cramped in my eight-by-eight-foot office, an open alcove in my New York City apartment. After a long time of deep breathing and trying to apply the concepts of mindfulness to calm what felt like a panic attack, I picked up the phone and dialed Suzanne's daughter Louisa's number. A man with a deep and raspy voice answered.

When I asked tentatively whether Louisa was there, he told me that she was out.

"Is this her husband?" I asked.

"No, it's David, her brother," he said offhandedly. This made me gasp. What did I say now? I hadn't even considered this possibility when I had gone over every feasible permutation of this conversation in my head. I mean, David lived in a nearby town.

After what must have seemed like the kind of pause you get when telemarketers call, I gathered some courage. "Oh, David! This is Dorothy. Dorothy Marcic."

"Dorsey?"

"No. Dorothy. Like in *The Wizard of Oz*. Dorothy Marcic."

"Who are you?"

"Your cousin."

"I don't have a cousin named Dorothy," he said almost defensively.

"Vernie's niece . . . from way back," I said, trying to find something he could connect to.

"Vernie? Who was Vernie?"

"Your stepfather. Back in the late sixties."

"My stepfather?"

By this time I was in a Kafka story. But I knew good communication under stress meant staying calm, so I continued. "Your mother's husband. Vernie."

What I wanted to say was "You know, the fourth spouse? The one you or your mother murdered," but I didn't think that would help me create a connection with David.

Long silence. I imagined his mind was racing through many memories, scattered thoughts.

He finally replied, "Oh . . . oh . . . Vernie. Vernie."

"I'm his sister's daughter."

"He had a sister?" he asked, and now I wondered why I even

bothered to go on. Was this the time to be persistent, or to cut my losses?

The conversation continued with David, who did not seem to know Vernie had any siblings, and me hopelessly giving him a family tree he doubtless had no interest in, because he quickly changed the subject.

"Have you accepted Jesus as your personal savior?" he asked hopefully, his voice elevating in pitch.

"I believe Jesus was the Son of God."

"We're going to have the Holy Spirit work on you," he announced with the kind of voice a boss uses when he promises to give a raise, but the employee isn't quite sure of the outcome.

I told David I was coming to Tennessee next Saturday and asked if I could visit, but he wouldn't give me any definite answer, and he seemed to pull back.

"I'll have Louisa call you back," he said with no emotion.

On the Thursday preceding my trip I still hadn't heard back. My mind kept suggesting that they didn't want me there, never wanted to see me again, were hoping I'd disappear like an annoying drip from the bathroom faucet. Where Suzanne and family were a recurring subject for us, Suzanne's family had seemingly Photoshopped us out of their lives in some kind of collective amnesia.

I thought about just showing up at their house; then they'd have to see me, unless they pretended not to be home. And I couldn't face driving four hours to find people who might not answer the door.

So I dialed Louisa's number. Again a man answered, who had a deeper, more confident voice. This time it was her husband, and I introduced myself.

"Oh, yeah, I see a note David left for Louisa."

Rather than politely ask *if* I could come, as I had last time, I began more confidently.

"I'm Louisa's cousin from way back. We haven't seen each

other for years, and I am really looking forward to seeing Louisa, David, and Suzanne," I began.

His reply shouldn't have surprised me, but it did. "Have you been saved? Do you accept Jesus?"

After some awkward silence I gave the same answer as I had to David. At that point I knew it wasn't just David. Evidently the whole house was *really* into Jesus, so I had to be diplomatic in how I responded to their desire to save me from eternal damnation.

"So you and David are both born-again Christians?" I asked.

"Oh, no. David might be," he said. "But Louisa and I are Messianic Jews."

"You mean like Jews for Jesus?" As soon as I said it, I wished I could take it back, because I heard a big sigh and a deep breath.

"We're not some hippie group. Our history goes back to 32 A.D., right after *the Resurrection*."

How do I get out of this? I wondered.

"I'd love to learn more about Messianic Jews, and it so happens I'm going to be in your neighborhood Saturday afternoon and would love to come and visit for an hour or two."

There was a pause and I worried he was trying to think of a polite way to tell me to leave them alone, but he said, "Saturday's our Sabbath and we don't work, but the afternoon is okay."

I left Nashville for their farm on Saturday by 12:30 and thought I'd get there around 4:30 P.M., but they lived out in the "hollers" of Tennessee, and I got mixed up between his directions and the GPS, which sometimes does not work correctly in rural areas. It was after 5:30 P.M. and I was still wandering around asphalt roads that wound back and forth, up and down hills, like a roller-coaster ride going nowhere.

It was February and already starting to get dark, and all I could see around me were gnarled trees with twisted roots and low-hanging branches that blocked visibility. It felt like I'd wandered into Sleepy Hollow. I passed shacks with loose shingles and porches cluttered with old stoves and furniture. The yards had one rusting and abandoned car piled onto another.

For about forty minutes I thought I was lost, and I was really scared. It reminded me too much of the neighborhood where I grew up in Pewaukee, Wisconsin, of our house, which was a former summer cottage on cinder blocks with a pump we had to plug in each time we wanted water. We had plastic sheeting thumbtacked on the frail wooden frames as a sort of storm window insulation, which did not help much when it got twenty below zero. Our tiny cottage was not designed for arctic winters, and it had only one space heater in the small living room. Many a night all of us crowded around that source of heat all night long and never slept.

Where was I? In *Deliverance* country? If I disappeared, would anyone be able to find me? Thank goodness I had told my daughters where I was going and why, and I had sent myself an e-mail with their address and phone. Maybe Shannon was right, I thought as I continued down an overgrown dirt road that was wide enough for just one car. Since one of them did murder Vernie, why wouldn't they want to eliminate anyone trying to find out the truth? I prayed they had no guns in the house, but that's not the kind of question you ask on the phone to someone you've not seen in more than forty years. "Oh, before we hang up, can you tell me if you pack any heat?"

Darkness kept descending, and this only increased the sense of dread from the overhanging trees covering up the decaying mobile homes that all seemed to have a streak of yellow running down the sides. How could Suzanne, who had once lived in the most elegant home in Oregon, Wisconsin, be domiciling in what looked like an abandoned part of the South that had once survived on some type of mining or industry?

I thought about calling Louisa's house to say I was lost, but remembered David had been evasive, and Louisa's husband defensive, so thought it best not to risk any more bad interactions.

Suddenly I turned a corner and there was a small and well-kept white house with a barn out back. This was the correct address, but I checked again and pulled into the newly paved asphalt driveway and noticed a tiny one-room log cabin in the front yard. Two cars were in the driveway and they were a few years old with no signs of rust, not like the cars I had been seeing for the past hour. Looking again at the address and the mailbox on a wood post near the road, I thought this must be Louisa's house.

I got out and tried to find the front door, because there seemed to be a lower level with a door as well, but I rang the bell on the upper door. No answer. I rang again, knocked several times. Then I went to the lower door and knocked some more. Maybe they didn't hear me. I went to my car and dialed Louisa's number and got the voice mail:

"Have a blessed day with your Lord Jesus Christ. Please leave a message. *Beep.*" I said I was there in the driveway and hung up. Then I called Shannon, who answered within half a ring. She was nervous, too. I told her they must have ditched me and asked if she had David's number. Maybe they went to hide over at his place. I dialed, but it was no longer in service. Just as I was looking down to dial Shannon again so we could develop a new strategy, I heard a knocking on my car window and jumped so high, I hit my head on the car roof.

Standing outside the driver's window was a woman who looked very tall, but I soon realized it was because she was standing and I was sitting. As I looked at her, the middle-aged face surrounded by red hair pulled back into a tight bun was smiling at me. She looked an awful lot like Suzanne had back in 1970.

"Dorothy? Is that you?"

I recognized Louisa's eyes, but she was no longer the thin, carefree artist from 1969, the one with the long red hair she must have ironed to get so perfectly straight. She had gone to university for a couple of years in Madison, and I had been to several of her parties, which had abundant liquor and drugged-out friends philosophizing about the advantages of insects having six legs. Instead of tie-dye jeans and paisley T-shirts, she now wore an ankle-length skirt—and not the hippie kind she used to wear—a starched white blouse buttoned up to the neck and a crocheted vest. I wondered if I had stumbled into *Big Love* country, except I was in Tennessee and not Utah. Her smile was real, though, and my fear temporarily eased as I opened the car door.

"We weren't sure what time you were coming and we took a nap and didn't hear the phone ring. So sorry."

"I got lost and it took me five hours to get here," I said, trying to make the situation more easeful. Awkwardness hung in the air like thick coal dust. "It's good to see you after all this time," I said in a way that assumed she felt the same.

"We are just happy you are here," she said so eagerly, and with such a radiant smile, I started to feel uneasy because of the real reason I had come.

Behind Louisa was a tall, stocky man with a full head of hair and a *Duck Dynasty* beard. That could not be David, I thought. And it wasn't. Louisa told me it was her husband, Bobby, and we exchanged pleasantries as she led me into the house, through the lower level. We entered what I imagined was supposed to be a recreation room, a large wood-paneled space with an old couch, lounge chair, and assorted footstools and chairs, all covered with crocheted afghans of many colors. Scattered around the room on chairs were magazines, Bibles, many Bibles, and other prayer/study books. Louisa showed me Suzanne's exercise equipment and explained how it had been used in the beginning when they'd moved there, but now lay untouched, as Suzanne had settled into the life of an invalid. An invalid? I'd have to find out more. My breathing was becoming heavier as I almost gasped for air, realizing the woman who confessed to murdering my uncle was just one room away.

I pulled out an old letter I had found from "Aunt Suzanne" back in 1981, in response to a birth announcement of my oldest daughter, Roxanne. She had written me about her doctoral work and the study she was doing on parents who kidnapped their children. Louisa read it carefully, but with no emotion. What was going on? I wondered. Was she surprised to see this letter from thirty years ago that gave so much information about her mother back then?

Walking upstairs, I noticed books and clothes on the stairway, not sure if these were on their way up or down. I was soon introduced to a young woman with a small build and beautiful brown hair pulled back in a bun. She wore a long blue dress and a white stiff apron, which went from her neck down to the edge of her skirt. She was the home health aide for Suzanne, who needed round-the-clock assistance.

Louisa came into the dining area, which was surrounded on two sides with wraparound windows. Then two—or was it three?—dogs were let in and jumped all over me with their paws dirty from all the mud outside. *There go my new Spanx,* I thought.

"Mother is ready to see you now," Louisa said.

I hadn't seen Suzanne in more than forty years, not since right after the murder. When my Uncle Vernie died, Suzanne got off on an insanity plea and spent eleven months in a mental hospital. No one on my side wanted to have anything to do with Suzanne, and they were not happy when I went to visit her, once, in the hospital. Because of their reaction I didn't go to see her again, and over time I understood why they weren't rushing to the finish line of the Forgiveness Game. Since there was no blood relationship with Sue, distancing ourselves from her was not too difficult.

Louisa continued, "She's been looking forward to your visit," and ushered me into a small room, perhaps ten by twelve, that was so crammed with furniture and knickknacks that there was hardly space to walk from the door to the stuffed chair and love seat in the opposite corner. In fact, it felt not much different from many New York City apartments, the whole of which might be the size of Suzanne's bedroom.

A collapsed black wheelchair stood behind the door and a room divider was folded up near the single wooden bed, which seemed to have an adjustable mattress, or else just lots and lots of pillows. On the wall and on every flat surface (also covered with white lace doilies) were pictures of Suzanne and an older man, who I assumed was husband number five. One of the pictures on the wall, though, seemed to be of someone else, a different older man.

Who were these men? Naturally, there was no photo of Uncle Vernie anywhere. A few large books were piled on top of the mantel above the gas fireplace. I thought this room was likely de-signed to be a parlor, since there was no closet, but there was the fireplace, and it was right next to the living room, a large, sepa-rate room that had an outside entrance, as did the kitchen. Such a blueprint was not uncommon in houses built back in the late '50s, as this one was.

Suzanne was sitting up on her pillows, her long blond hair, with hardly any gray, tied and hanging straight across her right breast. She had a pink robe presumably covering pajamas, and her legs were tucked under a chenille bedspread, though I noticed her shape hadn't changed much. Still short and frail. Still had those green eyes with brown or violet specks.

As I entered the room, a small and wiry brown-and-white dog jumped all over me, until Suzanne told him to quiet down, at which point he jumped on the bed near her and snuggled next to her legs. I got as close as I could to her bed, as the room divider was on one side, and on the other was a large bedpan/potty con-traption.

I leaned down to kiss her cheek. She didn't seem to register any emotion, but I could feel her watching me. Maybe I was paranoid, but during this whole conversation, as well as the later ones, it was as if she were boring into my soul, to figure me out and to ask herself: Why is she *really* here?

We talked about the relatives. She knew my grandmother had died back in 1995 and also that my mother, Leone, and stepfather, Pete Evert, were gone, but she didn't seem to know my brother had died in the 1980s. I asked about her youngest son, but she clearly did not want to talk about him, certainly not his suicide. We talked for a while about the grand old house in Oregon and how beautiful it was. Not much risk there, I thought.

Then I started asking her about Vern. What was it like being married to him? I tried to take what might be her point of view, saying I knew he'd had a temper—I was actually exaggerating for interview purposes—especially when he drank, which we all knew he did too much. During this conversation and the three subsequent ones, I spent fourteen hours talking with Suzanne and had to be careful what I said. My approach was to ask her questions, agree with her on opinions of Vernie or my family, and basically ingratiate myself. Having grown up in a family where speaking your mind could leave you bloodied and bruised, I had good training for this assignment.

I kept asking innocent questions about Vernie. All she kept saying were things about how she kept finding out husbands were boring and how she got tired of sending three husbands through school, so she decided to go to school herself. Suzanne was more than happy to talk about going back to college, getting asked to join Mensa, getting her master's, doctorate, and law degrees. I asked her whether Vernie had been abusive, and she tried to change the subject, but I asked again. He burned cigarettes on my back while we were dancing, and I thought it was an ice cube, she said. As much as I pressed, she wouldn't continue, but instead told me how her dissertation was a study of parental kidnapping, and that she had replicated a study that her stepdaughter, Alexandra, had done for her master's degree. What I didn't realize until much later was how this disjointed conversation was her style, and over time I started to remember how she had always been like that.

Since Louisa was in the room at that point, Suzanne had her get her dissertation off the mantel to show me. I oohed and aahed as I read through parts of it, as I read a few paragraphs that sounded interesting. She seemed pleased. When I asked about the pictures on display of the men, she told me several times what a "keeper" her fifth husband (Uncle Vernie had been number four) was. How did they meet? Evidently, the rabbi told them both they were meant for each other. Her mentioning the rabbi reminded me of her religious conversion, before her third marriage, way back when Louisa and David were little kids still going to the Presbyterian services, the same denomination in which Suzanne had her first wedding.

How was it she converted to Judaism? I asked. After all, she had grown up in the highly Christian communities of Mount Hope and Boscobel, Wisconsin, which might have never even seen a Jewish person. She just stared at me blankly. What was it that attracted you about the faith, about the teachings? She shrugged and said she couldn't remember. When I told this to a friend whose father is Jewish and his mother not, he smiled and said, "I know what attracted her. It had to be money." So I asked Suzanne, "Okay, so you became Jewish for husband number three, but why did you *stay* Jewish after the divorce? What was it about Judaism that was so essential to you?" Again no answer. Another friend, the cantor in his synagogue, thought it might be because she could then blame so much of what happened to her on being Jewish. I looked at Suzanne and asked again why she was so attracted to Judaism, but she just talked about how the rabbi had connected her with her last husband, the "keeper."

During our exchange Louisa had entered the room and at the end of Suzanne's story, Suzanne abruptly turned to Louisa and said, with no trace of sadness or apology, "There was a time I didn't see you for seven years, wasn't there? I didn't even meet your husband until then." She said these words so woodenly, and it seemed odd to me at the time. But it wasn't until days later that I realized she was reciting almost verbatim from the letter she had written me in 1981, the letter I had given Louisa a couple of hours before. Evidently, Louisa had shown that old letter to her mother. Looking back, I saw it was all staged for me. Why would Suzanne have to remind Louisa, just then, that thirty years ago they hadn't been together for a long time?

That's when Suzanne's son David came in the room. I knew his face, but he was now fifty pounds heavier with thinning gray hair. He had that same winning smile, which covered up a certain shyness, and he was dressed in jeans and a mottled brown T-shirt. He just kept staring at me, then came and hugged me and sat down on the love seat, apologizing for not coming sooner, but he had a lot of chores to do. I didn't realize the context until much later when I learned more about his relationship with Louisa, but David spoke about the work he did like some beleaguered indentured servant, and I felt sorry for him being forced into so much labor. Maybe that was the point.

Suzanne and I continued talking, and I kept trying to engage her about Vernie, with absolutely no luck. Then David kept looking over at me and started asking me about Jesus and the Holy Spirit and sharing stories about how God had helped him. No one was talking to Suzanne right then. Suddenly she lifted herself up on her hands a few inches and yelled, to no one in particular, "I have to pee!" Like Pavlov's dogs, David and Louisa got up. David headed toward the door, and Louisa toward her mother, at the same time she called out for the aide, who scurried in quickly.

Louisa grabbed me and led me into a room across the hall that was filled with a computer and printer, some clothes racks, and assorted furniture all crammed together, and asked if I wanted to see her artwork. Even though I had seen Louisa many times in Wisconsin back in the 1960s, I don't think I'd ever seen her watercolor and oil paintings, and they were amazingly lovely, in beautiful pastels and others with deep colors. It made me sad that her art career had been stalled by the murder. She had been a student at Pratt Institute in New York when "it" happened and she wanted to drop out, but her mother insisted she go back. Within two months she had a nervous breakdown and escaped to Alaska, the home of her birth father. Louisa didn't finish her degree for a long time and never really got a chance to be a full-time artist.

In Alaska she started calling herself Louisa Elmira Chappington. At first, I thought this had to do with Louisa being an artist. Louisa Elmira Chappington sounded so much more romantic than Louisa Briggs, after all. But then I discovered that Suzanne had been born Elmira Brandon and that Louisa's father and Suzanne's first husband was L. Harry Chappington. "Louisa Briggs" was never a legal name, but one used to obfuscate Suzanne's serial monogamy, with Briggs the last name of husband number two.

L. Harry married Suzanne in Madison, Wisconsin, in 1947, and after the divorce, he went north to Alaska. I found it interesting that Suzanne's first husband—and her daughter—fled to the farthest and remotest place in the continental United States.

Out of the blue, Louisa mentioned that her mother had had a psychotic break "that night." I noticed early on that no one in that family ever used the word "killed," much less "murder." It was like those writing exercises where they ask you to talk about an object or situation but never actually use that word. I asked her to elaborate.

"How else could she have loaded and hoisted up that heavy gun that even she says was too big for her?"

Indeed, I wondered. How else?

"Even her brother says she couldn't have done it alone."

Put the brother on the interview list, I thought.

Louisa continued, "It was because of the abuse from Vernie that she had the breakdown."

I don't think she remembered whom she was talking to. Had

she forgotten all the days I'd spent at their house and that I saw what went on? I guess she didn't know how aware I was of *real* abuse. When I was a little girl growing up in Pewaukee, Wisconsin, with my mother, father, and my siblings—brothers Johnny Ray and Raymond and sister Janet, with me as the youngest—I thought the reason people bought kitchen dishes was so the father could throw them at his wife, breaking them all against the wall. When all the dishes were used up, my father graduated to his fists. So when someone starts talking about abuse, I probably have a better sense than average to know if it really happened.

I remember Vernie and Suzanne arguing a lot. Such as one late September when I was eating breakfast at their wooden table, with carved spindles for legs. One side of the table was covered with mail, some envelopes opened, some not. A couple of pans with caked-on food were sitting on top of the white gas stove, and a pile of dirty dishes teetered in the sink. Vernie, in a blue shirt, tie, and suspenders, took a final sip of coffee and stood up quickly, looking at Suzanne, still in her pink robe, with her long hair down her back, who was pretending to read the front page of the *Madison Capital Times*.

"Where'd you put the car keys?" he'd asked in a quiet but controlled voice, pulling on one of his suspenders in a way that let me know he was covering up some anger. She ignored him and kept up the pretense of reading.

"I said, where are the keys?" This time the anger was more evident. "Sue! I'm asking you a question."

"You can go lick yourself, for all I care," she said, her voice mannered and quiet, never looking up from the paper.

David was on the other side of Suzanne, putting large spoonfuls of oatmeal laced with sugar in his mouth as he sat there in his boxers and white undershirt, his wild and curly hair covering up parts of his chubby face. The youngest, Danny, was blond, with hair as straight as the living room's leaded-glass edges, and whose slight figure could be seen beneath his striped pajamas, with a couple of buttons missing. He was sitting with food untouched, playing with a G.I. Joe and kicking his feet against the table leg.

"Sue. I've got to run by the office this morning." Now he stepped closer and was looking down at her. She didn't respond, so he took the paper.

"You think you can bully me around, Mr. Big Shot, Mr. Attorney General's Office?"

"I just want my car keys."

"What we want and what we get are two different things."

Vernie ripped the paper from Suzanne's hands and started rummaging around the kitchen, looking in drawers, under mail, under the piles of dirty dishes.

Suzanne just sat there with a Cheshire-cat smile. She picked up an emery board and began working on her nails. "My boss needs this report, Sue. In thirty minutes."

"La-di-da," she said, still not looking at him. "You think you can just stand up after the breakfast I cooked—"

"*You* cooked? When's the last time—"

"Goddamn it, Vernie. You never appreciate anything I do for you, do you? Always 'me, me, me, me.' Like your job is so important and I'm not. What if I had plans for today?"

"I'll be back in an hour," he said, taking a deep breath.

"And what am I supposed to do for that hour?" At this point she looked up at him. "Saturdays are for family, Vernie. *Family.* And all you ever care about is yourself."

"I'm trying to make a living for this family. That's what I'm trying to do."

"You don't fool me with all these trips to the office on weekends," she said so close to his face, a few drops of her spit fell on his nose. "Who is it, that Charlene, who's always wearing those short skirts? Or maybe Pauline, the one who talks like Marilyn Monroe?"

Vernie closed his eyes and didn't say anything for a couple of seconds. The others at the table pretended not to hear, and I was trying to be invisible, but it didn't work.

Vernie continued, "If I don't get this in, I might get fired."

"That's your excuse so you can go have sex with your girlfriend?" she said with eyes so angry, I thought she'd explode. "You think I don't see those short skirts and how she can't seem to expose enough of her cleavage."

"Sue, be sensible!"

"'Sensible'? *Sensible?* You think I don't know what goes on down there?"

"I go to work and come home."

"And you COME down there, too, don't you?"

By now, I wanted to slink out of the room. No adult I had ever known would say "sex" or other racy words out loud in front of their children. Vernie was lifting up magazines and looking inside the cookie jar.

"Where are the keys?" he screamed.

"All you ever do is yell at me."

"When you make my life difficult."

"I knew it," she said as she plopped down on the chair next to me and I turned and gave a weak smile, as if nothing was going on. "That's all you see in me is how bad your life is."

"It's sure a hell of a lot worse since I left my home."

"This *is* your home, Vern. And don't you forget it."

"How could I when you keep reminding me?"

"Because you keep wishing I was like that sugar-ass J-woman, who's so sweet you have to take some insulin."

"At least she treated me decently."

"Admit it. You still love her and wish I were dead."

"Be reasonable, Sue," he said unreasonably. "And give me those damn keys."

"You know when you'll get your precious keys."

"When I find them."

"Oh no, mister, you don't know how smart I am. You won't get them until you promise not to talk to *her*."

"She's my mother."

"Anybody who talks to Her Royal Highness—"

"Say her name. Jenylle. Who was my mother's daughter-in-law for many years and they live two blocks from each other."

"Anybody who talks to that sugar-infested J-woman . . . well, that person is off-limits. You get it? That's when you get your keys. And if you ever want sex again from me—"

There was that word again. I shivered inside and tried to figure out how I could wriggle out of the room without anyone noticing.

Just then, Vernie found the keys underneath the coffee grounds in the can and he held them up, triumphantly, like a soccer player does with the ball when the game is won. Suzanne came after him but he was out the door too fast, so she grabbed that coffee can and threw it hard against the door, cracking the glass. The can fell to the floor and grounds scattered everywhere. Next to her was the sugar canister David had been using. She grabbed it and ran toward the door, opening it and throwing the whole canister out toward the driveway, but it landed on the grass near the porch.

Suzanne came back in, closed the door, and turned toward the table, looking blankly at the three of us, as still as if we'd been turned into stone.

"Clear up the table, do the dishes, and clean up this mess. I have a headache." And she walked upstairs to their bedroom.

Such a scene was more and more common, but I never saw Vernie once raise a hand to Suzanne. With my mother there were frequent black eyes, bruised and swollen ankles from clocks being hurled, cut lips, and matted hair. Suzanne never had any of those signs.

By now, at the farm outside Chattanooga, it was getting late and it was pitch dark out. I had at least four hours of driving ahead of me. I said I had to go soon. Louisa looked genuinely disappointed and I could see the gentleness in her spirit, the sparkle in her eyes, the loving kindness. How do such angelic qualities come out of a family that murders, and maybe even a mother who murders? Maybe I had Suzanne all wrong. Maybe she was a wonderful person, a great mother, and just had that temporary break with sanity.

"We thought you would stay overnight. We have the space."

Oh, Louisa, I thought, *some person in this house murdered my uncle in his bedroom.* I had visions of lying under an Amish quilt in the recreation room while someone quietly crept up and aimed a rifle at my head. *Pow!* I knew there was no way I could get those images out of my brain and be able to fall asleep. I couldn't say that I was afraid of getting offed, of course, so instead told her I had obligations the next day.

At least stay for dinner, she insisted, because she was preparing their own organically raised chicken with some vegetables from their garden. I looked at my watch. It was 8:30 P.M. and I had only intended to stay for an hour or two, but I couldn't refuse that sincerity in Louisa's eyes. "Just until after dinner," I said. If I had known back then about all the other mysterious deaths surrounding Suzanne and David, I might have dodged the meal and trotted back to New York faster than a Tennessee walking horse.

It was a scrumptious dinner in the dining area with the wraparound windows, which offered some distractions. But the conversation was awkward, as Louisa, her husband, and David all took turns talking to me about Jesus, and Redemption, and the Resurrection. Louisa wanted me to know she was a Messianic Jew, not like David's born-again Christianity. Still, they were concerned about my soul and what would happen to me in the afterlife. It was touching in an invasive kind of way.

I listened politely, not wanting to get into any conflicts that might change the tone. *I believe in God,* I thought about saying, *and in Jesus and other Messengers of God, and my faith has sus-*

tained me through many tests, including the murder of my uncle.
But I kept those thoughts to myself.

I went to Suzanne's bedroom to say good-bye and we chatted for a while. Whenever I brought up Vernie, David would talk about Vernie's sense of humor, or his desire to help people. I realized David was the only person there who was willing to actually talk about my uncle.

When it was after 10:00 P.M., I got up and said I really had to go. They all tried to get me to stay overnight, but there was no way on God's (or Jesus') earth that was going to happen. David looked at me with some kind of eager longing in his eyes and offered to walk me to the car. My heart leapt, because I thought I might get some insights from him.

Outside in the cool, dark air of eastern Tennessee, surrounded by large trees, a looming barn, and the small guesthouse near the road, I asked him to tell me about Vernie. He stopped and looked at me. Floodlights attached to the house had been aimed at the driveway and I could see his face clearly. "I understand. You want some closure," he said as he drew a couple of paces closer.

At last! It had been ten hours since I'd left Nashville and I'd meant to head back four hours ago. What was I thinking? That I would just sashay in there, stay for ninety minutes, and then ask, *"So which one of you actually* did *kill my uncle?"* By the end of dinner I had felt I was on a mission of folly and that all I was going to hear were generalities.

Then David and I were there in the driveway and he seemed eager to tell me what had happened. We talked for about two hours, and I forgot that I was cold and we were in semidarkness, with three outdoor lights above the carport saving us from total blackness.

"What do you remember about Vernie?" I asked, wanting to start with lower-risk questions. He looked off into the dark for a moment, then turned back toward me, his face somber.

"I was just a kid when my mom married Vernie."

"Do you remember how old you were when they first got to-gether?" I asked, because the whole time frame of exactly when he and Suzanne got involved was pretty sketchy to me.

"Maybe seven or eight. Or nine. I don't know." He had been born in 1953, so that would make the original hookup around 1960 to 1962. David's younger brother, from Suzanne's third marriage, was born in 1960.

David continued, "I just remember him trying to teach me how to be a better person, making sure I did my chores and was polite to adults. He also taught me how to shoot guns. We'd go to the dump on Fish Hatchery Road in Madison and spend hours stand-ing between old baby buggies and broken TVs piled on top of mountains of garbage, aiming at tin cans or plastic bottles."

"Did your mom ever go along?"

"No. She never cared about guns. It was just Vernie and me. And I think Vernie liked that. He treated me like his own son and tried to toughen me up."

I was intrigued. "Toughen you up?" At this question David got more enthusiastic.

"He always told me stories about growing up and how he was the youngest kid and smaller than a lot of the neighbor boys. He had to learn how to defend himself against those big bullies. I think that's why he became a policeman. You know, watch out for the little ones who are defenseless. That was his reason for living."

By now, my body was shivering in the near-freezing tempera-ture, but I was afraid if I asked if we could move inside or sit in my car, I would break the spell.

"Do you remember that night?"

"The night 'it' happened, I was asleep in my room down the hall. Louisa was away at school in New York, and my younger brother was staying with a relative in Madison. They were yelling and it woke me up. Vernie was shouting, 'So shoot me, then. Just shoot me!' I was laying there in my warm bed, under the covers, so tired, and I just couldn't pull myself up to go stop their fight, which is what I usually did. David the mediator. But I just decided to go back to sleep. A little later I heard a loud bang and then my mother was knocking on my door. 'I shot Vernie,' she said. I got out of bed and let her in the room and asked her where: Leg, arm, or what? 'The head.' I ran fast to their room and saw blood and brains everywhere. Vernie was on the floor, all bloodied, with this gun lying next to him, and it looked like he had been shot straight on, in the face. I guess it was just instinct from all the times I've been hunting, but I picked up the rifle to see if it was still loaded and the spent shell popped out. 'This couldn't be happening,' I thought, and I threw the gun down. That's why the police found two sets of fingerprints on the gun, both my mom's and mine."

I didn't want to say anything other than nod, because David was on a roll, talking very fast. But my mind was racing. My uncle was a strong and proud man who had served as a soldier and then a police officer and at the time of his death was on an elite investigation team for the state. He had mob death threats against him and been in many compromising, scary positions in his twenty-five years in law enforcement. The uncle that I knew personally, and what I surmise professionally, would never have asked anyone to shoot him. He had told friends he was going back to his first wife and daughter. Why would he want to die?

Then David went on: "My mother asked if she should call the police and I thought, 'Heck, yeah, 'cause maybe we can save Vernie.' That's when I went into shock, because the rest is all jumbled up in my mind. I remember being in the police station all night and the police threatening to arrest me, unless my mom confessed, because they had my fingerprints on the weapon. Her lawyer was there and told her not to say anything, but after I don't know how many hours, she finally said she would take the blame if they could arrange an insanity plea."

Is that how it works? I wondered. You shoot somebody and

then negotiate with the police so they'll agree you're crazy? But I had to find a better way to say it to David.

"Looking back on that night," I started carefully. Here was a guy I barely knew as an adult who was only one of two living witnesses to my uncle's murder. How did I ask a difficult question in a way that would make it easier for him to tell the truth? "Do you think she actually did have a psychotic break?"

He stood very still, like an animal that doesn't want the predator to know it's there. As he looked down onto the impenetrable black asphalt of the driveway, he said, "I think my mother's been able to live with what she did all these years because she tells herself she was a victim, someone who became an alcoholic herself to stop Vernie from drinking, a woman abused by that alcoholic who begged her to be shot. But her thinking doesn't take into account that alcohol and arguments were a lethal combination for those two."

I was agreeing with David, that alcohol and arguments are not a good combination, but I also remembered lots of alcohol and lots of arguments in my own family, but no one ever pulled out a gun and murdered anyone. And what was all this about becoming an alcoholic to stop Vernie from drinking? How did she know he was an alcoholic? Lots of people drink heavily, but that does not make them addicts. And stopping him by accompanying him to the bars and loading up on drinks? No matter how hard I try, I can think of no reasoning that fits her strategy with the intended outcome. Wouldn't a Mensa-level woman have figured out that you don't get someone to reduce or stop alcohol consumption by becoming a drinking buddy?

My attention went back to David, who continued. "And my mom has this story, which I never heard about until recently, that Vernie burned cigarettes on her back while they were dancing. She says she thought he was putting an ice cube there and had done so several times previously."

Wait a minute, I thought, *this is the same incident Suzanne was telling me about.* If he had done it before, why did she *still* think it was an ice cube? If her story were true, wouldn't this Mensa woman have figured out he *wasn't* carrying ice cubes around to torment her? And that when she felt an ice cube on her back, watch out!

Almost as if he were reading my mind, David went on: "But I'll tell ya, I never saw any evidence of cigarette burns or heard her talk about it back then." He paused and I just stood there. Words would not come out of my mouth. "You know something else?" he said as I shrugged, having no idea what might be coming next. "Vernie was really different the last two weeks of his life."

"What do you mean?" I asked, thinking he was going to tell me about how Vernie had a committed resolve to change his life, or perhaps that he had instead given up on life.

"He found Jesus."

I did not see that coming. "What kinds of behaviors did he have that made you think he found Jesus?"

"He just laid around on the couch all the time and wouldn't talk much."

"That sounds like a depressed person to me," I replied, hoping I wasn't challenging him so much he'd stop talking.

"Yeah, Vernie was the biggest smartass on the planet, and when he finally faced the real *Big One,* that would make anyone depressed." It still didn't make sense, but I didn't want to spend more time on Jesus talk right then.

"The laws on insanity pleas were changed while my mom was in the mental hospital, so she wouldn't have to spend the rest of her life locked up," David said, switching topics. No kidding, as the eleven months she spent in the hospital was a huge difference from the rest of her life, I thought. He continued, "When she got out, she went back to school, finished her bachelor's, got a master's, a law degree, and a doctorate, none of which she'd have done otherwise." I took that to mean that murdering my uncle gave her a new lease on life, and she was finally successful in a way that had eluded her previously. This dichotomy between assassin and academic was intriguing.

David told me he had started college but bounced around, living in California, Florida, and other places. "My father died of a heart attack a while after Vernie's death, and I got an inheritance, which I lived off for some years. But I was really into alcohol and women and drugs and motorcycles. And it would have all killed me, except then I found Jesus and got salvation." He looked at me and smiled for the first time in a couple of hours. "And I'm going to work on you, Dorothy. Or, I mean, I'm going to talk to the Holy Spirit and He'll come into your life and change everything for the better."

I wasn't sure if my idea of "better" was the same as his, but I let him go on. "Then I moved to Tennessee, where my father's family was from, where I used to spend summers as a kid. I got married. We met at church and it was . . . Well, we got divorced later on. But I did have a successful business doing online marketing. Maybe I could help you in your work," he offered, but I didn't respond. Was he asking for money, or just wanting to connect with me? It was almost midnight and I couldn't deal with job concerns right then. "Everything really fell apart for me when I got chronic fatigue syndrome and couldn't work hard enough to keep the business going and it collapsed. A few months after Louisa and my mom moved to Tennessee, I lost my house, so I moved here"—he pointed to the house behind us—"and took over Louisa's basement bedroom."

This was a real dilemma for me. I could stay out in the dark, cold night and learn more from David, but I was really afraid that if I didn't leave right then, I'd fall asleep while driving back. If I had known this would be the last time I'd see him alive, I would have stayed all night long talking. Why is it we think we will always have another chance, when, in fact, we often do not?

"Talking with you brings closure for me, too," he said with

what I took as satisfaction as we cautiously hugged and I got into my car.

I noticed right away the light on the dash indicated one of my tires was low. Here I was in "Pithole," Tennessee, at 12:30 A.M. on a Sunday and had to drive four or five hours with a tire that might blow? Going toward the interstate seemed the best bet. I stopped at four gas stations, none of which had working air pumps. Then I found a semitruck garage and begged the woman behind the desk to have someone fix my tire. We only do trucks, she kept saying, no matter what I said. Finally, when I told her I was afraid I'd get in an accident, she took pity on me and filled the tire with air herself, even though she was dressed in a floral skirt and high heels.

Finally I felt safe enough to e-mail Shannon to tell her I was still alive and all had gone well, that I'd call her later Sunday morning. I could have called her then, because Eugene, Oregon's time zone is three hours earlier, but I was too physically and emotionally spent, and I had to pay attention to driving those four hours through the Smoky Mountains over what turned out to be roads so dark it felt like driving in the outer circles of hell. I got back around 5:00 A.M. Around noon I called Shannon.

"I feel pretty confident Suzanne shot your father," I said, more than a little proud of myself for what a great detective I was. I explained that based on David's detailed story about the argument and the shooting, and Louisa's version of the "psychotic" episode, and that they both had more or less agreed, I thought it was definitely Suzanne. I also mentioned Suzanne's claim about the cigarette burns, and Shannon got very upset, something I had never seen in her.

"My father never lifted a finger against anyone. Nothing that I ever saw or heard about," she said. I told her David doubted his own mother's story about the history of that type of abuse, which, I think, eased the pain for Shannon.

We talked about other possible scenarios. "I always considered the possibility that it was a 'hit,'" Shannon said somberly. "He'd worked undercover with the Mafia and other dangerous elements, and his life had been threatened more than once. But if that were true, then Suzanne and David would have had to be involved in it, so it just didn't seem as probable."

Shannon said she was relieved to know the truth, but was still bothered by the fact that Suzanne had spent only eleven months in the state hospital and then got out and cashed in Vernie's life insurance policy. Shannon had sued the insurance company, saying that by virtue of the fact Suzanne confessed to killing Vernie, she should not benefit from the death. Shannon lost. Her lawyer said they would probably win on appeal, but he needed a $1,500 retainer.

"George [Hecht] and I were just college students then and fifteen hundred dollars was like a million is to us now. But looking back on it, I wish we had borrowed the money, because it just wasn't right for the woman who murdered my father to collect the thirteen thousand dollars of his life insurance."

When I got back to New York a couple of days later, I researched what that $13,000 translated to in 2018 dollars, because by this time I had moved into heavy research and started to consider financial implications. It came to almost $80,000. I also started tracking down newspaper articles about the shooting. I bought a subscription to one of those archive services in order to get access. I was getting obsessed. Why? My mind kept going to the time I spent in Oregon with Vernie and his new family when I was in college, when Vernie would pick me up Friday nights after work and take me back to his home. He called me, asked me how my classes were going, and was always encouraging, in between his frequent teasing.

I think it was only after my frantic search through endless files of voluminous news clippings as thick as an old phone book that I realized why his murder had hung over me so unflinchingly all those years, why I just couldn't let go, and why I knew I was committed to investigating the crime no matter how long it took. Spending all that time researching and inquiring stimulated a great deal of self-reflection on my part. Not until months into my research did I realize how that one night changed everything for my family, as if the pH balance in the ocean shifted and all life forms were forced to adapt. For me, it was intensely personal.

Vernie had been like a father to me. My own father, who was always physically fit and looked like a top gangster when he dressed up and flashed his Franklin Delano Roosevelt smile, was a wife- and son-beating compulsive gambler who had to ask me how old I was. Though I did have a few positive memories of him taking me a couple of times to see the Milwaukee Braves (this was before they moved to Atlanta), or bowling, most of what I remember is two behaviors: how he wasn't there to notice we had no food in the house—forcing my mother, who was tall, thin, and quite beautiful back then, to beg from the neighbors so we could eat breakfast—and how he pummeled my mom and brothers, Raymond and the physically handicapped Johnny Ray, with a rage I have rarely seen since. He never touched my sister or me.

Thankfully, my mother divorced my father and remarried when I was ten. My stepfather was a good man, bald and several inches shorter than my mother, but no one cared. He was on the plump side, and I think his heart was plump, too, with love for my mother and us kids. He was kind and supported all of us, though we were still quite poor. At least we had running water, both cold and hot, whenever we turned on the tap. And there was a telephone on the wall in the kitchen and a toaster on the counter. But my stepfather and mother spent a lot of time in the taverns—especially after my brother Raymond died when I was thirteen—so I was left alone most of the time.

Vernie was interested in me as his niece. He picked me up when he said he would, which is something my mother never quite learned how to do, and he spent time at home, even if he and Suzanne drank a lot. With Vernie, I knew I could ask him to do something and he would actually do it. Did he feel more than an obligatory connection to me, too? I imagine he missed Shannon with a loneliness I cannot fathom, and he no doubt missed the whole family. He and Jenylle had lived only a few blocks from his parents and brother. Perhaps I was the stand-in for them all.

I also knew Vernie was especially close to my mother, eight years older, who had practically raised him. Because my grandmother was a single working mother (with an alcoholic husband) during the Depression, with five children to feed, two of whom were sick with diabetes and rheumatic fever, it was left to my mother to look after Vernie.

Since my uncle Vernie was a senior official in the state government, the killing made headlines all over newspapers in Wisconsin, Michigan, and Minnesota, not only that week but for years. Reports continued to appear about hearing delays, the judge and district attorney being changed, charges reduced from first-degree murder to manslaughter, and, with the final hearing, the court accepting her insanity plea. But one thing surprised me, and I wondered why I hadn't read these articles before. As the twelve articles the following day in various newspapers recounted what was deemed a first-degree murder, most reported that LaVerne Stordock had been shot in his sleep by a high-powered military rifle.

In his sleep? David had been adamant about an argument immediately preceding the shot, and Louisa had hinted at that, too. Had they all talked before I came and decided on a common narrative?

I thought some more about it. If David had been involved in the shooting and they had covered it up, what would be a motivation to tell the truth now? How could they trust me, not having seen me for more than forty years? Even though I told myself I had no interest in anyone getting arrested or going to prison, they didn't know my intentions and must have realized there is no statute of limitations on murder.

A few weeks later I called Shannon again and sheepishly said, "I think I was played, Shannon, and that makes me want to find the truth even more."

CHAPTER THREE

David's Communications

I got the first e-mail from David one day after my visit, telling me how amazed he was that the forty-year-old memories just poured out of him: I think it was good for both of us to talk about Vernie.

He then offered to answer any questions I had via e-mail. I wish now I had been less reticent in asking him those questions, and I can hardly forgive myself that it took me many months to get to the difficult issues surrounding the murder. Did I think I had years? Maybe it was the fear of talking about the really violent issues, which I learned from growing up in a battering household.

Because David reached out to me so quickly, I was touched, and it only made me feel closer to him. At the same time I knew how important it was to keep the exchange going.

We e-mailed a couple of times a week from then on. David wanted to talk to me by phone, too, but said Louisa wouldn't let him use the landline. At the time I thought that was stingy and maybe even mean, but I understood it in a different way some months later when Louisa said, "David can sink easily into his chronic fatigue syndrome victimhood and just lie in bed, which drives my husband crazy. So he has specific chores to do to earn his keep here."

After David told me how surprised he was with all the flooding of memories, I told him, You have no idea how important it was for me to talk about Vernie, and I was also surprised that some of those memories were even in my brain! There was a level of comfort in that communication, too.

David replied, Praise the Lord! A lot of good! And I got a real kick out of you saying it brought you much closure. Then he went on with what became a recurring theme: He wanted to work for me. He said he knew I had a doctorate in business, an area he was interested it, and that he'd been a computer guru for five years, followed by being a broker, during which time he watched the Wall Street Channel all day long for four years. Then he worked in the Green movement on finance deals up to $100 million, until the crash in 2008. During all this time he worked intermittently as a PR executive, personally scheduling over a thousand interviews. He ended with asking if he could send me some biz questions.

My answer was Sure, ask anything. And I wanted to know more about his illness, such as when had it started, and why? Then I asked him how he managed to be a computer guru, a broker, and a publicity exec, plus the bodybuilding career he had talked about that night. What was his secret? I tried to put it very sincerely, even though I was more than a little skeptical.

His reply:

It was great hearing back from you! It is now close of biz for me. I have to turn the computer off around 5 or 6 every day. It has to do with the CFIDS (chronic fatigue) and not stressing too much every day. God Bless you real good. I am praying that the Good Lord starts showing Himself more and more real to you all the time.

It hadn't taken David long after I'd seen him in Tennessee to let me know about his illness. I was starting to see his need to keep bringing it up, and he never did answer my questions about his careers.

The next day, though, he tried to smooth it over, telling how awful he felt that day and he'd have to answer more completely later on. His illness, he said, was the same feeling as when you get the flu. And he hoped he and I would become good friends.

It was my turn to share and I told him about the year I dropped out of college, from summer of 1968 to summer 1969. My room-mate and I had to buy furniture for the place where we lived in Milwaukee. We bought a stove and refrigerator from a small company, but they didn't deliver it. Always had an excuse. And living without those two appliances is not easy. After a few weeks, I called up Vernie and asked him if he could help. The next day, the fridge and stove were delivered. I asked him how he did it. He said, "I made him an offer he couldn't refuse." So he knew how to get things done.

In his reply David apologized again for not answering more fully, and went on with his own Vernie story about how he hated to get out of bed. Vernie warned him, and one day he poured a bucket of water on David's face and the bed. David got the point and learned the lesson. He then told me writing to me gave him "warm feelings inside," and told me how Vernie used to say: "May the Good Lord take a liking to you but not too soon," then he had to go lay down.

David clearly did not want to talk to me about the details of his business, but he had lots of energy to write in generalities about his illness and Vernie and how much he liked communicating with me.

E-mails back and forth weren't enough for David. He wanted to talk on the phone, and I wanted that, too. I hoped it was about more than making me a client, because he'd already mentioned several times about working for me.

After the CFS hit, I lost my career (I was a building contractor at the time). Wait a minute, there's another profession he mas-

tered? I lost my career, my house, wife, land, fortune and
health. So he had a fortune? I know there was an inheritance
when his father died. Or did he turn the inheritance into a fortune
through his Wall Street skills? I wish I had asked that question. In
the passing years, there have been good times financially, but
currently I am just surviving with a few dollars every month
from an annuity. Which, I assumed, was from his father, the insurance company executive. Louisa wants me to help her sell
her art online, which I've been doing. I learned months later
from Louisa that David had done a really good job with the online
art. Then David explained more about the technical obstacles of
our potential collaboration, because the operating system he had
would not take Skype and his computer was too old to upgrade,
so he was stuck, and he couldn't afford a new computer.

An hour later he sent me another message, answering at least
some of the questions I had asked about his illness and his jobs.

The CFID started 22 years ago. Which would have made it
sometime in 1992, right in the middle of his married life of 1988
to 1996, and the same year his brother committed suicide. It
looks like the reason it happened was mercury poisoning for
fillings. He talked about the toxicity of mercury and how it can
cause genetic mutations.

I gasped as I read this, because mercury *is* dangerous. But I
wondered if dentists still did that work in 1992. Wouldn't they
have figured out the dangers by then? According to the World
Health Organization, the American Dental Association, the Mayo
Clinic, Health Canada, the Alzheimer's Association, the *New
England Journal of Medicine*—and many others—dental amal-
gams (which have some mercury) have been used for 150 years
and are safe and effective. Can all those organizations be wrong?
Or was this more like his mother's invalidism, which I later found
out was supposedly caused by some unknown and untraceable
virus she caught in Africa?

He told me he survived by the grace of God and because he read statistics about suicide rates . . . Wait! Had he considered killing himself, as his younger brother had? . . . and how he learned to keep a positive attitude, largely with the help of God. In all the time I communicated with him, he did have an unusually upbeat orientation. Have a wonderful weekend and God Bless you real good!

We talked on the phone a few days later and among conversations about the Holy Spirit and Eternal Life, I asked him who Danny's father was, because I had not been able to find any information. Irv Gast, he told me, quickly saying he hadn't been in their lives long. And what about Vernie? When did he start coming around? David thought about ten years before he died, which put it at 1960, the year Danny was born. Could my über-responsible uncle have fathered a child out of wedlock and later adopted him? I called Shannon and asked her.

"That would make sense," she said. "My parents were having problems back around 1960. Maybe the affair started sooner than we thought." But when I talked to David again, he had spoken to Louisa, which I came to realize was his modus operandi on everything we shared. And usually it would include discussions with Suzanne. In a way it was really a four-way conversation every time David and I connected. And that was fine with me, because the more information I got, the better. Sometimes when David's story changed, I knew I had to be wary, because most likely Suzanne or Louisa had set him "straight." David gave me the revised version.

I was wrong when we spoke last time. Louisa said Vernie was only in our lives for six, maybe seven years. That meant Louisa was saying she was aware of their relationship in 1962. So where was the truth? Would I ever figure out this complicated web of marriages, affairs, and births?

I was grateful David loved to connect with me, and I was growing fonder of him each week. Why didn't I go there and see him again? I get angry each time I ask myself that question.

In our e-mails David kept trying to push working for me, and I wondered: Could someone with an obsolete operating system be cutting-edge in marketing and PR?

Around this time my first grandchild was born in Montana. During flights back and forth I had lots of time to think about the murder. As I reread David's e-mails and thought about the discussions that first night with Suzanne, Louisa, and David, floods of memories came back to me about my own family's experience with a sudden death and how it changed my perception of the living versus the dead.

I was thirteen and home alone on Wednesday, May 9, 1962, with my older brother, Raymond, the thin, six-foot-four, handsome, crew-cut-styled star athlete of basketball and baseball. In fact, the Milwaukee Braves had scheduled a scout to come and watch him pitch the following week. That night our parents were gone and I had no idea where my other brother was. My sister was out with her boyfriend. Raymond and I had just finished eating the dinner our mother prepared and left for us hours ago. I had little time to savor the memory of our favorite dish, chop suey and white rice, that was so sticky it seemed more like the three-hour-old oatmeal they serve at Shoney's.

Raymond was having an asthma attack. His face was tight and pale; his lips were alternating between pursed up and wide canoes as he tried to get more oxygen. Ever since I could remember, Raymond got these periodic attacks where he could hardly breathe, so he was never without the green inhaler with the round white mouthpiece. In between sucks on that contraption he gasped, "Put your hand over your nose, Dorothy" as he demonstrated for me and then quickly pushed the inhaler into his mouth again. "That's what it's like for me to breathe. I can't get any air. Please find Mama."

What could I do? There was no 911 back then. In fact, Wisconsin didn't even mandate it to be instituted everywhere until 1987, and this was all happening in 1962. There I was, a young girl, brought up in a home with serial and serious abuse. My mother had been battered regularly like meat being tenderized, and my brothers were often pounded into bloody and bruised bodies until my father ran out of energy or rage, whichever came last. What lesson did I learn from this? *In times of crisis, do nothing.* I know it is hard to imagine being like that, so dependent on my mother, who was eminently undependable. Why didn't I call an ambulance? Raymond had had plenty of asthma attacks before, and my mother would always come home and fix them. What reason did I have to think otherwise? And no one in my family had ever called an ambulance or the police before. In fact, until just before, we never even had a phone, so this calling around was a whole habit pattern, not part of my repertoire. Even though I was thirteen, because of all the abuse, poverty, and neglect in my family, my emotional age was much younger. I didn't have the faculties required to take meaningful action beyond trying to get my mother home from the taverns. That was one skill I had mastered and I did it that afternoon with the diligence of a soldier facing battle.

It took me several hours of dialing by memory every tavern in Pewaukee before she miraculously appeared the fourth time I tried the Shore Bowl. Within minutes she was home and called the ambulance.

When I woke the next morning, my stepfather told me Raymond was in a coma, but I should still go to school. All day I wondered how he was doing. That afternoon I got off the school bus and saw way too many cars in our driveway. I knew what had happened as I walked through the front door.

"Raymond died," my mother said, as if in a catatonic state, sitting with some friends around our brown Formica kitchen table. Her short hair was barely combed and she was dressed in an old white blouse with tan pedal pushers. I had just walked in the same door through which my brother had been carried out, and as I looked behind me, I remembered seeing him take those desperate breaths.

We found out after the autopsy that he died from aspirating the rice. Because of my brother's history the medics assumed he was having another asthma attack and treated it accordingly. My mother never cooked chop suey or rice again. And that summer I had to learn even more tavern phone numbers as my mother and stepfather sank further into the abyss of alcohol. Only years later did I learn that she had already lost one son, a boy born out of wedlock and handed over by the family to a barren aunt, a loss she suffered deeply, and quietly, until the day she died.

I found none of this regret or longing in Suzanne, Louisa, and certainly not David's cheerful remembrances of Vernie, though I did sense David really loved Vernie and wanted some redemption from all that had happened. He showed such an eagerness to connect with me. One of my friends said it was David's version of "the compulsion to confess," first described by the psychologist Theodor Reik. Later on, when I showed David's e-mails to a psychologist, she said David had a "strange attachment" to me. Was he working his way to telling me the truth, the whole truth, and nothing but the truth?

Within six weeks of my visit to their farm, David had his computer outfitted so we could talk, which we did every week or two. He started every conversation with something like:

"Has the Holy Spirit visited you yet? I've been talking with Him about you and you should feel it soon.

"Have you accepted Jesus Christ as your Lord and Savior? We pray for you every morning, Dorothy, so that your soul will be saved."

After a few Skype sessions I noticed David's newly posted bio on Skype:

I am new to Skype and looking for people in advanced sciences to chat with. Currently I am the Founder and Chief Science and Technology Officer at Special Time

Energy and Publicity. My science, engineering and
mechanics career started at the tender age of 16 years.

He was sixteen the year before Vernie was murdered. In David's
life I think you can divide all that went before March 1, 1970, as the
"tender" and innocent years, which came to a quantum-reaction
halt on that violent night, when he began his descent into hell.

CHAPTER FOUR
Suzanne's Strategy

Vernie and Suzanne met in the Congress Bar, where they both went for drinks after work, probably in January 1962, which would have been a frigid day, not unlike the weather the night he was murdered.

Suzanne had long since grown tired of husband number three, who, by all accounts, was not a good provider, relying on his wealthy father to give him jobs and bail him out financially. And except for his rich family, that husband did not offer Suzanne the chance to move up socially, so she must have been transported to another realm when she met this thirty-six-year-old, handsome, ambitious, longtime police chief, who now had his eye on a prestigious state job.

From what I have gathered, Vernie was well-known in Wisconsin law enforcement circles and was likely working as a consultant in Madison. He was charming, competent, and surely convinced of his ultimate success in the career ladder he was pursuing, so I am certain he exuded a kind of over-the-rainbow, winning-lottery-ticket appeal to a woman who wanted to live big and proud. And sure enough, before long, he would be selected to be part of an elite group of investigators for a new division under the Wisconsin Attorney General's Office.

Vernie dressed well and was tall, handsome, and full of personality and ambition—a man to latch onto, which Suzanne did, like one side of Velcro to the other. Before long, they were in a scorching adulterous affair. Suzanne, who many people told me "was not unattractive" and "didn't dress particularly sexy," somehow managed to have men constantly circle around. By her own admission she had been with many men ("You dated everyone," her fifth husband often told her), including three husbands before my uncle, and she evidently knew how to get Vernie to hang out his tongue when she looked at him sideways and took a deep breath. And the fact that he was married was not the kind of obstacle she couldn't overcome.

Another asset Vernie offered to Suzanne was status. Did Suzanne know this was once and for all her chance at some kind of fame? Because after the complicated divorces, when they became known as Mr. and Mrs. Stordock, she finally got her name in the paper for events other than marriages and dissolutions. Now she could be on the Society pages, with news of visiting relatives, or dinner parties, or her children's international trips.

Was she also calculating the demise of this relationship as well, or was she blindsided by Vernie wanting to go back to Jenylle (Shannon had been told by several of Vernie's Beloit friends that he had shared with them his plans to reunite with Jenylle)? Having been through three divorces already, it perhaps crossed her mind that having to share assets was tiresome. Wouldn't there be a way she could get *every*thing?

CHAPTER FIVE
A New Family Member— Dealing with the Unexpected

In summer 2014 I was on a four-hour train ride back to New York from Washington, DC, where I had traveled on business. Normally, I would read a book, or write, but that evening I was exhausted from conducting two days of intense training, so I searched the Internet for more clues about Suzanne and her history. Because I had recently purchased the subscriptions to archived newspapers and genealogical sites, I had more access than I'd ever had. But I was not prepared for the shocking information I found. In fact, at first, I thought I was mistaken and retraced my steps.

During those hours I searched for Suzanne Stordock, Sue Stordock, Suzi Chappington, Suzanne Briggs, Suzanne Brandon. After about two hours a 2009 obituary popped up for a "Jocelyn Brandon Freeman" of Madison, Wisconsin, whose parents were Norman and Claudia Rhoades and Suzanne Brandon. Right away it was confusing. How many obituaries have three parents listed?

I thought this must be a different Suzanne Brandon, but it listed her husband, Ronald Aaronson (husband number five), and some of Jocelyn's siblings as David Briggs and Louisa Chappington, so this must be Suzanne's "daughter." I dug around some more to find out who Norman and Claudia Rhoades were. The 1940 census showed them in Madison, with one son, aged fifteen. Scrolling down, I saw it listed their race as Negro. Other newspaper articles I discovered told stories about how they had adopted several children, including a "Jocelyn." Then I got it. Jocelyn was born in 1945, when Suzanne would have been sixteen. Was this some illegitimate daughter to Suzanne, who had found Suzanne later on, like in that movie *Secrets and Lies*? I had never seen an African American woman hanging around their house, nor had I heard any talk about her, so this revelation had to be post-Vernie, because this did not conform with how she had tried to portray herself.

I remembered Suzanne as someone always wanting to be admired. Looking back now, I can see she was her own PR agent, managing numerous times to get her and Vernie's names in the newspaper for hosting dinner parties or for visiting family in another city. Then she'd buy dozens of copies of the newspapers and send each of us all the clippings. One story was about a party for Louisa, who was setting off for several months in Europe, including Germany, and then also traveling to Israel. That was one write-up Suzanne did not share with the family. I only found out about Louisa's trip recently as I was doing research (in the archived service I subscribed to) on newspaper articles back then where Suzanne or Vernie were listed.

I remember desperately wanting to go to Germany for about ten years. One of my uncles was stationed in the army there for a long time and I thought it would be heavenly to visit and had chosen German as the foreign language I'd study. One winter day, when I was sixteen and in my brown wool coat, which was frayed in two places on the collar, I walked the three blocks from Central High School to a travel agency in downtown Waukesha. Surrounding the door were large windows filled with pictures of Bermuda, Mexico, London, and Spain. I pushed the heavy door open and walked up the four carpeted steps.

Two women were sitting behind desks, talking fast on telephones seemingly grafted to their ears. One of them was finishing up and she motioned to me to sit in the chair next to her desk. She wore a navy blue dress and a dour look. I'd never been in a travel agency before and felt very out of place, but my desire to go to Europe pushed me forward.

A woman who called herself Mrs. Radford hung up and turned toward me, the white lace peeking out from the edges of her black-sleeved top, with a kind of smile that let me know I did not belong in a place that sold tickets to people who actually had considerable assets. "Can I help you, dear?" she asked patronizingly, as a kindergarten teacher would address her new students in the fall.

"I . . . I . . . want to go to Germany," I stammered, not able to even look her in the eyes, because now I was feeling beneath her.

"Oh, you do, do you?" She looked down at me over her glasses, which had a beaded necklace tied to them so that they rested on her chest when she wasn't reading, or when she was staring at people who waste her time. "The cheapest way to get there," she continued, recognizing that I was in the lower-priced categories, "is by steamer ship. It costs six hundred dollars."

I barely remember anything after that shock, but somehow I managed to get back out on the street. *Six hundred dollars? How can I ever come up with that when I earn one dollar an hour babysitting?*

And my parents? Forget asking them for more than $50, which was how much they gave me for a wedding present seven years later.

When Louisa took her international trip, it was a time of escalating fights between Vernie and Suzanne, so I imagine Louisa was happy to get away. If my grandmother had known they were sending Louisa off on such an extravagant trip, she would have said they were spending money like a drunken sailor, a major reason we did not know, I imagine. And my grandmother would have ended her statement with something about "that tramp," which is what lots of people would have called Suzanne, had they known back in 1945 that she had an illegitimate child. And if that baby was what they used to call "mulatto," all the worse in those days, especially in totally white Boscobel, Wisconsin, which is still very Middle American and WASPy. No wonder they'd want to keep the birth quiet. I wondered if Vernie even knew about it. Maybe he found out about Jocelyn and threatened to tell everyone, as a means of motivating Suzanne to give him a divorce so he could go back to Jenylle. Even though attitudes were changing by 1970, Suzanne was of the generation that the people she was trying to impress could have thought less of her. Or at least that might have been Suzanne's assumption.

During my next talk with David, I brought up Jocelyn. He said she was some friend of Louisa's whom Suzanne had adopted. Louisa had found Jocelyn as a child when they lived in the same neighborhood, because Louisa had been fascinated by Jocelyn's hair. And then he told me Jocelyn was a recent widow in 1970, and that she and her children had moved into the Oregon house while Suzanne was in jail and in the hospital. Then I understood the adoption part. Here is this young woman, needy for her birth mother, who gets asked to help out and offered a chance at being adopted by her real mother. Take advantage of Jocelyn's vulnerability and basically get child care for free for a year. Actually the child-care part turned out to be much, much longer, as I found out later.

Then I wanted to hear Louisa's story. Louisa quickly began, "Oh, yes, Jocelyn. You know in Wisconsin, they allow adults to adopt other adults, so that's what Mom did." How did you all become so close? "I was out walking in the neighborhood one day and found this little girl who had black-springy hair, which I couldn't stop touching, so I brought her home. And we became friends the rest of our lives."

A month later, I brought up Jocelyn again, as if I had never heard anything. Louisa said, "I went out one day and found this little girl. She had black-springy hair that fascinated me, so I brought her home, and we've been friends ever since." I thought it odd that I'd never seen or even heard about her those years I hung around Oregon, but I didn't mention that.

I did some digging to figure out how Louisa and Jocelyn could ever have been friends. They never lived in the same neighborhoods to go to school together. But I did find them living about a block from each other, in a solidly African American neighborhood, during the time Suzanne was divorcing Louisa's father, which would have put Louisa's age at a curly-blond two to two-and-a-half. That's not an age a parent would let a child walk around alone, searching for potential friends. The two families lived at opposite ends of a very long block and across an extremely wide street, which had space enough for parking on both sides and two *double* lanes, meaning four lanes total.

The Rhoades family (Jocelyn's foster/adoptive parents) presumably had a whole house, but that building was torn down a while back and there is a large community center in the place where several homes used to be. Suzanne's building is still there. It's a three-story simple apartment building, constructed in 1918. Each apartment would be about 650 square feet. Not a bad size for a single mother back in 1950. But the walk from the Rhoades family's house to Suzanne's down the block and across that wide street would not have been easy for a two-year-old. A more likely explanation is that Suzanne kept in contact with the adoptive parents of her daughter, and during Suzanne's divorce from L. Harry Chappington, they found a nearby apartment where she could live. And the fact is that Jocelyn was much closer during her life to Suzanne than to Louisa.

Another person in the Rhoades family Suzanne talked about a lot was Carlotta Rhoades, whom Suzanne brought up at least three times, the woman who had been her best friend since Sue was 16, and for many years after. Carlotta was white and married Frank Rhoades, who was black, and they were related to Jocelyn.

Claudia and Norman Rhoades adopted Jocelyn as a child and brought her into the family that had Frank as a 15-year-old son. It occurred to me that perhaps Frank was the father and that's how Suzanne found the family, but I was never able to confirm that. I tried for months to track down Carlotta. Suzanne had thought she had perhaps moved to California. When I located another of Jocelyn's relatives, he told me Carlotta had divorced Frank, moved to California, then died some years ago.

How was it Carlotta became a close friend when Suzanne (who was still Elmira) was in high school, in such a small town far away from Madison? I asked Suzanne if she met Carlotta in Boscobel? No, in Madison, Sue asserted. I tried to ask more about how she could have met Carlotta. Boscobel was a two-hour drive on narrow roads to Madison. How was a 16-year-old to travel there by herself? I think Suzanne realized at that moment she had told me too much. She and I had never talked about her being the actual birth mother of Jocelyn, but she had certainly told me many times about her "daughter." After the gaffe about Carlotta, she looked at me funny and stammered a bit, knowing she had goofed. By telling me her friendship with Carlotta Rhoades started at age 16, she had essentially just admitted to the birth. How else in the world would those two find each other, especially considering Carlotta was four years younger? How do you explain a 16-year-old from the hinterlands of Boscobel becoming BFF with a 12-year-old in Madison?

Suzanne had told me that she lived with another family in order to attend high school in Boscobel. But maybe she was sent away to give birth. I tried several avenues to find Jocelyn's birth certificate, but was unsuccessful.

Then I remembered that Suzanne had called me up one day in Madison, when I was nineteen. I remember the exact day and where I was sitting on my bed in the psych ward when they came to tell me there was a phone call. I'd been seeing a psychiatrist for several months, and it was the first time in my life that I was aware of my deep feelings and all the turbulence that was buried inside my psyche. I know that sounds impossible, but when you grow up in an alcoholic house with domestic violence and your only salvation from beatings is to keep your mouth shut, you learn to stuff your feelings. Working with the psychiatrist helped me begin to unlock emotions that had been crushed and exiled for nineteen years. One day it was so overwhelming that my doctor and I decided it would be good for me to spend some time in the hospital. Three days after I was admitted, the call came and I went to the beige wall phone in the hallway, just outside the room I shared with a willowy woman who believed she was Jesus Christ. There was Suzanne, calling me when I was struggling with my own sense of self and the dysfunctional dynamics of my family. To agree to admission to a psych unit meant I was pretty desperate to find a way to exist and perhaps succeed in the world.

And what does Suzanne want to say to me? *"How are you doing, Dorothy? Just to let you know, I've struggled with emotional issues for years?"* Nothing of the sort. She announced that my mother had had an illegitimate baby during high school, which is why she never graduated. The son's name was Bob. I stood there with my jaw gaping, as Suzanne went on about how my mother's aunt Lilly had adopted Bob and raised him as her own. So I had a half brother I not only had never met, but didn't even know existed. A few weeks later I checked with my grandmother and my brother, who both knew about Bob, who evidently hated my mother for giving him up. My grandmother, ever wise, told me to wait until my mother died before I tried to contact him, because it would cause my mother too much pain.

Why did Suzanne feel it her obligation, even her right, to impart such sensitive information to me? And why at that moment? She'd been with my uncle about five years by this time, and I'd been to their house countless weekends. Why choose a time I was at my most defenseless?

*   *   *

And so many years later, in a circular fashion, as a train whisked me from Washington, DC, back to New York, I tried to figure out if Suzanne had an illegitimate child while she was in high school. When I called Shannon to tell her what I'd found out about Jocelyn, she was, like me, incredulous—and thinking there was some mistake, or other explanation. Then I sent her the online links and she got it.

"You can't make up this shit," I said, thinking back to one of my writer friends, who advised me not to look up what actually happened, but rather to use my imagination.

"You're right, Dorothy," Shannon replied. "You can't make up this shit." And that became our motto from that time on, because the story kept getting weirder.

CHAPTER SIX

Organizational Chart #1

As I continued researching Suzanne and her various husbands, children, and assorted relatives, I found myself losing track of important details. Which husband was the doctoral student? Whose father was he? How many times did husband number one remarry? What were Suzanne's brothers' names? When was her second divorce? Her third?

In order to minimize the confusion, I developed a time line that started with Vernie and Suzanne's births, in 1926 and 1928 respectively, up to the present. Suzanne's history on its own was fascinating. Turned out she was born in Millville, Wisconsin, as Elmira Irene Brandon, which is obviously the reason why her daughter was now Louisa Elmira. But somewhere between her marriage to Mr. Chappington, when she was barely eighteen years old with one semester at the University of Wisconsin, and her divorce from him less than four years later (for "cruel and inhumane treatment"), she changed her first name to "Suzi" or more formally "Suzanne." Daughter Louisa was born October 20, 1948. Then exactly one year after the divorce, the newspapers announced her "betrothment" to John M. Briggs, doctoral student. Two months later they were married. Son David was born January 11, 1953, and the divorce was granted in 1958 in Juárez, Mexico. At least the second marriage lasted a little longer than the first one. On June 27, 1959, she got married for the third time, to the father of her youngest son. And it wasn't just the complicated marriages—I was collapsing under the weight of data from the endless certificates of birth, marriage, divorce, and death, and the countless real estate transactions I had gathered. I needed something more.

I needed some mechanism to compile the endless, complicated information and relationships. Yes, a spreadsheet (see table below).

Before I found many documents, there was some confusion about when Vernie and Suzanne started their affair. David had changed the narrative from Vernie being in their lives from ten years to seven, which seemed to negate Danny being Vernie's natural child. I would affirm later from Louisa that she knew of their affair in 1962. And I also learned from two former colleagues at the Beloit Police Department that Vernie had resigned in 1962 because of some explosive family "impropriety," which agreed with whispers I'd heard as a teenager that he was forced to leave his job because of an affair.

(Elmira) Suzanne Brandon Chappington Briggs Gast Stordock Aaronson's Marriages

Suzanne's marriage to	Date of marriage	Children born
L. Harry Chappington	March 29, 1947	Louisa Elmira Chappington, October 20, 1948
John M. Briggs	April 16, 1952	David John Briggs, January 11, 1953
Irving B. Gast	June 27, 1959	Daniel Stuart Gast, September 16, 1960
LaVerne G. Stordock	No Wisconsin marriage record (see p.332)	Vernie adopted Daniel Stuart Gast, date uncertain due to sealed adoption records
Ronald Myer Aaronson	August 29, 1983	None; Ronald had 2 grown children from first of his three marriages

Shannon and I talked again when she was in Los Angeles visiting her mother. Our conversation was brief, which wasn't normal. Several hours later I got an e-mail:

> I am curious about this timing but did not want to ask because I am at Mother's house and she was listening. She asked me why I keep pursuing this. "Just let it be," she said. "It's all in the past."

Shannon, who loved her mother fiercely and drove all the way from Eugene, Oregon, to Los Angeles every two months to be with her, looked at the elderly but still beautiful Jenylle and said, "He was my father, and no one can take that away."

> Mother said nothing and just walked away.

An affair fifty years ago. A murder forty-five years back. How is it that those long-ago acts still keep us from moving in ways we might have otherwise?

Date of divorce or death	Length of marriage	Divorce granted to	When (ex-)husband died and where
Divorced February 7, 1951	3 years, 10 months	Suzanne Chappington	1995, Fairbanks
Divorced July 29, 1958 in Mexico	6 years, 3 months	Suzanne Briggs	1974, Maryville, TN, mysterious death
Divorced November 5, 1963	4 years, 5 months	Suzanne Gast	1977, San Francisco, suicide
March 1, 1970, homicide	5 years?	N/A	1970, Oregon, WI, homicide
October 2, 2010, natural death	27 years	N/A	2010, Minneapolis, MN

CHAPTER SEVEN
Shannon's Road Trips

Vernie was indeed Shannon's father, but the last few visits with him were not the kind anyone wants to look back on as the last connections. Instead they were the kind of interactions that stick in your memory like toast crumbs in honey. She told me in great detail about the family vacation they took in the spring of 1962, when she was fourteen, on a road trip to Texas to visit Uncle Don at one of his army assignments. It would be almost a year before she figured out why this family holiday turned out to be so unpleasant. The affair with Suzanne had already begun.

During the long trip Shannon wore her green plaid dress, with the bow at her collarbone, and sat in the backseat of the Chevy Bel Air red-and-white convertible, writing down the names of the states she spotted on license plates as they sped down the highways, and holding tight to the papers so they wouldn't blow away. Each night at the hotel she'd unfold a four-by-five-foot map and make color-coded markings to show the change in percentage of out-of-state cars as they drove from Wisconsin to Texas.

"Look at how beautiful the apple blossoms are, darling," her mother, ever gentle with the dark, wavy hair and that one strand of premature gray on the right side, said on the first day. She liked to comment on nature. Vernie just stared ahead at the endless road, which, by the time they were in Illinois, was flatter than a calico ribbon ironed hot. By the time Shannon had counted twenty-four state license plates, Jenylle had noted the geese flying north, farmers out plowing up their land, and several new houses being built where there used to be soybean fields.

"Jenylle, I can see all that without your help," Vernie said in a way that made him seem to be controlling his emotions. Jenylle's eyes looked down at nothing in particular, and it seemed as if she'd fallen off a wall and gotten the wind taken out of her, because she just took a few deep breaths and said quietly, "I'm just making conversation, Vernie."

Her father said nothing, and neither of them talked much the rest of the way. Shannon didn't remember them being like this before, ever. She was just a teenager and understandably didn't comprehend how relationships are so fragile and how feelings can stay suppressed until they burst out and hurt a lot of people. All she knew then was that something had changed. Vernie and Jenylle didn't have that easy way anymore. He wasn't laughing and teasing her, and she didn't pretend she wanted him to stop. He wasn't singing "You Are My Sunshine" endlessly, until she laughingly begged him to switch to another song, as she took her left hand and lovingly stroked the right side of his head, the part that would get shot off eight years later.

Shannon says now that the Bel Air was her favorite car. Perhaps because it was the last vehicle they all rode in together, as a family.

Some months after the trip to Texas, Vernie left the police department and began doing consulting in Madison. In January 1963 he took the job at the Wisconsin Office of the Attorney General in Madison and he was only occasionally in Beloit. So Shannon was thrilled that he asked to take her to Madison one weekend in early 1964. At last, a chance to spend time with her father, whom she adored and missed terribly. What would they do? She kept wondering, and she imagined he had some great surprise in store. Maybe he'd take her inside the immense white marble Capitol Building, or ice-skating on the lake. He definitely was trying to make up for the awkward trip to Texas. She was sure of it. Next he'd make it up to Jenylle. After all, hadn't all the relatives said, as far back as she could remember, what a great marriage her parents had, and how their house felt just like the Andersons' in *Father Knows Best* on TV?

As the car drove down Highway 14, she looked over at her father, who was in his casual attire and that easy grin he did so well. Just then, Shannon noticed a green sign announcing STOUGHTON, WISCONSIN: HOME OF THE COFFEE BREAK, which, back when she was a teenager, didn't mean much to her, except they were close to Madison.

"Mother showed me your report card," Vernie said, looking over at her as they entered the outskirts of Madison. "Your grades are good, but you could try a little harder in math," he said as he pulled on her hair, which she pretended to get upset with, and he egged her on more. See, he was back to his old self and everything would be just like it used to be, she thought.

"An A-minus is a perfectly acceptable grade in geometry," she responded with a smile to let him know she was in on the teasing.

"Oh, sorry, if I thought it was such highfalutin math, I wouldn't have said anything." He let go of her hair, but he tried to tickle her and get her to laugh. Maybe he didn't realize she wasn't ten years old anymore, but Shannon didn't care, just as long as she had her father back.

"Okay. I'm proud of my daughter. So shoot me!" he said with his famous Jerry Lewis grin. At the time neither one of them knew how prophetic that statement would turn out to be.

Vernie pulled into a Howard Johnson's parking lot and they had the Friday Fish Fry, plus some of the restaurant's twenty-eight flavors of ice cream; Shannon was feeling pretty good. That is, until Vernie got her suitcase out of the trunk and led her to one of the motel rooms. Were they staying here? she wondered. Where was *his* suitcase? He opened the door to room 32-B and led Shannon inside, turning on the lights and showing her where the solitary bathroom and lonely towels were, and how to work the TV.

"But, Father, w-what . . . w-where . . . ?" she stammered. It was completely out of character for him to just dump her someplace. Why wasn't he taking her to his apartment? He told Shannon he'd be back at eight in the morning; then he looked at her with the same stare as when she was in the hospital having her appendix out, as if he was never going to see her again. She spent the night alone and confused, barely able to sleep. Who was this man who looked like her father?

"Princess!" he shouted through the door the next day at 7:58 A.M. He knocked as if Shannon were two hundred feet away and could barely hear. She pulled the door handle and there he was, smiling and hugging her until she thought he would crush her. "C'mon, I'm gonna take you for your favorite pancakes and then I've got a surprise for you."

"What surprise?" she asked. She smelled the Old Spice he used after shaving. She wondered if her mother missed that aroma, too.

"If I tell you, knucklehead," he said while he picked up her suitcase and led her to the car, "it wouldn't be a secret, now, would it?" Then she saw that smile, the one that always made her heart expand, the smile that was him, filled with so much joy and love and hope. Maybe he had found a house for the three of them in Madison, so they'd all be together again. That *must* be the surprise. She was sure.

After the most delicious plate of chocolate chip pancakes she'd ever tasted, Vernie started driving out of town. Okay, she thought, so they'd be in a suburb or something.

"You're gonna love this place, Princess. Really love it." He was talking a mile a minute as he pulled out a cigarette and almost dropped it before he could light it. Why was he so nervous? Then they suddenly went from endless dried-up cornfields, with the brown stubs of the stalks sticking out here and there under the snow, to a small town with a sign that read OREGON, WISCONSIN, POPULATION 4,302. They were traveling down Main Street and Shannon saw one gorgeous old Victorian home after another. She wasn't sure if Mother loved these old homes, but thought she would get used to it, and make it as wonderful a place to live as they had in Beloit.

"This village was settled in the 1840s, and there's so many wonderful houses here. It's beautiful—and away from all the hubbub of Madison," her father said, pulling into the driveway of an unusually enormous mansion.

She was about to ask if Mother had seen this yet, as such a house might be too much for her. Their house in Beloit was a ranch-style home with three bedrooms and one bath, all on one floor, and Shannon knew how fastidious her mother was about having everything in the correct place. The house Vernie was showing her looked like it had at least six bedrooms, with three stories and a huge cellar with a big bulkhead door, the kind from *The Wizard of Oz*, where they had to go underground before the cyclone hit. Just when she was going to ask him where her bedroom was, he jumped out, ran around the other side of the car, and opened Shannon's door, escorting her to the back porch.

As they got to the top step, there was a thin woman, with a blond beehive hairdo, inside. She was dressed in a red cashmere sweater and pencil skirt, with high-heeled shoes and had a strange faraway look in her eyes. This was probably the owner of the house they were about to buy.

"Shannon," Father said, squeezing her hand tightly, "this is my good friend, Sue." Suzanne opened the door and they went in.

Shannon could see Suzanne was trying to smile, but the facial expression seemed somehow forced. Well, maybe she doesn't really want to sell, thought Shannon. Vernie didn't seem to notice as he bubbled around. He was so sociable. He was already on good terms with the lady of the house, Shannon thought. She resigned herself and thought it wouldn't be so bad moving to this place.

Shannon started to move through the kitchen, thinking they would go on a tour of their new house, but Suzanne showed them to the kitchen table, where there were some vanilla-sandwich store-bought cookies thrown on a plate. Her mother would be humiliated to serve such dross to guests. Several mismatched glasses had been filled with Tang, noticeable from its distinctive fake-orange color and acidic smell. On the counter behind, in no discernible order, were salt and pepper shakers, a jar of steak sauce, garlic, loose keys, two lightbulbs, a coffee can, a Lipton Tea box, and several candy bars.

Shannon sat down. Vernie let go of her hand and walked to where he was almost on top of Suzanne, or so it seemed. Then he kissed her. Not on the cheek like Europeans did in the movies, but full on the lips, and for more than a polite second. It was one of those passionate kisses that made other people very uncomfortable, especially a daughter who thought she was on a real estate excursion. Shannon froze as if strong electrical currents suddenly went through her body and she was powerless to move.

Somehow their coats got thrown over an empty chair. Maybe a son or two of Suzanne's appeared, but Shannon didn't remember anything. It took the whole weekend for the reality to coalesce in her brain. Her father had a girlfriend? Vernie didn't seem to notice how distraught Shannon was. Many years later, as Shannon and I discussed this, we realized he was in the flames of passion and was too completely overwhelmed by volcanic hormones to pay attention to her needs. After he drove her back to Beloit on Sunday, and gave her another big bear hug, Shannon cut off contact with him. He showed up at a YMCA party in Beloit where he knew she'd be, and she did talk to him for a while in his car. But that was the last time she ever saw him.

"When I was young like that, I thought I knew what was right and wrong," she told me later. "But as you get older, you realize life is more complicated, and I regret I did not see my father those last years of his life."

CHAPTER EIGHT

Another Death and More Planning

If she had been born fifty years later, Suzanne could have been a CEO. She knew how to plan for the future and how to maximize resources. Each of her husbands had more status and financial potential than the previous one. The tapestry of her life seemed to be woven around ambition.

She started out with L. Harry Chappington, who was a cabinet-maker, and doubtless someone who could get her out of Mount Hope, Wisconsin, population 218. When I drove to Mount Hope in 2015 and saw a clump of houses sticking out in the middle of mile after mile of corn and soybean crops, I understood why a smart and striving little girl would want more, would want to be where she would find action, challenges, and other smart people. Each of the four times I talked to her, Suzanne told me her story about how she got to Boscobel High School. She said she'd had longings most of her life, and when she was twelve, she finally convinced her parents, James and Annabelle Brandon, to send her to a better high school. They found a family she could board with and she started high school thirty minutes away in the thriving metropolis (pop. 2,400) of Boscobel, Wisconsin, best known as the home of the Gideon Bible movement.

It wasn't until much later that I started to doubt this account. Though I discovered fairly quickly that what she told me might not be the truth, somehow I didn't realize she might be covering up something in her youth besides an illegitimate child. I grew up in Wisconsin, about twenty years after she did, and in a rural area. Even though I was acutely unhappy at home and bored beyond toleration in my country elementary school, which had three grades in one room and one teacher, it never occurred to me to get my parents to board me so I could go to another school. And I never knew of anyone, anywhere in Wisconsin, besides Suzanne, who lived with another family, merely to attend another high school. Not back then, anyway. Generally, when a child was sent away like that, it was because of some behavioral problems. But this is all speculation on my part. However, I did find out later that Suzanne's mother told the police how selfish her daughter was, creating chaos everywhere, and how'd she do things such as break all the dishes in the house when she got upset. It's not such a stretch to imagine such a girl causing problems in her small grade school, which perhaps was the real impetus to get her out of Mount Hope.

After high school graduation, Elmira insisted on going to college, which was highly unusual in working-class families in 1946. Even finishing high school, which neither of my parents did, was a big deal. But Suzanne *always* got her way. In order to raise extra money for her, her father took on extra roofing work. After one semester she married Chappington and moved with him to Marinette, Wisconsin. Louisa was born eighteen months later, when Elmira was nineteen. Even though Marinette is three times the size of Boscobel, it didn't take long for Suzanne to feel like a caged chicken and realize Harry was not going to take her far. Within two years they were divorced. Before you could snap and shuck a bowl of green peas, Elmira was back in Madison, across and down the street from the family of Jocelyn Rhoades, the little black girl who played such an important role in Suzanne's life.

* * *

One year later she was engaged to John Briggs, doctoral student at UW–Madison, in what was then called the Commerce School. Someone on the verge of receiving his Ph.D. was definitely more suitable to her aspirations than a carpenter. After John's doctorate was completed, he taught at UW for a while and then worked as an executive at an insurance company in New York City. Around this time she was "sent away" to John's family in Tennessee (which included his brother Joseph, who had very important information for me when I interviewed him during my search), because Suzanne said baby David made John nervous. None of it makes sense. Why wouldn't she insist on going to be with her own family? I knew she was eminently capable of asserting and manipulating her wishes to family members. When I tried to get more information from Suzanne, I could never get a straight answer from Louisa or Suzanne about when they left New York and why, but John Briggs definitely stayed behind. Perhaps Suzanne couldn't make enough of a splash in the huge city of New York. Or she got so bored with "the Dumbbell" (her oft-used term for him), she could barely stand to be in the same room with him. Or maybe she just missed Wisconsin and what was familiar.

Not long after she was back in Madison, Suzanne found husband number three, Mr. Gast. It is commonly accepted among his family that he was never much of a breadwinner, but he had the attractive quality of having an extremely rich father, Abraham. Knowing Suzanne, she was looking ahead to her husband's inheritance. Abe was already old, and he took a shine to Suzanne, at least by Suzanne's accounts. She did have a way with men. She knew how to reel them in, and Abe was a big one.

During that first meeting I had with Suzanne and her family in Tennessee, I noticed a thumbtacked photocopied picture of an elderly man on her wall. His hair was slicked back and he had the

beginning of a smile. Was that Ronald, husband number five? It
didn't look like the same man as the one in the framed photo with
Suzanne on her table. That other man seemed more gentle, more
open. Suzanne said it was Ronald, "the keeper," and I could see he
had a long, narrow visage with gray curls that lined his face, though
I imagine the hairline had receded, and he had on intellectual-looking
round brown glasses. Naturally, there were no photos of Vernie
anywhere to be seen. I asked about the wall picture and she said it
was Abraham Gast, her former father-in-law. When she talked
about Abraham, she smiled more than during any other part of the
conversation. Abraham really loved Danny, she told me. Suzanne
was alone with Abraham November 17, 1962, the night he died.

After Abe died and she divorced number three, she moved with
her three children—around January 1964—to the most expensive
home in Oregon, Wisconsin, a place that easily made her a center
of attention, a 150-year-old Queen Anne mansion with gables and
a wraparound porch. Initially, it was part of a land contract.
Vernie couldn't have helped, because he was still embroiled in his
own divorce and property settlement, which took another eighteen months.

The torrid affair with Suzanne was way before no-fault divorce. Everyone in the family told Jenylle not to give him a divorce, that Vernie would eventually get tired of "that tramp" and
come back to her. But I think Jenylle was under a burdensome
pain that went on for several years, watching the only man she'd
ever loved fall hopelessly under the spell of a woman who'd already had three divorces, and one child by each of her husbands,
by age thirty-five. Jenylle had married her high school sweetheart
at age nineteen (Vernie was twenty) and likely never so much as
smiled flirtatiously at another man.

Vernie must have felt under a great deal of financial pressure to
give Jenylle a decent settlement. In the divorce decree he gave

Jenylle his half of their Beloit house, free and clear. That tells you something about his generosity, his idea of duty, or sense of guilt, or all three. I don't know whose idea it was, but Suzanne loaned him some money during the months around the divorce. Maybe in her mind it was a payoff to get rid of Vernie's wife, but I think to Vernie it was the lifeline he needed to compensate the woman he had loved for so many years and the mother of his beloved daughter. In a sadistic twist, Suzanne used the documentation on those loans as collateral to post bail after she was charged with first-degree murder. As I read about her bail in court documents, I wondered who would keep such careful files for six years on money exchanges between lovers who expected to be married soon? As she sat in jail and looked through the steel bars, how was she able to find that paperwork in such a short time so as to be out on bail within a couple of weeks? Was this all part of some plan?

I also wondered how Suzanne could have possibly afforded that house *and* given money to Vernie. She was working as a secretary, or a secretary supervisor, so she couldn't have been earning enough to buy the grandest house in town, and she couldn't have gotten much in a settlement from Briggs, because he had just started out in his career. Her birth family didn't have any money, so what happened? I can't confirm the scenario that makes sense to me in the face of all the data, but I'm going to describe it, anyway.

Her father-in-law Abraham Gast was under the influence of Suzanne, and I think there is a high possibility that he had an affair with her, but even if not, she had him wrapped as tightly as a milking machine grabs a cow's udders. But then along came Vernie, who was some big shot on his way to the attorney general's office, and he was a long way up from number three, who could barely hold down a job. Vernie was hot for Suzanne in a way she knew how to control, and she couldn't let this opportunity pass by, especially because Vernie was willing to divorce Jenylle—a life eruption that not all of her boyfriends would consider.

Just get rid of number three and move on, she could have pondered, because it sounded like a reasonable course of action. But Mensa-level, strategic-thinker Suzanne might have considered Abe's $90,000 estate, which is $744,000 in 2018 dollars. And she wanted that status-achieving house in Oregon, which was not cheap. What to do? Well, Abe was old and rather infirm, so maybe he'd be kind and die before she got divorced. Then she'd have enough money to live in her dream mansion. But really, how long could she wait for Abe to expire? Did she ask her sexual puppet, Vernie, for help? I'll never know, but I am certain he wouldn't have obliged, because there is no evidence I could find of him even so much as having a traffic ticket. And even as sexually obsessed as he was, I never saw any evidence of him going over a legal line for her. All of the kids in the Stordock family were almost overly honest. My mother might have lacked self-reflection regarding her alcoholism, but she was what they call "cash-register honest." I remember one time in a phone booth she found a wallet with a lot of money in it, tracked down the owner, and delivered it to him personally. Vernie was the same.

Perhaps Suzanne got impatient. She was alone with Abe that night in the hospital. As a convert, she knew that Abraham's family were observant Jews and would not allow an autopsy. So what if somebody would put a pillow over his face? Or maybe Abe just happened to die very conveniently for Suzanne's timetable.

Abe passed on November 17, 1962, and by April, Suzanne received $124,000 (in 2018 dollars) from Abe's estate. She waited a few months, maybe for decorum, to divorce number three and legally bought the Oregon house in March 1964.

All that was left was to marry Vernie and she'd have everything. But that's where my research got stuck. I'd been trying for more than two years to find any documentation for that union, and have tried everything, including subscribing to public record archives, searching on various state and national vital records websites, turning in written requests to Wisconsin, Minnesota, Illinois, Nevada, and other states, and I can find no record of Suzanne and Vernie ever marrying. No one knew when they got married, not Shannon, not David, not Louisa, whose answer to me was "I never knew when she married any of her husbands. She'd just show up one day and say, 'Oh, by the way, this is your new father.'"

I questioned whether I was ever going to find the answer. I finally got up the courage to ask Suzanne, "So when did you and Vernie get married?" She looked at me with that "gee whiz" stare as she played with her long plait of hair and said she couldn't remember. I persisted and asked if she remembered anything else around the time she got married, or even an approximation of a general time frame. Nope.

How can it be that Suzanne easily recalled tiny details about my brother's friend Kenny, who visited Vernie and Suzanne a few times back in the '60s, or incidents involving my brother Raymond, who died before she even met him, but she couldn't remember when she and Vernie got married?

CHAPTER NINE

Jenylle and Change

I've known Shannon and Jenylle my entire life and spent a great deal of time in their Beloit house before the divorce. And even after the divorce I'd see Jenylle on one of my frequent trips to Beloit to visit Grandma. From my personal experience and from all the things family members have told me, this is how I imagine Vernie broke the news of his affair to his wife of eighteen years.

It was a hot August day when Vernie asked for a divorce, the kind of day when you needed to press your large white puff on the talcum powder before patting it all over your body, which was sweating more than a lady was allowed to perspire.

Jenylle was dressed in a freshly ironed gray housedress with buttons neatly lined up from top to bottom, and she was wearing the silver locket that Vernie had given her on their tenth anniversary. She looked away from frying the chicken in the fresh Crisco, wondering if the crackling sounds had twisted the words—words that could not actually be coming from her husband, sitting there in his suit with the gun holster just under his right armpit, this man who might have looked at a woman now and then, but nothing more than any decent man would engage in.

"Jenylle, I'm in love with someone else," I imagine he'd said, using words that wouldn't quite connect in her mind. All she could think was, He knows how much concentration I need to make a meal in this humid Wisconsin sweltfest.

She was spearing the chicken breast and then the thigh, which was Vernie's favorite part, from the sizzling skillet, when he touched her arm ever so lightly, with his thumb and middle finger, in a way that signaled annoyance, something he'd done for years and she'd learned to ignore. But then he raised his voice: "Jenylle!"

That's when she dropped the thigh right on the floor she had waxed not two hours before. She abruptly threw the chicken into the tall garbage can, in case it was contaminated with chemicals.

"Jenylle, I'm moving to Madison."

What is he talking about?

"Vernie, we can all move there. I know the commute is hard on you."

"I wanna be with Sue."

She pulled the aluminum skillet off the stove, the new Tappan that Vernie had given her for her birthday last year, and she remembered what a thoughtful husband he was. For Christmas he'd gotten her the Philco clothes dryer, so she wouldn't have to stand outside in the subzero Januaries, pulling frozen blue jeans off the clothesline.

"Vernie, can you just let me be until I get the dinner on the table?" she said, worried the chicken would get cold. She pulled the macaroni salad with celery out of the fridge and laid the cotton place mats on the kitchen table.

"Sue and I are going to get married."

Weddings—ours was the most beautiful, she thought. Eighteen years ago, she in her white gown, with bouffant tulle, and Vernie all decked out in that striking dark blue U.S. Navy uniform, with the bright white belt. She remembered how in love they were, and how she couldn't stop staring at her movie-star-handsome husband. A year later their sweet Shannon was born, that little girl who brought a smile to Vernie unlike any others she'd ever seen.

"Jenylle, I want a divorce."

She plumped down on the kitchen chair and was grateful for the extra padding, even though the plastic would stick to your legs in the heat if you weren't careful to make sure your dress covered it all. Vernie had insisted on the new set two years ago, so he wouldn't have to worry about scratching the wooden surface of their previous chairs, because sometimes he still wore his handgun.

He never should have left the police department, but he was never specific on why he wanted to take that job in Madison with the attorney general's office. She knew it was a lot more money, but all that driving, and those crazy hours, when sometimes they had him stay overnight.

"Vernie, I think you should quit that job and get something back here in Beloit," she said, trying to get at the real issue. He just needed to be home more. He was forgetting what a good life they had with each other, close to his family in Beloit.

He went to the oak cabinet and pulled out a bottle of whiskey and poured some in that shot glass they got last year when visiting Wisconsin Dells. He drank two shots and she tried to put the bottle back, but he grabbed it and went in the living room and put the bottle on top of the TV. How many times had she told him to use a coaster?

"Jenylle, I can't take this anymore here."

"Take what?"

"You're too . . . too . . . perfect."

"I've tried to be a good wife, haven't I?"

"You're too good, but I gotta leave." He was pacing around the room, barely looking at her.

Where is Shannon? I don't want her hearing this nonsense, she thought.

"I can't live without Sue."

"Vernie, you don't mean this. You've got too much stress at work."

"She's everything to me."

"But what about me? And what about Shannon?"

"I'll see her on weekends. I'll drive back. And, of course, I'll pay child support. And you can have the house, the whole thing."

Through their picture window she could see the sun was setting and there were streams of orange-and-red light shining between the leaves of green poplar trees.

"I'm leaving now. I have enough stuff in the apartment they got for me to overnight."

"But Leone and her kids are coming to visit us and Grandma this weekend. It's your sister, Vernie."

"You can play cards with them. Leone loves Sheepshead."

She didn't want to say how much she disliked that game. *Why couldn't we play canasta?*

"And Janet and Dorothy can play with Shannon," he said.

"But you have to be here. It's your family."

"All the kids can go hang out at the farm across the road from Ma's. They'll have a great time."

Vernie took two more shots and just sat there, staring ahead. Maybe he'd pass out and then wake up from this awful dream, she hoped, even though she hated it when he even took one drink and was grateful he rarely had more. He just looked at her and started crying.

"I don't deserve you, Jenylle," he said, his words slurring. He got up and walked toward the bedroom, and she hoped he had come to some drunken sense, but he said he was looking for his overnight bag. By the time he got in the room, he collapsed on the bed and was out, right on top of the chenille bedspread.

Shannon came in the back door just then, and Jenylle ran to greet her. Shannon's shorts and top were sweaty and her tennis shoes were filled with sand.

"We had so much fun by the creek."

"Take those dirty shoes off, young lady," Jenylle said, helping her untie the laces.

"Where's Father?"

"He had a rough day at work, dear, and he's taking a nap. It's just you and me for dinner."

Shannon went on and on about all the rocks she found and the fish they saw swimming in the shallow water, while Jenylle tried hard to listen to her.

When she woke up at her regular 6:00 A.M., Vernie and his overnight bag were gone. The only remnant was the indentation on his side of the bed, which made the lines in the chenille look wavy.

CHAPTER TEN
The Rest of the Family

Early on, I called every person in my family still alive who had any memory of Vernie and his death. Well, almost everyone. Not Aunt Jenylle, who had suffered greatly from the divorce, including banishment from the family because of Suzanne's jealousy, and, of course, unbearable pain from the murder. I instinctively knew not to call her about my research, though she and I had talked quite a few times over the years and I visited her around 2009 in Los Angeles, and she always seemed so content, so emotionally together. I knew underneath there had to be lingering aches that appeared and faded away like beams of light from moving cars at night.

So I talked to every person but one. A bit of information here, some data there, and I could put together the giant jigsaw puzzle that was Vernie's murder.

I started with Aunt Maxine, who had been married to Vernie's brother, David, for more than thirty years, until his death from cancer. I talked to her several times on the phone. The first time I told her about my investigation, she spouted, "Well, it's good you are talking to me now, because who knows how much longer I will live?" I tried to make light of what she said with some loving joke, but, in reality, she knew better than I. Just over a year later her ninety-second birthday in 2016 was spent by the family as a memorial to her life.

Back in 2015 I was ecstatic when I was able to go to Florida for her ninety-first birthday. How lucky could I get? I flew down to Tampa to see her and her daughter, my cousin Donna, who is a psych nurse. I walked out of the airport to the car-rental area, feeling the warmth of the sun, which in May was comfortable and not yet humid enough to seem like the swamp Florida actually was. Generally, I rent from National, because I like to be able to choose my own car. And there I saw it, a stunning, shimmering, pearl-colored convertible, a Mustang. "How much extra?" I asked the clerk. Thirty dollars a day seemed worth it to feel natural solar beams on my head and the wind in my hair.

I threw my suitcase into the trunk, pulled down the top, and began the ninety-minute drive to the house where Maxine had lived for about thirty years. Because I don't usually spend that much time in the sun, I didn't realize until the next day how much I needed sunscreen. I ended up looking like a lobster, but only on the tops of my arms and the left side of my face.

The house was not new to me, because I'd visited a number of times over the years. It was in a development not far from the toll-way. I drove the circuitous streets filled with well-kept, mostly modular homes built around 1980 on average-sized lots. I saw many colorful gardens in small plots, decorated mailboxes, and golf carts being used as local transportation. One attraction for Maxine was the golf course, which she used a great deal in the first twenty years she lived there. She had stopped golfing in her late eighties, but was in good health and spirits. When I arrived, my cousin Donna came out and I barely recognized her, because she had lost thirty pounds since I last saw her.

It was the day before Aunt Maxine's birthday, so she, my cousin, and I went out to eat at Ruby Tuesday. Aunt Maxine was still the tall and graceful woman of years gone by. She might have added some wrinkles and moved more slowly, but her wardrobe was as handsome as ever. Slim white pants and white formfitting blouse. I had asked what kind of cake she wanted and brought a fresh-baked apple pie from one of the premier bakeries in New York City, which we all enjoyed with vanilla ice cream when we got back to their place. Then I turned to Maxine, who was sitting in her brown-and-white-plaid swivel rocker, with her legs up on an ottoman, her gray hair short and stylish. "Tell me what you remember about Suzanne," I urged.

From the beginning I had a strange feeling about her and then she did things that made me realize why I felt that way. I guess she must have admired me or something, but everything I did, she did. Like bridge, which I played all the time. Pretty soon I heard Suzanne is starting with a bridge group. Then they told me she was taking swimming lessons, which I'd been doing for years. It was like she was trying to be me.

I noticed that Suzanne never showed any love or affection toward her children. She always acted like the kids were in the way. The youngest, Danny, always kept to himself and didn't seem to have any skills socializing with other kids or adults.

The one emotion she did show was jealousy. You know, when there's a divorce, generally the new wife finds a way to include children from the previous marriage, but Suzanne did everything she could to exclude Shannon, and I imagine that was part of the reason for the estrangement with Shannon and Vernie, which I know broke Vernie's heart. He got himself caught between Suzanne and his daughter.

About five years after Vernie died, David came to our house in Waukesha and he and Bill spent the afternoon together. When he was leaving, I walked him to the door. He turned to me and said, "I don't want you to think my mother killed Vern, because I did it." So I told him he

didn't have to cover up for his mother, and that we
would never speak about this again.

As I listened, my heart felt like it dropped to my stomach. David
had confessed to the murder? How could this be the first time I
heard about it? Was this one of the reasons the family thought for
years that David did it? Right then I decided I would wait for the
right moment and confront David. But how do you bring up such
a topic? *"Oh, by the way, do you remember confessing to the murder to my Aunt Maxine?"*

Maxine went to bed at midnight, leaving me with my cousin,
three years older than I, and a real night owl. I remember my
cousins most vividly as kids, so it takes me back every time I see
one of them and realize how old I am. My cousin Donna had always been "the smart one," and after having four kids, she went
back to school and got her bachelor's and master's in nursing.
Every time I talked to her, it was like chatting with one of my academic friends. "Tell me your impressions of Suzanne," I said.

Suzanne never seemed quite right to me and then
when I started nursing school—and this was way
before the murder—we came across a description for
sociopaths, and I said, 'Oh, that's her.' Someone who has
no regard for anyone else's needs or feelings. They
manipulate and lie and don't have any guilt or remorse.
They're impulsive and aggressive. That's her completely.
Always attacking Vernie or any of us in the family.
Blaming us for everything. She had the characteristics:
antisocial, narcissistic, and extreme possession of others.
Suzanne was very jealous and wouldn't let anyone in
the family talk to Jenylle. If she heard some family
member had had a conversation with Jenylle, Vernie was
told in no uncertain terms not to talk to that person.
Consequently, he wasn't "allowed" to talk to his own
mother for six months, because his mother

communicated with Jenylle, who, by the way, lived just
two blocks from Grandma Stordock. They had been
close for twenty years and now it had to be stopped, as
far as Suzanne was concerned. I remember at Grandpa
Stordock's funeral in 1968, Jenylle had asked if she and
Shannon could go and pay their respects. They would go
early, so they wouldn't run into Suzanne. When Suzanne
got to the funeral home, she looked at the guest book
to see who else had signed, and she saw Jenylle and
Shannon's name. She started shouting and ran out of the
building, going all over the parking lot until she found
Jenylle and Shannon in their car, pulling out of their
space. Suzanne shrieked at them and told them they did
not belong there. It didn't matter that Shannon was
paying her last respects to her grandfather. Jenylle was
her normal, dignified self and did not respond, but
Shannon said something to the effect that he was her
grandfather. The funny thing was, though, that Suzanne
insisted Vernie be friends with her three ex-husbands.
Who does that?

Sociopaths mimic other people, like what she did with
my mother, by copying her. Then consider the way she
confessed to the murder, knowing the evidence was
confusing. Both she and David had fingerprints on the
gun. She then had to call someone she knew, the sheriff,
so she was in control of the situation. And why wasn't
Danny home that night? Isn't that just a little strange? I
remember Vernie and Suzanne arguing all the time and
him saying on a number of occasions, "I never should
have left home." That's not something a sociopath can
tolerate. It really struck me when you said Suzanne was
bedridden with no medical condition. What a great way
to control people, to have them at your beck and call.
And that stuff about marks on her back. Let me tell you,
as someone who has been a psych nurse for three

decades, Suzanne is not the type of woman who would let *anyone* burn a cigarette or whatever else *anywhere* on her body.

The stories my cousin told about jealousy were not new. I had seen it too many times at family gatherings in Beloit when Vernie wasn't talking to her every single minute, when he might turn to his mother or sister or brother and talk for a few moments. Suzanne would start screaming at the top of her lungs.

Donna went on to tell me, as she had several times previously, that Suzanne got away with murder because she likely was having an affair with some high-level official. Or perhaps Danny was the child of some big-time Wisconsin guy.

When I talked to my sister, Janet Mittelsteadt, she reminded me about a time in the very early days of Vernie and Suzanne's relationship, when Suzanne was about 36. It was a crisp autumn day when Vernie and Suzanne, my parents, my sister, her husband, Richard, and I were standing around in a loose circle on one side of my mother's Formica-topped table in the kitchen. Smoke clouded the room as bottles of Pabst beer emptied almost as fast as they were pulled from the cardboard case near the front door. Vernie was teasing my sister, something he enjoyed, but my sister hated. "Hey, sweetie, why's your hair so perfect all the time? Is it a wig?"

My sister has always been extremely attractive and well-groomed, which everyone noticed, usually in a positive way. She was medium height, perfect figure, and always had her blond hair done in the perfect coif and wore unusually stylish clothes. Looking at her was like flipping through *Vogue* magazine. But she was also very shy, and Vernie probably thought he needed to open her up to the world more. This tactic did not work.

Suzanne didn't like it, either, for other reasons. Maybe because my sister *was* so beautiful. Suzanne became angrier as her jealousy intensified. With every new "tease" of Vernie's, Suzanne would kick him on the side of his leg with increasing force. At one point Vernie commented to Janet how lovely her skin was. Suzanne shrieked and then yelled to him, "Well, what do you expect, dummy? She's in her twenties. Of course her skin is like that." And then she kicked again. After Vernie's leg was surely bruised under his brown slacks, he finally stopped paying attention to my sister. After she got her way, Suzanne finally sat down at the end of the table, her neck long and her face tilted in a way that allowed her to look down on the rest of us, like a queen directing her court. Everyone else followed her to the table and sat in their chairs.

My sister had to remind me about another situation a few months later. It was Christmas, a big deal in the Stordock family. We often went to Grandma Stordock's house for a meal and sharing of presents. Generally adults gave children and young adults presents, not the other way around. Suzanne came that year brimming with packages. All of us cousins got presents from "Suzanne, Vernie, Louisa, David and Danny." All the cousins, except one. And that would be my sister, Janet.

And I've tried so hard to understand Suzanne. During the three years I've worked on this project, I've had to do research and collect documents in a number of areas. When I was putting the final touches on my first draft, I was looking at my bookshelf one day and thought if I died tomorrow, my three daughters (Roxanne, Solange, and Elizabeth) would have the ominous task of wondering why their mother had so many edgy books. Most likely, they'd understand all the titles on murder and serial killers, but what about all the volumes and movies, including Netflix viewings, on sexual obsession, prostitutes, and kinky relationships? So I made sure to tell them I was trying to comprehend the nature of the sexual hold Suzanne had over Vernie. What did she have that could be *so powerful* he would essentially destroy the rest of his life to get it?

CHAPTER ELEVEN
Louisa's Courage

For the first two years I investigated this story, I spent more time with Suzanne's daughter, Louisa, than with anyone else in that family. I learned so much from her. One story she told me on several occasions was about her trip to the Oregon house. Later I spoke to the couple that owned the Mansion when Louisa stopped by in 2000, and got more details about that visit.

Louisa told me about driving into Oregon, Wisconsin, after so many years, and seeing again the well-maintained concrete street lined with tall oak and elm trees, gently swaying in the summer breeze, which gave relief during July heat waves. Her car was pulling a heavy load of antiques stuffed into the U-Haul trailer, furniture she had long since forgotten about due to the many years she'd lived in Alaska. Somehow her mother could not let go of these possessions from so many lives ago, from times Louisa was trying to forget. Why had she been the only one who could transport this heavy cargo from Madison, where Jocelyn had been patiently keeping it in her basement, up to Minneapolis?

As she pulled the car over, she realized that she herself carried a heavy load and that seismic tremors within her psyche were erupting along fault lines from places so old and covered over with stories and explanations and denials and fears that even a geologist would have trouble locating the source.

She didn't *have* to go to the house. But it seemed as if a giant magnet, the kind used to gather up metal from construction sites, pulled her to the Mansion, where it had happened. Where their lives had changed forever in one night.

Turning right from Main Street to Lincoln, she parked the car and got out. The driveway was no longer gravel. Now it was asphalt, and the house seemed so terribly *white*. Had it always been that stark, just calling out to the heavens that it existed and better be noticed? She pushed herself toward the back door and smelled lily of the valley and saw beautiful pansies and daisies growing, formed neatly around the house.

"My name is Louisa and I used to live here about thirty years ago," she said to the woman who answered the door. The woman's hair was cut like Mia Farrow's in *Rosemary's Baby*, and she wore one of those tailored running outfits that was never meant for running, and she smiled sweetly, but with questions in her eyes. *She must not know who I am,* Louisa thought. *Maybe she doesn't know what happened here.*

The woman's name was Alice Seeliger and she and her family had lived in the house since 1977. Louisa followed her inside, feeling as if she was a small lamb being led to a scary place by a kind stranger. Entering from the porch to the kitchen, Louisa thought they were in the wrong house. There was an extra door on the other side of the room. The ceiling was lower. Appliances and cupboards were new. In the living room and den her senses were startled. When Louisa's family lived there, everything downstairs was white—walls and ceiling and neutral floors—and now it was decorated with colorful wallpaper. She had to pull back because it felt so strange, so different, like someone else had inhabited the space. And then she realized that this was the second family to live here since her own had vacated in 1973, or rather since her mother moved out, because Louisa had left—maybe escaped is more accurate—to Alaska in 1970, just a few months after *it* happened.

They walked through the living room, up the beautifully carved staircase, the one her mother had had refinished to its original elegance. Louisa turned to go into what had been her bedroom and froze. How many nights had she lain there, listening to the arguments, the hurtling of words she never, ever wanted to hear again?

Alice asked if she wanted to see the other rooms and Louisa walked behind her until she entered *that* room and stopped. "No," she said, "I can't." She couldn't tell her why. Couldn't make the words come out of her mouth. Just "no," that's all. And she couldn't go into the bathroom where Vernie used to shower. If she did, she might see him shaving his face with that Remington razor and wiping off the shaving cream with the blue towels that she had washed and folded so carefully.

She tried not to remember the time her mother attacked Vernie with the broken bottle. Or where her mother must have stood when she called Louisa on the phone right after "it" happened.

Louisa looked at Alice. "Can I see the attic? It's where I went to paint, and to hide." How much should Louisa tell her? She sensed the woman knew what had transpired. Alice said some comforting words and seemed to know not to ask too many difficult questions and instead inquired about her family.

"One of my brothers lives in Tennessee with his wife. Our youngest brother passed nine years ago." Alice told Louisa how sorry she was, but before she could ask how he died, Louisa started telling her about her mother. "She finished her law degree and is representing battered women in Minneapolis. I'm taking our old antiques up to her place in one of the suburbs." Louisa walked toward the back porch and saw the car waiting for her. "I didn't think I'd be able to come inside," she said. "Thank you for helping me."

Because of the attached trailer Louisa couldn't back up and instead went around the whole block, past the cornfields and back onto the highway, heading for the long ride to the Twin Cities, where her mother waited for the furniture.

In the summer of 2015 I got various and sundry court documents, including Vernie and Jenylle's divorce decree, where they both stipulated that the only piece of furniture Vernie would take was his Aunt Anna's antique rocking chair. I wondered if Aunt Anna's keepsake was part of that arduous U-Haul journey, and if that chair now resided in Tennessee.

CHAPTER TWELVE
The Law and Openness to Learning

I tried to be open to new information as I researched about Suzanne's court case, so that I wouldn't close myself off to new insights. What more was there to learn about the insanity plea? And then I came across state documents that made me gasp. In Wisconsin the legal view of "insanity" changed with two events. The first, and perhaps most important, was a change in the Wisconsin legal statute about how to treat defendants found innocent by reason of insanity. Whereas previously it was very cumbersome and difficult to get out of a legally ordered mental institution commitment, the new statute—Assembly Bill 603, chapter 967–976—allowed more latitude for such people to be able to petition for release within the first year of hospitalization. They needed to assert that they were completely healed, with some backup by hospital personnel. This law was passed December 1969, less than three months before the murder.

Secondly, a landmark case was decided that allowed someone to claim they were overtaken by an insane delusion that led to a criminal act, and it seemed to allow the defendant greater leeway in self-diagnosing such a condition. This case was decided February 3, 1970, less than a month before Vernie was killed.

Are these merely coincidences? One might argue that Suzanne, not being a physician or an attorney, would have no knowledge of these changes. But Suzanne, by her own admission, was a genius Mensa member, and she was married to a powerful man who worked for the State of Wisconsin. Vernie's work allowed her to develop other powerful relationships.

Take for example the case of the Dane County sheriff. After Vernie was shot, the first thing Suzanne did was call the sheriff on his private number. She bragged to me about this, saying she didn't call him at the station, but at his home. Court documents depict him testifying that the ringing woke his wife, who then handed the phone to the sheriff. She identified herself as "Suzi," which indicates a personal relationship.

Do I think that is the only powerful person she felt comfortable calling on? I do not. She mentioned to me during one of our conversations that she had met one woman to whom she felt very connected and how they understood each other. It was another woman who had murdered her man. Hope Thomas Privett was ultimately convicted and sentenced to life in prison.

"I really felt I could help her," Suzanne said in her usual unemotional speech pattern. It wasn't until some subsequent research that I discovered Hope Privett was the only other female murderer in Dane County during that time period. Privett had also tried to get off on an insanity plea, but she had been convicted of first-degree murder and given a life sentence.

While Suzanne was talking, I was sitting on the chair at the foot of her wooden bed, while she was stroking her small brown-and-white dog, Holstein, and looking past me, as if she was pretending to be gazing my way. "I sent her money and cosmetics. I even talked to the judge about getting her out of prison."

Wait! What confessed murderer had the kind of relationship to talk to a judge about another murderer? Why didn't I ask her which judge she meant? Suzanne went on, "She changed her name and was living somewhere in Wisconsin." Another comment I failed to follow up on. If she changed her name, it had to be after she got out. After I dug for weeks, I lost Privett's trail at 1980, when the last newspaper article had a Church of Christ minister pleading to let her be released in his care, because she was transformed and was now close to God. When I called the prison, they said she had been released in 1980. I called several of her distant family members, one of whom told me she had nothing to do with Hope anymore, because Hope was mean to everyone, even her own mother, to whom she caused a lot of pain in her final years. When I got hold of the current pastor at the Church of Christ and told him about her, hoping he had some information, he said, "Well, I guess she didn't really transform, did she?"

After weeks of hunting down any possible lead, I discovered the location of Hope's daughter, who was only two years old when her mother was arrested for murder. I tried to call the daughter, but she wouldn't pick up her phone or call me back. So I sent a text, explaining what I was doing and why I wanted to talk to Hope, if possible, but got no response. It did not surprise me. Why would this woman, who seemed from my research to be living an exemplary life, want to bring back painful memories?

Bonnie Privett called back about two weeks later and we talked for almost ninety minutes. "I do know where my mother is," she stated with a disarming warmth in her voice, which seemed to erase the distance between New York City and Maryland, where she lived. "But I won't tell you, because I want to protect you." I wanted to say, *"Please don't protect me,"* but I felt that would be violating a boundary with this woman who had obviously had more pain in her life than I could imagine:

> My mother is a bitter, nasty woman who carries deep resentment for all that happened and hatred for everyone in her life. She didn't raise me. My sister and I were brought up in foster homes, though I know when I was with my mother it was endless neglect. I didn't meet my biological father until I was twenty-one.

When my mother got out of prison after eleven years, when I was fourteen, I got scared that maybe she'd come after me. Still, she was my mother and I was curious. Maybe she wasn't as bad as people said. Maybe I needed to give her a chance. Eventually I moved in with her. What I learned was that she is someone with major temper issues who angers quicker than an atomic reaction and will take whatever objects are in her reach— dishes, books, steam iron, pool ball—and throw it at the person she is raging at.

I know little to nothing about the stabbing back in 1969, but I do know she is capable of murder. Picking up a knife and plunging it into someone is on her normal continuum of violence, and she wouldn't have any regrets.

As Bonnie and I talked, I saw the similarities of both Hope and Suzanne having vicious tempers, yet both were able to charm when needed. They both saw themselves as victims of abuse and felt completely justified in the murders. Both women had hurt their mothers deeply and had left toxic chaos in their children's lives.

And this was the woman, Hope Thomas Privett, whom Suzanne had felt closest to and had evidently kept up with for years, since she knew she had changed her name and was living somewhere in Wisconsin. All that had to be after 1980. The daughter told me that after Hope murdered her lover, she successfully pleaded with her recently divorced husband to hide the murder weapon, a knife.

Bonnie Privett, who had a wonderful husband and six children, said with great strength, "I was told as a child that I would grow up to neglect and hurt my children and be a lousy person, but I prayed to God and told myself that I was going to make my children have a much better life than I did. And I feel proud that I was able to accomplish that goal." While talking on the phone with her, I was brought to tears at the courage of this woman, whom I would later meet. Even now it makes my heart swell when I think of how she has built a life, starting with such overwhelming hardships. She has so consciously made her life pure and good. It reminded me of Suzanne's daughter, Louisa, who found God and has tried so hard to be a loving and thoughtful person. She followed this life path, even if she didn't consciously see that she was being the opposite of her own mother, as Bonnie was able to conceive.

"My mother got away with murder," said Bonnie. "Even though she served eleven years, that is nothing compared to taking someone's life." And I'm thinking, well, what about serving only 11 months? What I also didn't tell the daughter was how I'd contacted a number of family members of the murdered man, a father of seven. After all these forty-plus years, they were still in too much pain to want to talk about what had happened.

It was lore in my family that Suzanne got away with murder. Another Madison attorney said it was very clear from reading the court transcripts that there was some behind-the-scenes deal made. We had always assumed so, and thought she walked away for one of the following reasons: She knew secrets that high-ranking officials did not want divulged, or else she had an affair with someone very powerful, someone who she knew would protect her. But how could I prove either of these?

Though I felt very certain that Suzanne had engaged in extramarital affairs when she was with Vernie, I needed evidence. Suzanne would never admit to it. And how do you find documentation of something so hidden that happened forty-five years ago?

CHAPTER THIRTEEN

David and Connections

I knew I had to build a strong relationship with David. As I got to know him and could see the good and honest person he was inside, this became more and more pleasant. It did cross my mind more than occasionally that this might be the guy who shot my uncle, and I don't even know how to explain it, but I loved him and felt no need to even work toward forgiveness. It was already there.

My psych-nurse cousin Donna's theory was that if David pulled the trigger, it was not of his own volition, that Suzanne had somehow manipulated him. But even if he did it on his own, he was young and immature and later had decades to reflect on it. But then again, he actually wasn't reflecting on it much, or he might have remembered my uncle or me sooner when I called that first time.

David always initiated the calls with me. At first, it was just e-mail; then when he got his computer fixed, we did Skype, every few weeks once we got started.

The last few months of 2014, David mentioned often how pretty I was, and how much he enjoyed talking with me. In a December 4 e-mail after a Skype session, he said he loved me, but then quickly said he was not pushing for romance, but just that the connection from so long ago touched his heart, and how he'd love to come visit me in New York, if God would give him that million dollars he's been praying for.

Around that time he got really enthused as we talked about living in Wisconsin. "Let's go back and buy that house in Oregon," he said, "we can get married, and I can run my business out of the basement. Wouldn't that be great?" I just laughed, hoping I could turn his serious comment into something we both saw as a humorous remark.

He did mention in early December how lonely he was. "I'm the only Christian in this house," he said. "My mother is Jewish, and Louisa and her husband are Messianic Jews, so I am alone. A minority."

He talked about how difficult it was for Louisa to have to take care of his mother, who would wake up every hour having to pee, and only Louisa could help her. So Louisa never got any sleep. They did have a home health aide, but she wasn't there during the nights. Louisa told me later that her mom complained of having a urinary tract infection, but they'd tried many medications and nothing was helping. This meant Louisa was never able to sleep more than sixty minutes at a time.

During that time period I was starting to gather background information on the case, because Shannon and I were still trying to learn who had been the actual murderer. In early November I went online and sent an electronic request for police records of the murder to the Oregon Police Department, and I contacted Dane County Courts on December 2, 2014, to get court transcripts. By December I hadn't heard anything from Oregon, Wisconsin, so I called the police station. It took several telephone calls for the clerks to figure out that their new digitized records did not go back that far. They had recently updated their computer system and could not retrieve anything before 1990. I was crushed. How in the world would I ever know what happened without the police reports? Why had I waited so long?

*   *   *

That same day, December 12, David sent me an e-mail, really pushing for a Skype session that weekend. It was a superbusy time for me, as I had Saturday completely booked, morning to night, and Sunday during the day, and Monday I was flying across the Atlantic Ocean to be part of a theater panel in Berlin, Germany. David and I found we could talk at 8:30 P.M. on Sunday, December 14. Normally, I wouldn't schedule something late on a Sunday, especially after two intense days, and I thought about asking David if we could wait a week until I got back, but I did enjoy talking to him, and it seemed really urgent for him.

"Dorothy, I want to talk to you about two things. God and Vernie." I told him I was too tired to talk about God, but what was it about Vernie? "You need to know, Dorothy, that Vernie and I fought a lot, I even ran away a few times. That's one of the reasons the police almost arrested me that night, because they knew about me and Vernie fighting."

Having just spent considerable time on the phone with the police, I mentioned something about the Oregon police.

"It wasn't Oregon. It was the Dane County sheriff that came." He didn't realize it, but at that moment my spirit leapt with joy. Maybe I could get the police reports, after all. David kept going on about how both his and his mother's fingerprints were on the gun, and how he almost got arrested. I decided to challenge him, something I hadn't done before, as I'd previously tried to be the nosy but pleasant cousin. Confrontation was what I intentionally avoided. But that night it was different, and I can't tell you what happened inside me. Maybe I somehow sensed this was my last chance.

I talked to David about blood splatters and gunshot residue. Those were as important as fingerprints. Which of you had them? I queried.

"Well . . . my mother . . . of course," he said, and stopped for a moment. I could hear him breathing hard. When he spoke again, his voice quavered.

"Dorothy, you don't understand how traumatic it was that night for me and my mother!" he spouted, and if he'd been in the same room, I know I would have gotten little droplets of spit all over me.

Yeah, I thought, *and how traumatic do you think it was for my uncle who'd just gotten half his head blown off?* But I didn't say it. I considered another revelation: Though he'd confessed the murder to my aunt Maxine, I decided he'd had enough stress for one night. He seemed overwhelmed in some post-traumatic stress disorder moment and I did not want to make it worse. I could always bring up his confession when I got back from Berlin.

David died three days later. I got a Facebook message December 18 from Louisa, telling me about the upcoming funeral and: *Much of his last thoughts and prayers were about and for you and your eternal destiny. Please call if you choose.* I immediately picked up the phone in my small art deco hotel room in Berlin, where I was staying with my daughter, Solange, and got her on the line. They thought it was likely a heart attack, as he'd had heart problems as a child. The memorial service was the following Tuesday. I thought it impossible for me to get there, as I didn't get home from Berlin until Monday night and changing the ticket was going to cost more than $1,000, since the return flights were now very expensive. But I realized this was the one and only funeral of David and I *had* to go. So I kept the transatlantic plane back and booked a flight at 5:30 A.M. Tuesday to Tennessee, coming back to New York the following morning. That meant getting home Monday night, unpacking, repacking, and getting two hours of sleep before I had to leave for the airport at 3:30 A.M.

I arrived early enough to go to Louisa and Bobby's house before the service. Everyone had sadness in their eyes. I went into Suzanne's room to give my condolences, and she looked at me once again with that piercing gaze. When I told her how sorry I was that David was gone, I think I saw a tear starting to form, but I wasn't sure, because I felt no pain coming from her, not like everyone else was feeling. Suzanne was collected and calm and talked a little about how much David liked to discuss family history.

Louisa's three grown children would be there. One of them had recently moved into the house and was working nearby, one had come up from Florida, and her son was due in from Alaska any minute. All of us went to the grave site, in a nearby town, where the funeral was to be. That's the town David's grandparents and his father had grown up in, and where David had lived until a few years earlier. Maybe it was because of the rush of getting from Berlin and New York, or maybe because I'd lived in Tennessee for more than fifteen years, but I hadn't paid attention to the weather. Even though Tennessee has generally milder weather in the winter, it was still December 23 and that day was chilly, hovering in the high forties and low fifties. So there we all were, about thirty of us, standing (not a chair in sight) outside in the cemetery, waiting for the service to start. I had only brought a light jacket, as I never imagined being outside for the funeral. Louisa got a call saying her son's plane was going to be another forty-five minutes late, and we, of course, had to wait for him. I finally asked to sit in the car to warm up, as we'd already been outside for about a half hour, but I noticed most people stayed near the grave site. But they were wearing warmer clothes than I was. It was mostly people from David's churches, the one in the town where he'd once lived, and the one he'd started going to about a year ago when he'd moved here.

Finally Louisa's tall and good-looking son arrived and the service began. A stocky man in a black suit and white clerical collar walked carefully up to the casket. The pastor at David's Methodist church gave a lovely talk about David, his love of Jesus, and his fascination with science, particularly quantum physics. After this, Louisa introduced the rabbi, who looked very similar but was just slightly taller than the minister. The rabbi was going to speak in honor of David's Jewish mother. But where was the mother, by the way? I knew she was an invalid, but I'd seen her stand up and take some steps both times I'd been there, and there was a fold-up wheelchair in the corner of her bedroom. And why was this all suddenly about Suzanne's religion? It felt awfully uncomfortable for me, and I imagine for the other mostly Christians there, who were too loving to say anything, when the rabbi took over the service and talked longer than David's pastor. His thoughts were inspiring and he told us about how Jews used the back side of a shovel to show reluctance in having to bury a loved one, which was so touching that most of us were in tears. Or were we just crying because we had lost someone we loved?

It made me wonder if the funeral was really for David. Then I remembered reading Danny Stordock's obituary and looking at his gravestone, which was all written in Hebrew, despite my understanding that Danny was not really Jewish. Louisa had told me something about Danny accepting Jesus toward the end of his life. And in the obituary there was no mention of the man (LaVerne Stordock) who gave Danny his last name, which would have allowed Suzanne to collect SSI survivor's benefits from Social Security for Danny, and more benefits as his mother.

Vernie is absent from any obituary listing of Danny I could find, even in the official death certificate from Dane County, where Ronald Aaronson is listed as Danny's father. Ronald never adopted Danny, who was twenty-three and had been out on his own for years when Suzanne and Ronald got married. When I met Danny's half brother (an older son from the first marriage of Suzanne's third husband) and his wife in Madison, he talked wistfully about the brother he'd never met. "Do you have any pictures of him?" he asked pleadingly. His voice broke from pain when he recounted the shock he'd experienced when reading Danny's obituary and how no one from his birth family was mentioned at all.

Even if Suzanne never showed up at David's funeral, she made sure her stamp was on it. The same as it was in her fifth husband Ronald Aaronson's obituary, which listed David Briggs and Louisa

Chappington as his surviving stepchildren and predeceased step-children as Danny and Jocelyn—neither with last names. Did she not want anyone to see the name of Stordock, lest it send off some signals she wanted no one to pursue? And would Jocelyn's last names (which came in so many different varieties) cause people to ask too many questions?

Later, when it was just family, and we were all sitting around the family table, one of Louisa's kids asked me how I was related. Silence as Louisa and I looked at each other. I had no idea what Louisa's children knew and did not want to be the person who told them their grandmother was a confessed murderer, so I just replied, "Your grandma used to be married to my uncle Vernie."

Louisa's three children all looked well-scrubbed, though I found out later one of them was battling with personal problems. At the time I just marveled at how well-balanced they seemed. Then I started telling some funny stories about Vernie and how much he loved being a cop. I could see the relief on Louisa's face. She later told me how grateful she was that I had reminded her how Vernie had some good qualities, because she mostly thought of him as a monster who tortured her mother. Bobby asked Louisa later if her children knew what had happened with Vernie, and Louisa said yes, but she did not sound convincing.

I asked Louisa what was wrong with Suzanne that she was confined to her bed. Louisa said no one was able to find any med-ical reason. After her fifth husband, Ronald, died, she moved to Alaska so Louisa could take care of her and she started walking with a cane. Suzanne was so insistent they move to Tennessee to be near David, Louisa finally complied and gave up her forty years of life in Alaska with her three kids, who all lived there, Bobby left his grown children, and they moved to Tennessee. Louisa told me at a later time that she would have never heard the end of it from her mother if they'd stayed in Alaska. By the time they had moved to the farm outside Chattanooga, Suzanne was gradually spending more time in bed. I asked Louisa if doctors had tried to cure Suzanne, but Louisa said many had, with no success. Suzanne had some story about how she and Ronald were on a Doctors Without Borders trip ten years previously and she picked up some bug that no one else in the group got, and she blamed it on her unwillingness to drink the firewater that the witch doctor had offered everyone. And that led to her being an invalid, from no apparent medical cause. Louisa had told me previously about a urinary tract infection of Suzanne's that would not be healed, because the doctor could not find any infection. Louisa had taken her multiple times to the clinic, to no avail.

That night after the funeral I thought it was a good time to get more information. So I asked Louisa when they had moved to Oregon, Wisconsin, and she said it was the school year that Kennedy was shot, after she had already started in her Madison high school. Based on research I did at the Oregon Historical Society and local newspapers, I think they moved into the Oregon mansion between December 1963 and January 1964.

It was getting late and very dark outside. Louisa and Bobby were pressing me to sleep there, but I still was skittish to be unconscious in the same house as my uncle's confessed murderer. Whereas I saw her as a murderer or, at minimum, a conspirator/instigator of the killing, to them she was the beloved mother who was cruelly and unjustly confined to her bed. So I made up some excuse about preferring to sleep in hotels. I sensed I was hurting their feelings, but I couldn't get past my fears. Was I being unreasonable? I didn't really care. I just wanted to sleep without any worries. Fear creates unusual ripple effects, which I was not interested in exploring that evening.

That night in Tennessee, as I was heading for the door to leave, I asked Louisa about Danny and how he died. She said he'd come out as gay and had a boyfriend who was really into drugs, something they did together. Then the guy broke up with him, and Danny wanted to scare him and took what he thought was only a slight overdose, so that he'd survive and be taken to the hospital and his boyfriend would come back. How she knew this was in Danny's mind, I forgot to ask, but she did say she prayed with Danny not long before he died, so she felt his soul was saved and close to Jesus.

Louisa then said I could ask her anything, so I thought I'd better take this opportunity. What about the cigarette burn, I asked. Was there a pattern of Vernie abusing your mom?

Louisa said she'd never seen any physical abuse. On the contrary, one time Vernie had come downstairs for breakfast with bandages over his face and she asked what had happened. Suzanne said he'd cut himself shaving, but Vernie hesitated before recounting how Suzanne had come after him with a broken bottle. Suzanne did not contradict him. Another example Louisa gave was when Suzanne took all the dishes out of the kitchen cupboard and vigorously threw them against the wall, breaking them into bits. After hearing all the crashing, Louisa came running downstairs and tried to stop her mother. Vernie told her to please ignore what was going on, that they would work it out themselves. David had also told me that the stories of abuse were things Suzanne had told herself to live with what she had done. Nobody in that family ever used the words "murder" or "killing."

Then I said David had told my aunt Maxine, maybe forty years ago, that he'd killed Vernie. Louisa became a motionless statue for a couple of seconds, then looked at me and said: "This would explain so much, about how my mother had always protected him and said, 'We have to make sure David is all right, especially when I'm gone.'" Louisa said that Suzanne was relieved when David died, something neither she nor her husband could understand. About an hour after this comment, when I was standing next to Bobby, he made the same observation: "Suzanne was so relieved when David died."

As I drove through pouring rain toward the airport at 1:00 A.M. to find a hotel, I was grateful I'd pushed myself to get there for the funeral, and grateful I'd established a connection with Louisa, who had tried valiantly to be a person who loves abundantly, who lives out her religious principles, and who is good. I had mostly remembered her as an artistic hippie and was gratified to see how she'd managed to build a life. She had told me the tragedy of her first marriage, saying she'd realized one day that she'd married a carbon copy of LaVerne: a Swedish alcoholic. I didn't correct her, because he was actually Norwegian, but I think it showed she didn't know him well, because Vernie wore his 100 percent Norwegian heritage with great honor. I think from various comments Louisa made that she saw Vernie as just another one of her mother's string of husbands. Why bother to learn anything about him?

Was Vernie an alcoholic? Definitely not when he was married to Jenylle. His drinking increased during this marriage to Suzanne. Did that make him an alcoholic? Coming from a long line of alcoholics, and having a brother who was in treatment so often that he was on a first-name basis with the intake nurses, and being in more Adult Children of Alcoholics workshops than I can even recall, I think I have some discernment on who is this type of addict. So I can speak with some confidence that Vernie was more likely "alcohol-dependent" than alcoholic. I believe his drinking would have subsided if he had lived long enough to go back to Jenylle.

The rain was relentless the night of the funeral, so I stopped at the first inn I found. A few minutes after I got to my room, a large brown cockroach walked across the smelly, worn-out carpet, and I decided I didn't want to stay in this place, either. While driving down the highway to find another abode, I wondered some more about why David died just three days after I had confronted him about the blood splatters and the gunshot residue. Turning in to the drive for a more upscale hotel, I realized David had surely told Louisa and his mother about our conversation, because that was his usual practice. And then why was Suzanne so relieved when he passed? What kind of mother is happy when her son dies?

CHAPTER FOURTEEN

Court Transcripts

It took three months to get the court transcripts. The few surviving forensic pictures didn't reproduce well, and the psychiatrists' reports had disappeared, but with those forty-year-old transcriptions of every hearing, including the final one, as well as the probate documents and those from the suit involving Vernie's life insurance policy, I got much of what I needed.

By the final hearing Suzanne was found not guilty by reason of insanity "at the time of the shooting," and she was committed to the state hospital. While waiting for the hearings and later to go to the hospital, she had the mental alertness to file for his life insurance, which she got, and to petition the court to give her Vernie's half of the house as his "widow." On all the probate documents, where she asked for bank accounts and other assets, she listed "widow," and I wondered, well, who made you a widow? She got everything. Shannon, Vernie's only natural child, got nothing.

Vernie's will listed Suzanne and Danny as the heirs. Knowing Vernie, I have a hard time believing this was his idea. He loved Shannon, and had tried several times to contact her. Because Suzanne would fly into a rage if any of Vernie's relatives talked to his first wife, Jenylle, I feel certain Suzanne was only too happy to have Shannon out of the way, too. Shannon did sue the insurance company, on the grounds that his confessed killer (Suzanne) was benefiting, but lost the case. It's hard to imagine such a thing would happen, but the case was described in the December 28, 1971, issue of the *Madison Capital Times* and the final judgment came three years later, giving all of the insurance money to Suzanne. After reviewing the court transcripts, I found the result to be more complicated. From the transcripts I found Danny was supposed to receive half of the insurance money, as well as half of Vernie's State Retirement Fund. But still, I wondered, how could the person who admitted to blowing off half my uncle's head be the very person who got half his life insurance money *and* most of the other assets?

I want to take you through the transcripts. The first one is March 2, 1970, one day after the murder, which was about 2:15 A.M. on Sunday, March 1. Early on, one of Suzanne's attorneys, Jack van Metre (the other was Kenneth Orchard), recounts how Suzanne's longtime family physician, Dr. Walter Washburn, showed up at the police station and immediately determined that she was "mentally ill." After I read this, I looked up Dr. Washburn's record and found a general practitioner who graduated from medical school around 1950, with no evidence of any psychiatric training. In addition, there is no information on how Dr. Washburn happened to appear at the police station. It was only months later, when I finally got the police reports, that I learned that Suzanne had made many calls from her home while the police were there, telling everyone she'd shot Vernie, and I surmised that Dr. Washburn had been on her call list. Or perhaps she had asked her attorney Orchard to call him, as one of the officers reported she talked to her lawyer while the police were in the home investigating the crime scene. Evidently, her psychotic break had ended.

District Attorney James Boll told the court on Monday morning he had spoken to Dr. Washburn the night before, and that Washburn had recommended Suzanne be examined by Dr. Leigh Roberts, a psychiatrist, and that she be transported from the jail to the university psychiatric hospital, where she stayed until leaving for court that morning, March 2. At first, upon reading the few sentences that described the appearance of Dr. Washburn and his essentially appointing Roberts as the psychiatrist, it all seemed like a normal procedure. Little did I know how the seeming innocence of Dr. Washburn's behavior would infect the case with a virus from which the district attorney chose not to recover, and that Roberts had a few secrets of his own that would eventually be laid bare.

DA Boll said the prosecution anticipated an insanity defense and, therefore, thought it would be the best for all concerned if she was examined as close to the event as possible. The preliminary hearing would normally have been within ten days, but Jack van Metre requested a delay, because of the time needed for several psychiatric examinations. Everyone agreed on one month hence, with the date of April 7. A court order on March 10 proclaimed that Dr. Leigh Roberts determined Suzanne was legally insane, though the transcript of that hearing has disappeared. I found the court order, but not the transcript.

As for bail, DA Boll said that because this was a serious charge—in fact, the most serious charge in Wisconsin statutes—he recommended no bail. Van Metre said that under the Eighth Amendment, everyone has the right to bail (a prosecutor friend of mine later told me this is preposterous) and he would ask for $25,000. Boll countered that if there had to be bail, it should be $65,000, as it had been in the recent Virnell Hunt case. That translates into about $425,000 in 2018 dollars. Judge Russell Mittelstadt said he would rule on it later.

Newspapers in Wisconsin, Michigan, and Minnesota were all over the murder case. One of the first articles to appear was in the afternoon *Madison Capital Times,* which not only listed the crime, but also described Suzanne as appearing in court in a three-piece dress suit and red high heels, and how she was a "tall, willowy blonde who wears her hair on a bun at the top of her head." This had to have been written by a man, I thought (and I was correct), because I don't think other women would find someone like Suzanne attractive. I've known a number of similar females whom men circle around like planets in orbit. They're not *un*attractive, but you wonder, *Hey, really?* And why would anyone think a five-foot-three woman is tall?

How is it possible that she spent the entire day, March 1, at the police station, then was taken to the state hospital that evening, and showed up in court the following morning in a suit and high heels, as was mentioned in one article? Did she pack a whole suitcase before she was arrested? If she really had been in a psychotic state as she claimed, how could she have managed to choose an outfit that seemed to coordinate and was surely designed to get attention? Which it obviously did.

How about bail? On March 11, Judge Mittelstadt set bail. Remember the DA had asked for $65,000 and her own attorneys requested $25,000? The judge set her bail at $15,000. I find it strange that in a capital case the judge would grant bail below what her own attorneys asked for. The judge evidently took pity on her, even though he immediately defended himself, saying he'd probably be criticized in some quarters, but that in such "domestic crimes, the chances of repetition are negligent." How many other husbands did she currently have whom she could kill? Defense attorney Orchard said Mrs. Stordock's financial situation was in a "muddle" because "she is accused of killing the individual from whose estate she would stand to benefit." So that's your defense, counselor? That she should be treated with care because she might get a heap of money from killing someone? It took her just thirteen days to raise the money and she was out of jail and back into the hospital on March 24.

Her attorney requested a delay (which the DA opposed) for the April 7 hearing, saying that some unnamed psychiatrists opposed subjecting Mrs. Stordock to the "trauma of a hearing." When I first read that, my heart stopped. *What about the trauma that my uncle experienced?*

There were more delays. The preliminary hearing went off on April 21. It started with Suzanne's attorney demanding copies of forensic photographs, which he claimed were taken at the request of the defense. In the hearing DA Boll objected, saying they were police photographs, but he didn't know, six weeks later, if they were even developed. Suzanne's attorney said some of the pictures were taken without Suzanne's permission. I thought, What? Sue just killed her husband, and when the police showed up, she kindly asked them to take pictures from a certain angle, so she'll have her Kodak moment?

Next we hear from Dane County's sheriff, Vernon "Jack" Leslie, who testified that the phone rang in his house at 2:30 A.M. (he knew this because he looked at the clock) on Sunday, March 1, and he let his wife answer. She handed the phone to him across the bed and he heard a female voice say, "This is Mrs. Stordock and I just shot my husband." Sheriff Leslie asked her to repeat her words and she said, "This is Suzi and I just shot Vern." The sheriff said he jumped out of bed within one to two seconds and headed toward the crime scene. But when he called the dispatcher from his car, he was informed that Mrs. Stordock and the detectives were on their way to the City-County Building. This makes it sound like perhaps Suzanne called *both* the sheriff's office *and* his home. In one of my interviews with Suzanne, she was immensely proud of herself that the first call she made was to Sheriff Leslie's home, as if no one else would have been that smart or that bold. According to police reports I got later, Sheriff Leslie phoned the dispatcher at 2:23, so Suzanne must have called him some minutes earlier, as he was outside already. Police reports have Suzanne calling the station at 2:19, so I surmise she called the sheriff at 2:17.

Later in the hearing an Officer Krupke (I am not making this up) said he got the call from the dispatcher around 2:20 A.M. and proceeded to the house with Officer Kenneth Pledger.

Krupke and his partner, Pledger, arrived at 2:28 A.M. Suzanne and David were waiting by the back door and let the officers in, and because the kitchen is the first room from the back door and the porch, I assume they stood in that room. Krupke asked where the person was and David said upstairs, so Krupke asked if it was a gunshot wound and Suzanne responded affirmatively. When Krupke asked if it was in the arm or leg or where, there was no response. So the officer said, "Take me to the person," and David started leading them up the closest stairway, the one right off the kitchen.

Now, it's important to understand that this house was the grandest home in town, placed on the Historic Register of Homes in 2007. An ornate Queen Anne with lots of original woodwork, its back stairs are very plain, with hardwood stairs and plain white plaster walls. Most likely, these were servant stairs back when the home was constructed in 1906. But if you walk through the kitchen and then the hallway that divides the dining room and the den, you enter the living room and, around to the other side of that room, you find the elegant half-open stairway bordered by a series of intricately carved spindles all the way up to the second floor. So, when Officer Krupke asked where the injured person was, and David took him to the closest stairway, Suzanne said, "No, you use the other stairway. It's better."

In the house, which I've visited multiple times in the past three years and many times before the murder, the two stairways are not close. You can see on the crime drawing (Figure 1) that the back stairs, shown on the top of the drawing, are quite close to the kitchen. In order to get to the front-room stairs, someone in the kitchen would have to walk around past the kitchen stairway, into the dining room, go all the way through the living room, to the other side of the house, to get up the ornate stairway. You'd need a guide, which they had in David.

You can interpret this behavior in a number of ways. If you don't know the people, it would be reasonable to assume Suzanne

First-Floor Layout

SUPPLEMENTARY REPORT

Case No. _____36189_____ Report By. _____Klein_____ Date _____3-1-70_____

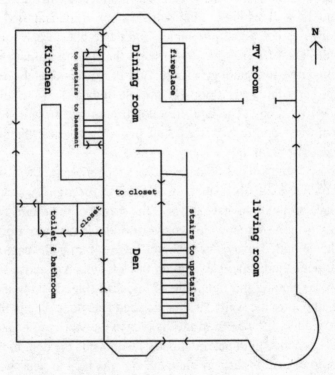

Ground floor room arrangement (not to scale)
357 North Main Street
Village of Oregon
Dane County, Wisconsin, 53575

Figure 1. (Re-creation of police diagram by Maxim Zhelev)

was in a state of shock. But remember, this is the person who just a few minutes previously had the mental capacity to look in her address book for the sheriff's home number and call him. This was a woman who cared about status and appearances. In this moment of absolute chaos, what prompted her to direct the police to the beautiful staircase?

Upstairs in the master bedroom the officers found the nude body, in a heap next to the bed, with a bullet hole in the headboard and the wall behind it. They saw no signs of life and tried to get a doctor to come and pronounce him dead, but no one was available. The officers spotted a rifle on the floor, a military weapon converted for hunting, with its bolt drawn completely back and one cartridge on the floor. The muzzle of the rifle was pointing toward the body. The bed, headboard, and walls were splattered with flesh and blood. Even the laundry basket near the door had pieces of brain in it.

According to police and coroner's reports, Vernie was sitting at the edge of his bed, looking slightly to the right, which would place him with his face towards the corner of the room. The only things in the corner were two chests of drawers whose front edges almost butted up against each other. One 8mm bullet came from a 30-degree angle and hit him on the left side, just above the temple, exploding the right side of his head (blood, skull and brain tissue) over the walls, headboard, bed and floor. The police estimated the distance from the shooter to the victim to be at least 8 feet, which would put the shooter just outside the door to the bedroom or a little farther. The weapon was held at what would be hip-height, which means the shooter either had to hold the gun below the waist or crouch down on one knee.

Under cross-examination Krupke said he got the call from the dispatcher at 2:20 A.M. This fits with the theory that Suzanne called the sheriff at 2:17, the police at 2:19, and then the sheriff called the dispatcher at 2:23 and learned the officers were already on their way.

After Krupke talked about finding the weapon, defense attorney Van Metre asked Krupke if the rifle wasn't in fact an 8mm Mauser. In my research I learned this was an extremely exact weapon, sometimes referred to as a "sniper's rifle." Vernie was a former cop and kept guns around. My aunt Maxine, Vernie's sister-in-law, explained to me that Vernie kept everything locked up in a gun case, and only he knew where they key was, though Maxine was pretty certain Suzanne knew where to find that key.

The coroner testified that a high-velocity missile (translation: bullet) wound to the head caused death, that the bullet entered the left side of the head, pretty close to the temple, and it went out in the same place on the right side, though much of that side of the head was blown off in the process. He was able to determine the angle from parts of the skull that remained. No powder burns were found, so it could not have been close range, and he estimated the rifle had been several feet away when the trigger was pulled. Death was instantaneous, and Vernie would not have been able to even move slightly after the shot. The coroner said the officers had informed him they found Vernie dead at 2:15 A.M.

Finally they called David to the stand. He testified he had been out that night on a date, getting home at 1:30 A.M., at which time his mother let him in the locked back door. He went to bed and couldn't sleep because his parents were arguing about a cigarette burn. So he called his girlfriend at 1:35 A.M., in bed, in his underwear. He said he was "on top of the bed with the covers over me." How can someone be both on top of the bed *and* with covers over him? It might sound innocuous, but the question of whether he was actually *in* bed was crucial to knowing what happened that night, though the DA never explored this aspect.

Then David went to sleep and the next thing he remembered was his mother coming into his room and waking him up, probably at 2:05 A.M. She said something about Vern, and because his parents had previously been arguing, he went to the bedroom and saw the body. He bolted downstairs, where his mother had gone, and she said something about a gun, so he ran back upstairs and saw the gun on the floor, picked it up to eject the shell, then went back downstairs, where his mother was on the phone. The DA asked David where the ammunition for the gun was kept, but he wasn't sure, which was not the same answer he gave to the police, but I didn't know that until months later. David was asked if he made his bed after all the commotion, and he replied that he hadn't.

I remember being a teenager and getting on the phone with my friends, male or female, and staying on for hours, so long that my stepfather threatened to pull the wall phone from its socket. So it makes no sense to me that a seventeen-year-old boy got home at 1:30 A.M., went all the way upstairs, took off his clothes, and got into bed within thirty seconds, then decided after five minutes he couldn't sleep. So he called his girlfriend, but he didn't talk for very long. He hung up, and fell so deeply asleep that he didn't hear a rifle blast that was more like cannon fire from the room right across the hall? All of this occurred while he was in his underwear, but not really under the covers. I remember that frigid Wisconsin night all too clearly. The howling wind, the temperature so cold your breath would freeze. And there was David, in that huge, old, drafty home that was built before anyone knew the word "insulation," and he didn't do anything to keep warm? And why did the DA ask him if he made his bed, but then did not follow up with it? How could David's bed been perfectly made, as the police (and Suzanne's brother to me) reported, when he testified he had been sleeping in it when his mother came to his door, after the shooting? Wouldn't they want to know *why* he evidently had not been in his bed? If he hadn't, that would call into question his testimony about the phone call while in bed. And where was any evidence about fingerprints on the weapon, gunshot residue on hands, or blood splatters, or angle of shooting to get a position on where the murderer was standing?

The final question DA Boll asked David was "You didn't shoot your father, did you?" To which he replied, "No, I didn't." A man is murdered in cold blood and the DA asked the only other person in the house that night—who, by the way, was known to have a facility with guns—whether he was the shooter, and then took him at his word.

The next day Boll was quoted in the *Capital Times* as saying that David answered that last question in such a hateful manner, he had to be telling the truth. I guess I missed that show on *Law & Order* where the DAs start assessing someone's guilt by the tone of his voice. Maybe they call it the "Modulation Defense."

After the preliminary hearing there were four delays, including one to change judges and another to change the prosecutor to an assistant district attorney (ADA). Boll was going off to army reserve camp and couldn't handle the case. My stepfather went to those summer camps and they were always two weeks long. With all these delays so far, he couldn't wait two weeks? ADA Victor Mussallem took the case. At the same time the DA dropped the first-degree murder charge down to first-degree manslaughter. The law had changed to become easier for mental insanity pleas, but only for cases charged from July 1, 1970. So dropping one charge and bringing another allowed Suzanne to fall under the more lenient guidelines. There were more delays until the final court session was scheduled for January 1971.

As I was going through the voluminous reports that I have in notebooks, and these take up one whole bookshelf in my office, I kept coming upon dates in July 1970. First was the idea that the law changed on July 1, as mentioned above. A motion of prejudice was filed against Judge Bardwell on July 13, resulting in Judge Norris Maloney being appointed. I spent two years puzzling over why the attorneys filed that motion against Judge Bardwell, and why did they wait months, until July, to do so? After rereading most of the court documents in 2017, I saw a new connection. Judge Bardwell had been the presiding judge at the murder trial of Hope Privett, mentioned previously. Despite two psychiatrists testifying that Privett could not have formed an intent to kill, on June 6, 1970, she was found guilty of first-degree murder and sentenced to life in prison.

One month later Suzanne's attorneys said she could not have a fair trial under Bardwell, the reason being that seven psychiatrists had evaluated her and that they were going to get charges reduced to manslaughter. Let's unpack this. What do the number of psychiatrists and an alteration in charges have to do with Bardwell? The court documents gave no reason that made any sense. Was it because Hope Privett had not received the insanity plea she had hoped for? And if her lawyers already knew the charges were to be changed, what deal had been made behind the scenes? As much as I searched, I never could find out why the original presider, Judge Mittelstadt, was replaced by Judge Bardwell.

Then on July 31 the case was turned over to Mussallem and the charge was reduced. What a good month July was for Suzanne. After some time, the final hearing was set for the following January.

At the end of that short twenty-minute capital-case final hearing in January 1971, Grandma and Aunt Maxine sat, waiting for the trial to continue, as everyone else got up to leave. They couldn't believe that the fate of someone's murder conviction would be so quickly resolved. My grandmother told me many years ago that right before the judge ruled, Suzanne went up and whispered something in the judge's ear. Grandma thought it was probably Suzanne telling him how her son really did it and she was protecting him, which only reflected our family's deep suspicion that David had actually pulled the trigger. A minute after that interaction, Suzanne was declared innocent by reason of mental defect at the time of the shooting. Her diagnosis was chronic paranoid schizophrenia.

During the hearing Mussallem said he interviewed all of the police officers who were at the murder scene and they said she was in a trancelike state (a determination not supported by the police reports), which bolstered the conclusion of mental insanity. Again, then, we've got key evidence in this case being decided by tone of voice, or *modulation*. Mussallem also tied his conclusions to the fact that she had between three to five cigarette burns on her back (the sheriff had testified several months previously that he had seen *one* burn on her back). Plus he had four psychiatrists (none of whom testified) who agreed with this, and one who did not. Dr. Joseph B. Brown—DA Boll's choice for evaluator—disagreed. He did not think Suzanne exhibited any of the characteristics of schizophrenia. Mussallem must have felt compelled to discredit his boss's selection, because he spent about half of the twenty minutes showing why Brown must be wrong. Mussallem argued Brown came to this diagnosis because he did not see Suzanne until March 10 (nine days after the murder), and, also, Brown could not possibly be correct, because the officers said she was not sane (this was not what was written in the police reports). But the most compelling reason for Mussallem was that Mrs. Stordock was taken Sunday night (same day as the shooting) to the university hospital for mental evaluation *before* she was arraigned on Monday morning. He did not think the state could overcome such a detrimental incident.

Even with more psychiatrists on the side of the defense, the biggest problem ("an extremely damaging element") seemed to be the obstacle that on the day of the shooting the defendant was transferred to the psychiatric hospital. And then trying to overcome the defense psychiatrists, Mussallem stated he had all the officers re-interviewed to see if their experience with Suzanne the night of the murder matched what the psychiatrists reported. Below is an excerpt from the transcript. (Note: Capitalization has been adjusted and italics have been added for emphasis.)

> MR. MUSSALLEM: . . . [A]ll of their statements are quite consistent with the diagnoses reached by the psychiatrists that the defense would offer, particularly that her behavior was not appropriate to the situation, that she seemed to be unusually calm, almost in a trance-like state. I don't feel that the testimony of any of these officers would in any way benefit the State's case. Indeed, it would probably be quite detrimental in that this would bolster up the conclusions reached by the defense psychiatrists.

All the officers said she was in a trancelike state? Which means, I suppose, she had no *modulation* in her voice. And the case depends, once again, on voice tone? And how about his excuse for not having the officers testify? Because they would bolster the defense case? Isn't that precisely what Mussallem was doing? How much worse could it possibly be to have a real, live witness who had been on the scene minutes after the murder? I discovered later, in the police reports that officers had described Suzanne as polite, calm, rational, cooperative, in charge of her faculties, and sane.

Musssalem did admit that Dr. Brown found no evidence of schizophrenia. And then the Assistant DA proposed the officers were more knowledgeable about schizophrenia, and by altering their reports to say she was in a trancelike state, he tried to argue she was schizophrenic. But that wasn't the worst.

> We are left in the . . . with *the very damaging fact that the defendant was removed from the jail on the very same day of the shooting and transferred to a mental facility.*

So I don't believe that the State has any chance
whatever of prevailing or being able to destroy or
overcome the case that could and I am sure would be put
on by the defense, and I don't really believe that any
function would be served by a trial.

I have tried for months to get my head around this concept,
how the transfer of Suzanne to the mental hospital for evaluation
became the reason they *must* grant insanity. Consider it: Dr. Washburn showed up at the jail the day of the murder and said Suzanne
needed psychiatric treatment, called in Dr. Leigh Roberts, and DA
Boll agreed to let her go be evaluated. Then, ten months later, that
transfer was used as an excuse for giving her the insanity plea?
We sent her for evaluation to see if she was sane, and because we
allowed her to be evaluated, she definitely is insane? A prosecutor
friend of mine said this was one of the most unsupported court
conclusions he's ever seen.

That was it. Case over. Suzanne was innocent and was transferred to Winnebago State Hospital. Under the new law she could
petition within a year whenever she thought she was cured. She
must have convinced the staff she was better, because they let her
out November 1971, after eleven months. It took another year for
the court to agree with her that she had "fully recovered her mental health," and then she evidently filed some final petition in
1973, when the court determined there was no likelihood of her
committing a serious crime again.

After further research, I discovered a legal requirement for periodic psychiatric reevaluations, as part of the initial verdict and
sentencing. However, when she was let out on parole in November 1971 and was declared mostly cured in March 29, 1973, it
was without any further reexamination since January 6, 1971, the
date of the hearing and her verdict.

The law did require some further exam, I assume, because she
petitioned the court in September 1973 to have a final exam and

to require only one psychiatrist instead of the normal two. The District Attorney at the time, Humphrey J. Lynch, approved her request. They got Dr. B. H. Glover, who had been the psychiatrist recommended by Suzanne's attorney back during the case in 1970, to now declare her without any mental defect, which was done in court January 29, 1974, less than three years after the murder. Did anyone think Glover would say she had a current mental defect?

One caveat, by the court. Suzanne was not supposed to have any guns in her home, but her son (presumably David) was allowed to borrow weapons from the Dane County Sheriff when he needed them, as long as they were returned.

What to make of this all? On March 2, 1970, Suzanne Stordock was arrested for first-degree (premeditated) murder, moments before she apparently told the police she would confess if they would consider her insane. As I look back on it now, the real thing that was premeditated was her insanity plea.

CHAPTER FIFTEEN
Family, Once-Removed

Finding people connected to Suzanne's past became an obsession with me. Lots of them were dead, such as her youngest son, her parents, two brothers, and others. She had one living brother, and there were two stepchildren from her fifth marriage. I felt I had to wait to talk to the stepchildren until I had interviewed Suzanne a few times and let her and Louisa know I was writing a book about the case.

When I first started this venture, I told myself I only wanted some answers, but as I started gathering all the evidence, I realized there was a story that was begging to be told. I researched with more focus and began writing, gradually telling Louisa about the project as it was actually developing *into* a real project. I let her know I was researching the old house, and as many things about Vernie as I could find, and that I was also interested in her mother as part of the story. Why was I hesitant to tell her the outcomes of my research and all the information I'd gotten from the police files? Maybe it was from the many times I'd seen her mother overreact when people did not behave as she wanted. So I didn't talk about what I'd found in the coroner's report and probate documents, worrying about the reaction of Louisa, who had only shown me a welcoming attitude and love. But I frequently suffered severe bouts of self-recrimination for not being completely open with Louisa, by asking so many seemingly innocent questions when I had an agenda. How could I live this way and pretend to be someone who values credibility? Don't I teach authenticity in my management courses?

I wasn't eager for them to know I wanted to contact Suzanne's only living brother, Franklin, but I was pretty sure there was no contact between him and Suzanne, according to things David and Louisa told me. Yet I didn't want to take the chance. I knew Franklin was in his eighties and could die at any time. It was a risk either way. I decided to wait.

I started looking for relatives of Suzanne's previous husbands. I spent scores of hours on the Internet after buying subscriptions to various heritage sites, looking for clues on relatives from her earlier marriages. L. Harry Chappington's other kids were not an option, because of the connection to Louisa, as I not only didn't want to spook her, but I also wondered if they would tell me the truth. But what about Irving Gast, her third husband? Turns out he had two sons (now in their sixties) by his first marriage. After a few weeks of sleuthing, I tracked them down—one in Madison, Wisconsin, who'd returned a couple years ago to get a doctorate in computer science, and the other a retired MD/health executive in Pennsylvania.

First I called Jim Gast, in Madison. His wife, Anne, answered. When I explained who I was, her voice perked up and accelerated, and she immediately told me the murder had been a subject of conversation in the family for many years. I found this fascinating, because they were only tangentially related to Suzanne, and even Suzanne's family had not talked about it much in the past forty years. I asked the wife about Jim's mother. "Oh, a horrible person," she said. "Back then—and today."

When I phoned later on, Jim answered on the first ring and started talking right away. His voice was deep and held a great deal of emotion, much of which I soon understood had been with him for a long, long time. He spoke at length about memories and stories he'd recounted over the years:

> Irv was never a good provider. When my brother was just two weeks old, Irv ran off to California, right after emptying the bank accounts, so my mother (Carolyn) had nothing. A year later she followed him out to California, hoping she'd get some money to support the family, but she had no idea where he was. The only clue Carolyn had was the address of a bookkeeper where Irv's father had wired him some money. She found Irv. His father, Abraham, encouraged him to give the marriage one more try. So, they got back together just long enough for me to be conceived and then got divorced. Afterward, my mother went back to Milwaukee and we moved in with her parents, who lived in one of the wealthier suburbs. My one and only memory of Irv was when he came to Milwaukee when I was two or three years old.
>
> One story I've heard a lot was about Abraham's estate. Suzanne had moved on by the time Abraham died in 1962, but she was still legally married to Irv. At the heirs' meeting in spring of 1963, Irv went there, expecting to get one-third of the generous estate. Little did he realize that his ex- and current wife would both materialize. Carolyn said she was owed a lot in child support, though Irv claimed he had paid her in cash. [*Author's note:* Jim was not sure who was telling the truth.] The meeting was taken over by Suzanne challenging Carolyn, and the two of them had a high-pitched and intensely high-decibel conflict, not paying any attention to Irv at all. In the end each of the women got half of Irv's share, and Irv got nothing.

Jim later told me Carolyn considered Suzanne her "arch-enemy," and it is likely because of this exchange, as well as Suzanne taking over Irv's life, when he should have been a better father to Mike and Jim.

Jim urged me to call his brother, Mike. Mike was evidently also waiting for me by the phone and probably had a little more time to think about their history than Jim had had earlier in the day. He answered on the first ring and I felt an instant rapport with him, as I had with his brother. How was it the three of us so circuitously related to Suzanne should feel such instant affinity?

I didn't know my father, only from stories from my mother and other family. My mother told me around 1955 Irv came to Park Forest, Illinois, where we were living, in order to try and strike a deal. But my mother already had an arrest warrant out for him for lack of child support. Suffice it to say, they did not reach any agreement, and Irv took off to Texas and perhaps got married and divorced again. No one knows for sure.

He came back to Madison in [the] late fifties, married Suzanne in 1959, and Danny was born in 1960. Suzanne converted to Judaism and joined the Jewish Congregation with Irv. Abraham had been brought up very conservative, so the congregation they belonged to was conservative, with women separated on one side, something Suzanne let everyone know she hated. Suzanne put forth some effort, but she was not well-liked by the other ladies at the temple. In truth, they despised her. There were reports of her trying to take charge and take credit for events and meetings. Sometimes she'd lose control and yell, and that didn't set well with anyone. The ladies were also scandalized by the way Suzanne treated Irv. She treated him badly in public and would denigrate him in front of others.

The marriage didn't go well, either. Irv was not a good provider, and he had problems with depression. Abraham had a very successful dry cleaning and tailoring company, and he kept giving Irv various business opportunities. None of them stuck. Irv got by in life by being good-looking and charming, tending toward the slick side.

Around a year after Danny was born, Irv showed up unannounced with Suzanne in Illinois and wanted us boys to meet our new brother. Carolyn did not agree. I remember seeing them for a few minutes before my mother sent us to a neighbor's. The last time I saw Irv or Suzanne was during the dispute over Abraham's inheritance back in 1963. Mike found out Irv had died in 1977 and later discovered he'd had two or three other marriages. One was a half-year before he died and only lasted a couple of months.

In 1980 I got a call from Danny, who, by the way, I hadn't seen since he was a year old. He was twenty and had driven down to St. Louis with three friends and wanted all of them to move into my house. Here was a kid I didn't know, who just showed up and expected me to take care of him. But I was a poor medical student at Washington U, with three young kids and no money. I couldn't take him in. Plus I'd heard too many stories about all the drugs and alcohol he was into. Danny said if they didn't stay with me, they were going to live out of his car. I had no idea how they intended to support themselves, but I had heard growing up he was a kick-around kid with no stability in his life, that he was in foster care for a while and then ended up being raised after the murder by some kindly black woman named Mrs. Freeman. Danny referred to her by that name, Mrs. Freeman. He spoke of her very lovingly and referred to Mrs. Freeman as his sister, though one of a different generation.

At this point I was thinking that Suzanne probably had what is now referred to as "attachment disorder," because she had divorced or discarded four husbands, had essentially abandoned her youngest kid, and evidently had issues in her relationships with the other two children.

Now I had to put my attention back to Mike Gast:

> You mentioned Suzanne had five husbands. Well, my mother had four. She changed husbands and boyfriends weekly. I saw her use sexuality with husbands, coworkers, and friends. Even late into her forties she wore provocative clothes and miniskirts. When I was in college, she came to campus to be housemother, but in those few weeks she blew through a series of affairs, even though she was married at the time.
>
> Her style could be described as reactive, with frequent blowups. She was very controlling of Irv, also high-strung and quite difficult to deal with, which sounds similar to what I've heard about Suzanne. My father was evidently attracted to women who did not treat him well.
>
> As to your uncle and why he left a kind and loving woman for Suzanne, it reminds me of a cop friend I had in St. Louis. The stresses of his job did not lend themselves to a stable marriage. He had a simple life with two kids that he threw away and went after more edginess with a sexually libertine woman.

When I later recounted this to my cousin Shannon, she seemed to stop breathing on the other end of the phone wires and then spoke haltingly, telling me what an old Beloit friend of hers had said. To paraphrase the exchange, Vernie needed a woman who was controlling and would tell him what to do. Shannon's mother was not that kind of woman. Shannon murmured she never understood her friend's comments before—not until I shared the Gast brothers' stories.

And what happened to Irv? Louisa had told me Irving surfaced in the 1970s as a born-again Christian. But Jim Gast told me he had never heard anything about his father and a religious conversion, and he'd only found out his father had died in San Francisco in 1977 when looking him up on Google in the early days of the Internet.

Two and a half years after our first interaction, I called Mike Gast again, to make sure it was all right to use his name in the book. We talked for nearly an hour and I once again felt the connection with a decent and kind man, who was willing to chat with me about various incidents in his family. I had come across photos of Danny since we last talked. Would he want some? Oh yes, definitely. As I was thanking him for his cooperation, he became quiet for a moment and continued, "Both Jim and I want to thank you for doing this research, because you've helped us fill holes in our childhood, aspects we knew little about, and it is been very healing for us. We really appreciate your work."

His comment caught my attention. I had not realized the degree to which what I was uncovering would be helpful to those outside my immediate family.

Then I moved on to husband number two, John Briggs, the father of David. My research showed he had died in 1974, and he had a brother who was evidently still alive, but try as I might to find his current location or phone number, or that of two previous wives and children, I kept getting, "This number is no longer in service." Then I found a real estate transaction recording his sale of a house. After more digging and wrong numbers, I finally got someone to answer the phone and asked if she knew where Joseph Briggs was. He's right next to me, she said, and gave him the phone. I gave my name and my relation to Suzanne, his brother's wife, and asked if he remembered anything about the family, or had heard anything about the murder. He kept saying things like, "not really," to any questions I had. After about four minutes he suddenly energized and said, "Oh, you're talking about my brother's *first wife*." And then went on:

> I only saw his wife once, back when I was eighteen, and took a bus from Tennessee to Madison, where my brother was studying, and I don't really remember anything about her. I was just a kid. And then the divorce and her later marriages, my parents protected me from all of that. But I will tell you that I got a call back in the early seventies from David, my nephew, asking if he could stay with me—with us—for a while. Naturally I said he could and then later regretted that decision. Things didn't work out. I was a pastor of the Baptist Church. I was married with two daughters, and David would be out drinking, chasing girls, hanging out with the motorcycle gang. So he had to go. But he did talk about the murder, saying he had witnessed it. I have no contact with them now.

So, despite Suzanne telling me she was close to Joseph, he barely remembered her and mostly recounted the problems with David.

When I researched Suzanne's fifth husband, Ronald Aaronson, I discovered his parents were Holocaust survivors and he had married a woman who had evidently emigrated from Austria as a young woman. Susan Weisz and Ronald remained married until her death in 1974, when their two children were in high school. I learned that Ronald was an innovator in the field of optometry and spent many years on eye-health service projects around the world. His heart was as big as the continent of Africa, where he often traveled and worked.

Surely his wife's death in 1974 was a painful blow to Ronald and his children. Four years later, he married Patricia Murray, who was from Bemidji, Minnesota. The marriage did not work out and they divorced later. Suzanne told me several times that she met Ronald because the rabbi said they were two lonely people who should meet. All very touching and romantic, until I remembered two things: (1) Suzanne had told me on that first visit that her dissertation on parental kidnapping had been done as a replication of her stepdaughter's research; and (2) An old letter I found from Suzanne dated May 1981 was partly about her research project on parental kidnapping.

Putting this all together, I deduced that Suzanne made a move on Ronald sometime in late 1980 or early 1981, and I assume more like 1980, because I know how long it takes to get a research project under way, and funded even, as Suzanne reported in the letter. Ronald was in his second marriage in 1980 and '81. Suzanne wanted him, so she found a way through his daughter to get his attention. It took maybe a year to get wife number two out of the way. The divorce went through on September 25, 1981, and then she and Ronald were married in August 1983. I don't know why they waited two years, except that Suzanne told me Ronald would never confront anyone, so I imagine him getting his two grown children to accept a third wife must have been a formidable task.

Louisa told me about Ronald's children. Jeremiah, the oldest, was a rabbi in the Northeast, and Alexandra was a therapist in the South. They were close and were more than a stepfamily. I looked them up and found the twenty-fifth-year scholarly honor for Jeremiah from rabbinical school. It listed his parents as Ronald Aaronson and Suzanne Brandon. No mention of his departed mother. Further searching gave me a website that Jeremiah had put up himself about his family tree, listing his parents as Ronald Aaronson and Susan Weisz, never listing Suzanne Brandon.

Louisa mentioned a couple of times about how wonderful it would be if I happened to visit at the same time as Ronald's daughter. The second time she said it, she just stopped, looked at me, and said, "You need to understand that Jeremiah and Alexandra don't know anything about what happened [code for the murder]. Mom and Ronald thought it was best to make a fresh start in their new life." Her face registered a sternness that was not normal for the tenderhearted Louisa. I got her message: *If you want to meet Alexandra, you have to accept our version of reality.* I didn't say anything. But I wondered: *What if my father remarried a woman who had murdered her previous husband? Wouldn't I want to know his new wife was a confessed killer?*

CHAPTER SIXTEEN
Franklin, with Key Information

After fourteen months into my research I realized that I *had* to talk to Suzanne's brother. My heart beat fast as I dialed Franklin's phone number, the one it had taken me months to find. Franklin had lived in numerous places after Wisconsin, including Las Vegas, Montana, and now, Washington State, but there were also various other Franklin Brandons scattered around the country. His wife had died, but I had no idea if he had a girlfriend, or had remarried, and I certainly did not know if he'd want to talk about a crime his sister admittedly committed some forty-five years previously. What if he started cussing at me and hung up?

Franklin lived in the Pacific Time Zone, which was three hours earlier for me, so I waited until very late at night to call, thinking I could catch him even if he'd been out and about during the day. It was May 1, 2015, and he answered on the third ring. His voice was deep and smooth, and I imagined in other circumstances he could have been a radio announcer, and that he surely must have had women swoon just by hearing him speak. He knew right away who Vernie was, and we both had some faint recollection of meeting one another at a family gathering ages ago. I told him I was doing some research for a writing project about my uncle and his murder. He did not hesitate and answered readily, but in a

slow, deliberate voice that suggested he was not covering up anything. Here are some of his comments:

> That murder's been a mystery ever since it happened.
> And the killing was so unexpected. Vernie and Suzanne
> seemed to get along great. I went and visited her in the
> hospital and asked her why. She said he burned her with
> a cigarette and that was the last time he was going to hurt
> her. Well, I never even knew they had any problems, but
> I'll tell you this. She didn't shoot him. It was that simple.
> David did it. He was always a renegade kid and Vernie
> was a narcotics officer. They didn't get along at all. And
> that day Vernie told him he had to get a haircut, because
> he had this big, bushy 'do. When I asked what happened,
> Suzanne told me she had gone and got the rifle off the
> gun rack in the den, came up, raised the gun, and then
> shot him. But I knew she was fibbing.
>
> I went over to the house the next day with my brother
> Bob. I got out of the car and asked him to wait for
> me, as I wanted to go there alone. Sometimes I just get
> a feeling about things. I went upstairs to the master bed-
> room. Straight across from the bedroom door was the
> door to another bedroom, which belonged to Daniel, who
> had not been home that night. In the doorway of that
> bedroom was a chair with several pairs of pants lying
> over the back. I walked over to the wall where the bullet
> had lodged, took a pencil and stuck it first in the head-
> board, and then in the wall, so I could see the angle the
> bullet traveled. Then I walked into Daniel's room and
> had to step over the seat of the chair to get in. And I just
> lay my hand down across those pants and held my finger
> out there. I was looking straight at the pencil. I knew that
> was where the shot had been fired. My sister claimed she
> went to David's room after she shot Vernie, to wake up

David. The hall in the upstairs was maybe twenty feet long, but it made no difference, because he could not have slept through the blast from a Mauser 8mm rifle. And I know they took my sister and David out of the house pretty quickly, so nothing had been touched. I went to David's bedroom and there were so many wine bottles I couldn't count them. But his bed was perfectly made. No one had slept there.

Later on, David came to visit me in Las Vegas and I sat on the porch and accused him. All he said was he wouldn't deny it. I supposed my sister took the rap for him because she is his mother, and she was trying to protect him. My brother told me a few years later that we've seen two murders that people got away with. The other one was our oldest brother, Jimmy, who got out of the navy after World War II and was working for some wealthy woman in Michigan, who was going through a divorce. Her story was that Jimmy came to wake up the husband at six A.M. and the pistol fell out of his inside pocket, hit the floor, and accidentally fired and took off the bottom of his heart. I saw the autopsy reports and there was no way the trajectory of the bullet matched her story, but they were rich folks in Crystal Falls, Michigan, and they could afford expensive attorneys.

You know, I have a hard time calling her Suzanne, because her given name was Elmira, and it broke my parents' hearts when she changed it as soon as she got out on her own. Elmira was one of my dad's favorite aunts.

Franklin continued:

Well, Elmira always was uppity and too good for us. Forced my dad to work extra jobs to pay for her to go to

high school in Boscobel, because Mount Hope wasn't
good enough for her. She boarded with a family who
owned a drugstore and did some work to help pay for
her room. She always got mad at me when I called her
"Elmira," but the hell with it. But Elmira was always
going to school and it was our responsibility to pay for it.
That's why my dad got crippled for the last twenty-four
years of his life. She needed to pay college tuition in
Madison, and dad wasn't earning enough money on the
farm, so he took a roofing job, and right at the end the
ladder came unhooked and he fell down thirty-two
feet and mangled his foot. So he gimped around for
twenty-four years.

My sister got married, I don't know, four or five
times, but when she married Vernie, we all said, finally
she's got a regular guy, a good guy. They both came out
to Las Vegas and I took them out on my boat. We had so
much fun.

But her kids, well, David was heavy into drugs.
Even when he got married—to an older woman—in
Tennessee, his wife tried to get him off drugs, but then
she finally gave up and divorced him. He was useless.
And Danny, well, he never had a chance. He was one
troubled kid.

Then I told Franklin I had been searching for eight months,
looking for a marriage license for Vernie and Suzanne, coming
up with nothing. I had checked with the State of Wisconsin Vital
Records, twice, having them look between the years of 1963
through 1970, even though Vernie wasn't actually divorced until
1964. Shannon had told me she heard they got married before his
divorce was final. And I also checked with Dane County, just in
case, even though the records were from the same database. I
looked everywhere, including Las Vegas, where Franklin had pre-

viously lived, and in Minnesota, where Suzanne later lived. Neither David nor Louisa could tell me exactly when the marriage took place.

Louisa did remember one time, though, that Danny had found Vernie and Suzanne naked in bed when Louisa was fifteen, which puts it in late 1963 or early '64, but the kids were told it was all right, because they were already married. When I told this to Franklin, he said, "I never heard anything about a wedding from either of them, so maybe they just told people they were married." I told him I had asked Suzanne, but she couldn't remember when they got married, despite the fact she could recall very specific details from that time period about my mother being a school bus driver and details about my aunt Maxine. Franklin's response, "Memory was never a problem with anyone in our family. Louisa told me recently about all the memories Suzanne tells her, and our brother Bob was sharp right until the end."

In a second call to Franklin a few weeks later, he reiterated much from the first time, but I asked him this time if he thought Suzanne was mentally ill or insane. "Absolutely not. No one in the family ever was. And when I heard about her insanity plea," he said, "I realized she had conned the system. She's always been smart and tries to fool people. This time it worked." When I told him some of the reports said Suzanne had described herself as coming from an abusive family, where her parents fought all the time and got divorced, Franklin got upset:

First of all, my parents were married up until my father died in 1974. Second, she was always telling people our family was violent and I told her those four years you were there before I was born must have been pretty intense, because those aren't my memories. The only time I remember my father raising his voice, or a hand to my mother, was one day when she kept complaining over and over about money and wanted to go and buy something. He raised a newspaper up to her and swatted her, just once. I never saw him do anything like that again.

Then I told Franklin that Suzanne had told the psychiatrist she had tried to kill herself in August 1966. Had he ever heard about it? At this one, he laughed. She knew what to say, he noted, to get an insanity verdict.

CHAPTER SEVENTEEN

The District Attorney, Lawyers, Judges, and Sheriff

The newspapers reported on Monday, March 2, 1970, that District Attorney James C. Boll was in charge of the investigation and made an announcement the day before he would seek first-degree murder charges. He stayed on the case until August, when he turned it over to ADA Victor Mussallem, who ended up with the quickly dispensed insanity plea.

Who was this new guy? I saw pictures of him in the newspaper and he had this gangly, nerdy appearance, with black curly hair and glasses. He looked like someone who was smart in school but perhaps socially awkward. He graduated from UW–La Crosse in 1965. Back then it was called Wisconsin State University at La Crosse and was pretty much a backwater school. Mussallem did get admitted and graduated from UW–Madison Law School, which is impressive, and he went into private practice for a year until he got hired as assistant district attorney in Racine, Wisconsin, one of the medium-sized cities in the state, and the original home of Golden Books, one of the earliest and most successful children's publishers. Right after his stint in Racine, Mussallem became ADA in Madison, which would have been a much better position. His first day on the job was March 2, 1970, the day Suzanne was arraigned.

Here we have a capital case of a cop killer, as my uncle had been in law enforcement his whole life, and it got turned over to someone two years out of law school, who'd only been on the job five months. And as soon as Mussallem took over, the murder charges got dropped and changed to manslaughter so that Suzanne was then under the more lenient revised state legal statute and she ultimately got off. This part has been really difficult to get my mind around, because Boll was such an upstanding guy. He was so clean you'd think he had a squeegee man following behind him on the occasion of his retirement from being district attorney and going into private practice.

It only gives more weight to what most of my family believed, there was some behind-the-scenes deal. Perhaps someone was pressuring Boll and he had too much conscience to go along with it himself, but not enough to prevent it.

So he gave the case to an inexperienced ADA, who gladly took over. And why wouldn't someone like Mussallem bend the law a little? He got fired from his position two years later in 1972 for appropriating porno films that had been seized in a raid and showing them at parties. He challenged the firing and it dragged out for more than a year with the subsequent DA, who said Mussallem had poor attitude, poor performance, and created a morale problem in the office. Mussallem was taken to court in 1980 by the Wisconsin Board of Regents for $4,630, plus $1,100 interest on his law school loans. Mussallem argued that since he hadn't paid them off in six years, he didn't owe any more. The court did not agree.

Time was not kind to Victor Mussallem. The Wisconsin Supreme Court suspended his license (meaning he was disbarred) for three months in 1991, citing instances in 1988 and 1989 where he forged prescriptions for controlled substances and was subsequently imprisoned for three months in a federal medical facility, where he participated in a program for drug abuse. He died in 1999 at the age of fifty-six.

Mussallem was unavailable for an interview, but what about Boll, the original prosecutor? It took me weeks to track him down.

During that time I learned that Boll's wife of fifty-five years had died in 2012, some years after they'd moved to Florida. Then it was more weeks before he finally answered his phone. There was no voice mail option, but I wouldn't have used it, anyway. I wanted to hear the immediate reaction to me asking about the case. And I wished I could see his face, too, which from newspaper pictures appeared intelligent and kind, with a rectangular shape, strong jaws, and dark, straight hair, as you'd expect of a stalwart hero.

Finally, the night of March 8, 2015, I heard James Boll's voice on the line. I told him my name and that I was the niece of LaVerne Stordock, who was murdered on March 1, 1970, and that Vernie's wife, Mrs. Suzanne Stordock, had confessed, and that Boll had originally prosecuted the case. Did he recollect it?

Without the hesitation of even one-half second, he replied, "No, I don't remember anything about it." There was no pause, no asking for me to repeat the names or the dates, just, "No, I don't remember anything about it." He went on to tell me he had three other murder trials that summer, which, by the way, he had no difficulty recounting. We talked very pleasantly for forty-five minutes, with him telling me about all the challenges of being district attorney in Madison during the student riots. There was nothing wrong with his memory, as far as I could tell.

He asked me details about the case and then expressed surprise that Suzanne got off on bail.

"We usually didn't give bail in those kinds of capital cases," he said. Did I have the police reports? he wondered. Not yet, I told him.

"So, when you get them," he said, "feel free to call me back."

"Really?" I said.

"Oh, yes, I'll help you with those. That's what DAs work with, police reports."

When I got the police reports the following week, I thought I'd fly down to Florida and have a meeting with him. I called James Boll and noticed he now had voice mail. I didn't leave any voice mail the first few times, kept hoping I'd just catch him; then finally I left a message that I got the reports and was coming down to Florida to visit some friends and would love to meet him. He didn't call back. I left two more messages over the coming week, then tried to call him while I was in Florida, but never heard back. I guess he wasn't so eager to talk to me, after all.

Still, DA Boll has a snow-white background. Untouched by scandal, always fighting for justice, he's completely admirable. Then why did he turn over the Stordock prosecution and then distantly supervise this murder case that looked nothing like the other ones in Dane County at that time? I can't answer that. But I do know that Victor Mussallem, who took over the prosecution, was less admirable, as described earlier.

I tried to find other major players who might be corruptible. If there was some behind-the-scenes deal and cover-up, there likely were several people involved. Using the database resources at my disposal, I started doing background checks and newspaper searches on the major players. I looked at Sheriff Leslie, the first person Suzanne called (according to her and Officer Pledger)—at his home—after the murder. And how was it she happened to have his private number? As I researched Leslie, at first all I saw was the fact that he and Franz Haas had traded positions as sheriff and undersheriff since 1953, and how Leslie was a family man with eight kids and had two sons serving in Vietnam. He looked like a cross between Jack Nicholson and Gary Busey, and had nothing of the "heroic" quality Boll had in his pictures.

Around June 1968, when Franz Haas decided he wanted to remain sheriff and was not going to hand it back to Leslie as they'd done for fifteen years in their usual go-round, Leslie got mad and said he was going to run against Haas. That's when the first cracks appeared, because in previous elections, Leslie never had any real competition. I mean, consider that 80 percent of the newspaper articles about the sheriff involved property foreclosures, and most of the rest about traffic problems. The pay wasn't that great. So perhaps that's why there was not a long line of applicants for the job. As soon as Leslie announced his candidacy, Haas fired him.

One problem in this bureaucratic uncoupling for Leslie was that both he and Haas were Democrats, so Leslie switched parties, claiming that he was completely in favor of the Vietnam War and could not abide by the Democratic Party's position.

The University of Wisconsin newspaper broke a story in late 1968 about how one of Leslie's sons, a returned vet, had been beating up antiwar protestors, and Leslie had kept it secret.

Worse problems surfaced in the following campaign, in 1972, against William Ferris. News started leaking out about the twelve— no, fourteen—and then, ultimately, twenty-three accidents in which Leslie had been driving an official county car, and many times under the influence. Somehow he'd managed to squelch this news. Then there was the time he joined with brewery companies to oppose the state's proposed increase in the drinking age from eighteen to twenty-one, even with solid evidence that the age increase would drastically reduce highway deaths.

As sheriff, Leslie claimed he didn't want to hire more officers. Then it came out he had violated campaign laws in recent campaigns, and his private security company was protecting ticket buyers attending entertainment that the Dane County DA had alleged was obscene. There were many more indiscretions, but one notable one was how he appointed one thousand special deputies with badges, who were authorized to carry guns, many of whom were bar owners who used their special status to wiggle out of legal offenses.

It got so bad that a large group of Republicans started a "Dump Leslie" movement in September. The tide had turned. Not only did Richard Nixon win on November 7, 1972, by a landslide, but so did Democrat William H. Ferris for sheriff. While Nixon carried forty-nine states and got 61 percent of the popular vote, Ferris got 63 percent of the votes in Dane County, with a 2–1 lead. Taking away the other five candidates who trailed them, Ferris got 72 percent more than Leslie. The public had spoken.

Can we conclude from this evidence that Leslie was corruptible? Definitely. Was he involved in the obfuscation in Suzanne Stordock's case? Perhaps, but I haven't yet proven it. So far, I've established two major players in the Stordock case had serious ethics violations and censures.

If you think of this case as a three-legged stool, of law enforcement, district attorney, and medical experts, what about the doctors involved? I found in December 2015 that the state's main psychiatrist, Dr. Leigh Roberts, was notorious for granting insanity pleas to anyone and everyone. He looked a great deal like Ned Beatty in *Deliverance*, only Roberts was even chunkier and had thick, black hair. Roberts later lost his medical license for having sex with a patient, which says to me he is not only corruptible, but especially vulnerable to women who employ what they used to call "feminine wiles." And we already know Suzanne used sex to get what she wanted. How many times did I hear her announce Vernie would not get any more until he did what she wanted? A psychiatrist I consulted about Roberts's license forfeiture noted, "That's all you need to tell me and I then discount anything he says."

So *every* leg of that stool was ethically wobbly. What I am saying is that each of the three main law-enforcement players had corruption issues. Sheriff Leslie, whom Suzanne phoned right after the murder, was run out of office because of ethical abuses. The assistant district attorney, who ultimately prosecuted the case, was later disbarred, and the state's main psychiatrist, upon whose assessment the insanity plea was based, lost his medical license some time later.

I next started to think that I should look beyond ethics. Maybe that wasn't the whole story. What about Boll and his office and the context of where the law was in 1970? Maybe one of the reasons Suzanne got off so easily is that Wisconsin and much of the country was going through a period of feeling more empathy toward the accused. Lighter sentences, more sympathy for extenuating circumstances, for difficult childhoods, for effects of poverty, and so on. It was this sort of leniency that was criticized by the right wing and got much attention from President Reagan onward, when candidates would become more popular if they ran on a "law and order" platform.

I decided to look at the evidence, specifically those three other murder cases DA Boll claimed he had the summer of 1970. Fortuitously, any murder case in Dane County was reported in the two Madison newspapers, so I had no trouble researching them. He had remembered almost accurately. Actually, there were four other cases that summer, but I am thinking Boll wasn't counting one of them, because it was adjudicated by the very beginning of June, and maybe that didn't seem quite summer yet. The other cases were:

1. Mrs. Hope Thomas Privett, thirty, mother of two, who murdered a Sun Prairie coworker/lover, Harold Vernig, thirty-five, on November 23, 1969, and went for the insanity plea. Privett was recently divorced, and Vernig was going through a divorce. Privett was held without bail. Parents and wife of Vernig were the first round of witnesses, called by the defense. Privett was represented by attorney Darrell MacIntyre, who came with a long and impressive list of defense counsel successes. James Boll prosecuted and spent five days in court proving his case. Judge

Richard W. Bardwell presided. Hope Privett was found guilty of first-degree murder on June 6, 1970. Sentenced to life imprisonment in Taycheedah Prison for Women.

2. Odell White, thirty-three, pleaded innocent to murdering Robert Borchardt, on June 27, 1970, in a traffic dispute between two strangers at a stoplight, with White insisting throughout that the gun had gone off accidentally. Bail was set at $50,000, which he was never able to raise, so he stayed in jail. White was found guilty of first-degree murder (which meant the jury thought intent was present) on November 12, 1970, and sentenced to life in prison with hard labor. He fought back sobs as the verdict from the jury came in. White's attorney was Harold Jackson, with Judge Bardwell presiding. ADA Andrew L. Somers was the prosecutor.

3. Virnell Hunt, twenty-five, pleaded insanity in the murder of Jeanne Francis Schroeder Broomell, twenty-two-year-old housewife found in her bed by her husband, on January 20, 1970. Hunt was found guilty by a jury of first-degree murder on July 29, with a mandated life imprisonment, according to Wisconsin statute. James Boll led a five-day prosecution, followed by attorney Richard E. Lent's defense. Hunt was originally held without bail, but that was changed and bail was set at $65,000, which he was not able to raise, so he remained in jail. Norris Maloney was the judge.

4. Russell Buckner, nineteen, was charged with first-degree murder (of Robert O'Donahue, twenty-two) and robbery for an August 17, 1970, holdup in a bar. He was held on $100,000 bail. His "partner in crime," Rodney Beales, twenty-one, was charged with third-degree murder and robbery, also held on $100,000 bond, with Jack van Metre as defense counsel. Buckner was found guilty of second-degree murder and sentenced. Two others were arrested and they turned state's evidence, one of whom

was sentenced to eighteen years in prison and the other
offered immunity for testimony. Prosecutor was Assistant Attorney General Andrew L. Somers, who was com-
pleting a case he had as ADA. Defense attorney was
William Coffey of Milwaukee. Buckner was found guilty
of second-degree murder on January 23, 1971, and
sentenced to forty years, with Judge Bardwell presiding.
Since Rodney Beales's case was delayed for so long,
until February 1972, his bail was mercifully reduced to
$5,000, which he was able to raise. Almost eighteen
months after the murder and robbery, Beales was found
innocent, as some witnesses testified he never even
entered the tavern.

5. Suzanne Stordock, forty-one, charged with first-degree
murder of husband and lifelong law enforcement
professional LaVerne Stordock. First judge was Richard
Mittelstadt, who set bail at $15,000. Then Judge
Bardwell got the case. A few months later attorneys
requested a new judge because of prejudice, and Judge
Norris Maloney was assigned. Original prosecutor was
DA James Boll, who turned case over to the assistant
district attorney, Victor Mussallem, at the same time the
charges were dropped to first-degree manslaughter. Her
final hearing lasted less than thirty minutes. She got the
insanity plea.

Here's a table with the summary information regarding the
other Dane County first-degree murders prosecuted in that same
time period of Suzanne Stordock's case of 1970 through 1971
(see table on pp. 152–153).

What does it all add up to? Not counting the two men who
turned state's evidence, there were, including Suzanne, six people
charged with murder and five of those with first-degree murder,
three of whom sought the insanity plea. Only one of the five had
killed a cop, and that same person was the only one who got out

Murders in Dane County, Wisconsin, in Same Time Period as Stordock Case, 1969–71

Dates, murder–final trial	Name of murderer & gender	Victim's name & gender	Charged with
November 1969–June 1970	Hope Thomas Privett, female	Harold Vernig, male	1st degree murder
January–July 1970	Virnell Hunt, male	Jeanne Broomell, female	1st degree murder
June–November 1970	Odell White, male	Robert Borchardt, male	1st degree murder
August 1970–January 1971	Russell Buckner, male	Robert O'Donahue, male	1st degree murder
March 1970–January 1971	Suzanne Stordock, female	LaVerne Stordock, male—the only cop among the victims	1st degree murder, dropped to 1st degree manslaughter, July 1970

on bail, the only one found not guilty, the only one who got the insanity plea, and the only admitted (or judged) killer not sent to prison, and that fortuitous person was Suzanne B. Stordock.

Perhaps some could argue that a white woman being tried would tend to be treated more favorably back in 1970. If that's true, let's compare the prosecutions of Suzanne Stordock with that of Hope Privett. Both were accused of first-degree murder.

1. Both killed a lover (alleged husband, in the case of Suzanne) who was threatening to leave.

Murder victim	Plea	Bail	Verdict	Sentence
Coworker, lover	Insanity	No bail	Guilty, 1st degree murder	Life in prison
Stranger, broke in house	Insanity	No bail; later changed to $65,000, but couldn't raise	Guilty, 1st degree murder	Life in prison
Stranger in traffic dispute, road rage	Innocent	$50,000, couldn't raise, stayed in jail	Guilty, 1st degree murder	Life in prison with hard labor
Stranger in bar during robbery	Innocent	$100,000, never raised, stayed in jail	Guilty, 2nd degree murder	40 years in prison
Husband, police officer	Insanity	$15,000, set after 8 days, out of jail 3 weeks after murder	Innocent by reason of insanity	11 months in mental hospital

2. Both went for an insanity plea.
3. Only Suzanne got out on bail.
4. Despite two doctors testifying that Privett could not have formed an intent to kill, and despite the fact she was barely saved from a suicide attempt not long before her trial, Hope was denied her insanity plea, and convicted of first-degree murder.
5. Total pages for Privett's hearings and trial were 635, with Suzanne's ninety-seven. Whereas DA Boll spent five days on Privett's prosecution and the final trial

transcript was 423 pages, Suzanne's final hearing produced fourteen pages of transcript.

6. Hope was sentenced to life in prison at Taycheedah Prison for Women. Suzanne was judged insane at the time of the shooting and spent eleven months in the state mental hospital and was free for the rest of her life.

I realized at this point in the Stordock research that I had a bias I was not even aware of. Despite Wisconsin being the home of Joseph McCarthy and McCarthyism, I also knew it was the place where the La Follette family and William Proxmire had practiced progressive and clean government. Isn't that how I would describe the land where I grew up? And yet, even though I went into this research believing Wisconsin was a fair and honest state and not *really* accepting my family's contention that there had been some backroom deal, I started to think the Wisconsin judicial system in the 1970s was looking a great deal like I imagined Mississippi was back in the 1930s.

Accepting this new reality caused such dissonance inside me, forcing me to challenge deep beliefs about the integrity of Wisconsinites, that I questioned whether I could continue my quest. Would the price I had to pay inside myself be worth it in the end?

CHAPTER EIGHTEEN

Asking Questions with Suzanne

I ventured into the country called "The Suzanne Formerly Known as Psychotic" in hopes of understanding what had happened the night of the murder.

I posed a lot of queries to Suzanne during the four times I went to visit her, and I tried, very consciously, to ask open-ended questions, which have been scientifically proven to elicit longer responses. In the beginning I just wanted some answers, and I had some abiding hope that merely knowing what had happened that night could balance the injustices everyone in my family had felt. Looking for any legal justice was not my aim, or so I had convinced myself, that is, until months later when I came face-to-face with three Dane County detectives. But at that time I remember deciding that I was hoping for some confession that would give me a sense of justice and, in the end, some answers.

During that first visit in February 2014, I walked into the house of a family that had blacktopped over the cobblestones of family history for decades, having conveniently forgotten, or at best sidetracked, the fact that one of their members was a murderer. Enter Dorothy, with a compulsively optimistic, naïve belief that somehow these former relatives would open up the truth, a commodity that had been welded over with steel-girded stories in a kind of collective loss of memory.

As much as I tried to engage Suzanne in conversation about Vernie, the most I got from her was "Husbands. What I learned is they are all boring." She told me that numerous times during our visits, and I came to understand that men would be enthralled with her sexual energy at the beginning. However, once they started to see the real Suzanne, they ceased being captivated by her, and she lost interest.

But I never really understood why men were drawn to her. She wasn't particularly pretty, just sort of decent-looking and thin. Perhaps it was pheromones. I've tried to look up articles in scholarly journals, and I've interviewed psychologists and asked many men to give me some insight. Part of what I've learned is this type of woman has a nonverbal way of letting men know she is obtainable. We can call it the "Availability Factor." Maybe it's the way she looks at him, or touches her own breast, or fingers a drinking straw, or how she pretends to, at the same time, be out of his reach. "Someone like that is irresistible," declared a male friend.

I got an even better answer from a writer friend. He went into emotional overdrive when I explained how Suzanne would sit next to Vernie in the front seat of the car, with me on the passenger side, as her left hand would quietly remain on his right thigh, with her pinky touching the crotch area. "You told me everything about her in that one action," he said explosively. He continued:

> A woman who would practically grab a man's genitals in front of his eighteen-year-old niece, back in the 1960s, was an alpha woman and someone comfortable with overt sexuality. Any man who might have challenged her would have been discarded. The fact that your uncle accepted her aggression tells me he was the passive one in the relationship. Your uncle thought he was being a sexual bandit, because he thought he was stealing her attention from everyone else in the car. But, in actual-

ity, she had drafted your uncle and you into her erotic army. Being part of this ongoing titillating experience was why he left June Cleaver.

Then he stripped away any doubts I might have secretly harbored about Suzanne's persona: "Where I grew up in the Bronx in the sixties, women who were 'loose' all had beehive hairdos." I shrieked and everyone in the room stared at me.

"Suzanne had a French-twist beehive," I whispered, my mind racing through many memories. It was true, as the newspaper reporter indicated, she sometimes wore it in a bun, but often it was a French twist with some height on top, which made it more like a beehive.

He went on, "I can state with almost one hundred percent certainty that the murder was committed from pride. He wounded her ego in some way, and I'm sure her hitting her forties and having the blush of youth recede gave her more motivation."

When I told this writer friend that the family had heard Vernie was trying to leave her, he just laughed. And when I further explained how Vernie had adopted Suzanne's youngest son, he just about fell on the floor chortling.

"You mean she not only dominated him through her sexuality, but she managed to obtain a secondary support for her son? What a mastermind!"

I mentioned that her fifth husband was the son of Holocaust survivors.

"Of course, she chose another male who would abide by her bidding. Holocaust children are known to be avoiders of conflict."

I knew I needed more information from Suzanne, but during that second visit in December 2015, I got nothing. She was withholding information better than the Russian KGB. It didn't help that I felt duplicitous in my role as friendly cousin, even though at that point I wasn't completely sure this would become a writing project. Answers. I was after answers.

Shortly after the funeral, I decided to pursue the writing and see where it would take me. A month later I called Louisa and mentioned to her how I was working on a few writing projects, one of which was a book about my family, including Vernie's "situation," which I knew she understood to mean the murder, as they always talked in code about the killing. Some weeks after I told Louisa, I had my third visit to Suzanne and family, and I was worried this new information would cause Suzanne to withhold even more, if that were possible. *Au contraire.* Whereas in the first two visits Suzanne was polite but tight-lipped about anything having to do with my uncle Vernie, in this third interview she went on and on and on, sitting tall on her invalid bed, her words pouring out, but her face still showing no emotion Our time together was only broken by pee breaks, but then she'd ask me to come back in. She wanted to be interviewed. She wanted to tell me oh-so-many things, and she evidently expected her statements to appear in a book. Total for that one visit was more than four hours of questions and answers.

During the first few minutes Suzanne started telling me—once again—how she was able to go away to Boscobel High School so she could take business courses, how she did so well on a typing test (128 words per minute) the teacher didn't believe her. Suzanne ranted to me, "I don't lie! That's what I typed." So, even back then, people suspected she was unencumbered by the truth?

Because I had been mirroring her nonverbals and treating her with near adoration, she just kept talking, and she said she had some "issues" with Vernie. "Later on, I had a difficult situation that I resolved. And I think in that one shot, I took out Vernie and my mother." I was stunned, as she continued. "It was like getting a release of some kind."

Was she just admitting to the murder? And she was telling me she knew the fatal shot was her means of solving a problem? And perhaps the "difficult situation" was a man finally wanting to ditch her? And did she mean by taking out her mother (who lived for another ten years) that her mother became even more negative towards her?

But maybe I misheard her, so I asked her about the shot that took out Vernie and her mother. She replied with no emotion, "Well, he deserved it more than she did." Her words described intentional behavior, not a psychotic breakdown.

Knowing the attraction Suzanne held for men, I wanted to see if she knew this, but she feigned ignorance. She never thought she was pretty. I wasn't asking about "pretty," but rather about men's desire for her. You ask any woman what it feels like to have men interested and they'll tell you how powerful they feel. Even a low-IQ relative of mine noticed that as her breasts developed, boys suddenly were giving her attention. Surely, a Mensa woman, smarter than 98 percent of the population, isn't going to be less aware than my female relative with an IQ of 68.

What were you drawn to in Vernie? I asked. Blank stare.

Why did you love him? She stumbled around with some confusing words about his worldly ways and then said she *must* have liked him. Though, she added, she did get to where she did not like him.

What attracted her? Was he smart? She didn't think that would have been high on the list. And what was he enticed by? "I don't necessarily think my intelligence would have appealed to him," she declared with great confidence.

Was she perhaps more exciting than his first wife? Yes, she said. Suzanne only met Jenylle once, she claimed, at a court hearing to reduce child support. Suzanne's attorney had chided her that day: "Do you have to look so damn wealthy?" So what if she was wearing a mink coat? And could she help it that she looked so damn good in everything she wore?

Suzanne spent a great deal of time during the four hours of the third interview telling me how Vernie had no integrity, no values, no conscience, and would have had affairs with anyone, and how he was cruel, cruel, cruel, beyond what she ever thought was possible, how she feared for the safety of her children, and how she hated herself for what she had put them through, and what she did to them with that one bad judgment. There it was again, the "bad judgment." Not an out-of-reality psychotic break. At this point my research skills helped. When you've gathered a great deal of data and begin to look at the numbers, it can seem like just so many unrelated, scattered pieces of information in the beginning. But when you see a measurement reappear, you've got two instances and you can draw a line and begin to see a pattern, perhaps even a trajectory. Suzanne had already twice mentioned her "judgment" that led to the murder, and she had never given me any details or evidence there had been a psychotic break.

Suzanne described how Vernie wanted more excitement in his life, especially if it involved doing bad things. She said he needed an exciting female and she (Suzanne) filled the bill, but then she got *too exciting*. At this point she laughed explosively, and then tried to explain. "Well, I was the one who ended his life, if I remember correctly," she noted without any irony. How much I wanted to get up and look her straight in the face and ask, *How in the world can you laugh about killing my uncle, the man who took care of me, the father of Shannon, who's never gotten over this loss?* I thought about Alice Gregory's work on the shame experienced when someone accidentally kills another person. Since Suzanne claimed to have been basically in a trance, one could argue that her story involved not an intentional killing but an accidental one. However, Gregory discovered that unlike Suzanne, the accidental killers were unable to rid themselves of shame and remorse for the rest of their lives. If only I could have brought that up with Suzanne. But I had to maintain my professional demeanor, the unbiased management consultant, who nonetheless must appear to sympathize with Suzanne.

After the laughter she went on boastfully. "Then I called the sheriff, the actual sheriff. Not the sheriff's office, but the sheriff's home. Afterward, David came downstairs and told me, 'I had a dad. And I don't have one anymore. Goddamn you!' so I started to tell him how Vernie had burned me, but David just looked at me and said, 'It doesn't matter.' He was right. Anything I said would be like an excuse, and there is no excuse for what I did. I did so much for my kids and look what I brought on them."

When I told Suzanne that David had confessed to the shooting to Aunt Maxine, Suzanne scoffed and said he was covering up for her, even though it was dumb, because people would know the truth, but I couldn't get any details out of her on how people were supposed to "know the truth."

She waxed on about all her difficulties, how she'd gotten herself in trouble, and she'd learned a lot—which has made her reasonably well-balanced—but she would rather not have had to learn.

So, killing my uncle helped her gain mental health, is that what she was trying to say? I thought.

One lesson was that she'd become a better and more important person than she had realized. Even if the schoolkids would knock Danny down (he was, by this time, about eleven years old and slight of build) and say his mother murdered his father, she wasn't going to leave her beautiful mansion in Oregon, Wisconsin. And what about the people who stared at her when she was out? Let *them* walk across the street. It was a tough time for her.

For *her*? What about Danny and all he had to endure? Did she ever consider moving and starting anew for her son's sake?

Her life was harsh back then, she continued. Only three people visited her in the hospital, and I was one of them, a visit that created an enormous amount of negative feelings from my family. My grandmother was particularly hurt.

"You're associating with the woman who murdered your uncle,"

she said with such pain in her voice it now makes me want to pros-
trate myself in front of her. But back then, I was so certain of right
versus wrong, I just shot back, "Jesus said to forgive!" Oh, how I've
come to regret that interaction with my beloved grandmother,
whose life was seared with pain.

Was part of Suzanne's strategy to take away any blame toward
herself? She recounted her hospital psychiatrist's admonition:
"You have been driven to the point it was either suicide or homicide, and whether you want to hear it or not, you chose the healthiest."

I came to understand how much she wanted me to hear this, because she repeated the same quotation twice that third visit, and at
least two other times during my interviews. "I didn't want to hear
that I chose the healthiest," she said, "because my heart and soul
and mind, and whatever, protected me. I didn't know anything
about guns," she continued, "except I had been with Vernie when
he'd bought that gun for deer hunting." When she said "that" gun,
she really meant *that* gun. With multiple weapons in the house
she never talked about why she picked *that* gun, and I lost my
chance to ask.

People wondered how she could even load the rifle, she reported. "But I did it, somehow, I did." It scared her, having that
stuff in the house. At one time he had a machine gun, she said.
There were so many crooked people he knew through work, so
who knows where he got it? That job he had with the State of
Wisconsin Attorney General's Office was such a dream job. "But
you know, his uncle Gil Stordock [one of the top officials in Wisconsin's Department of Veterans Affairs and the American Le-
gion] got it for him. Gil had a lot of influence." What did Uncle
Gil, who was big in Veterans Affairs, have to do with the state attorney general? Or maybe that tells us more about how Suzanne's
mind worked. Use people and relationships to push your way up
in the world.

After she got out of the hospital, she decided to go back to school and make up for all the time lost. People called her selfish, but she didn't care. She finished her bachelor's, a master's, a doctorate, and finally a law degree. When she attended a hearing to be admitted to the state bar, they asked her if she'd ever been arrested or convicted. She said, "'Yes. Of murder. Hasn't everybody?' Then the judge told me I'd make a good attorney. So when people asked me what kind of attorney I was going to be, I said a good one. So all the things that have happened to me, all the good, all the disaster, everything, has been a total blessing, because look how far I have come."

At first, I was stunned. She killed my uncle and that made her life take on the kind of positive turn that nothing else had? I sat there trying to sound eagerly impressed with her intelligence, her sophisticated ways, her cunning approaches to life. I knew such adulation helped her open up, because I've spent a good part of my life living with narcissists.

This reminded me of a 1998 article about her in *The Wheel,* the College of St. Catherine newspaper. Suzanne was an adjunct faculty member there. It listed her accomplishments with glowing praise and admiration at how far she had come, since starting college in the 1940s, but taking time off to "raise her family." She returned to college full-time in 1972, when "all but her youngest son" had graduated from high school, though she said nothing about getting out of a mental hospital in late 1971. The final sentence, on the second page of the article, said it all: *"Most of all, keep in mind that you are doing something for yourself, and you deserve it."*

Then Suzanne talked with me about her "place" in northern Wisconsin (which she actually bought jointly with Vernie), which they purchased, she said, when she was sick and hadn't worked for a while. Later I discovered that was a few months after one of her alleged suicide attempts, and also after the child support court hearing. Vernie stated in October 1966 court documents that he felt it "an undue financial burden" to pay child support because he'd remarried since the 1964 divorce and the cost of maintaining [an expensive] house in Oregon, his car payment, etc., was too much for him. (Suzanne usually worked, but she was unemployed at this time.)

When Vernie and Jenylle were divorced in 1964, the age of majority was twenty-one, but in 1966 the law changed the age when a child was no longer considered a minor to eighteen. Shannon turned eighteen in February 1966, which just happened to be the year Vernie and Suzanne took Jenylle back to court in the fall, not long after Suzanne's August suicide attempt (which she had told one of the court psychiatrists and appeared in his report). Though in the divorce decree he had agreed to support Shannon's college expenses, he now claimed not to know which institution of higher learning she wanted to attend and how much it would cost. Vernie won the suit and only had to give one more nominal payment of child support. The next month Vernie and Suzanne bought the thirty-five-acre spread, plus cabin, in northern Wisconsin.

I think getting out of paying child support was one of the items Suzanne was after when she would withhold sex from Vernie, and I think the other two were cutting Shannon out of the will and removing her as one of the beneficiaries of the life insurance. In the original divorce settlement with Jenylle, it was ordered that Shannon be kept as a beneficiary on his life insurance, but when they went back in 1966, the requirement for Shannon to be a beneficiary was deleted. A new will was drafted in April 1967 without any mention of his only natural child, Shannon. It is clear that removing Shannon from Vernie's assets was completed between 1966 and 1967, which is the time frame I remember Suzanne frequently announcing the conjugal refusals.

She continued with me on one of her favorite topics: how she had put three men through college and got sick of working to educate a husband. When she wanted to divorce Briggs, her attorney told her to wait until he had more assets, which she evidently did. Then she met a hairdresser, who had this wonderful father, the wealthy Abraham Gast, whom people often told her she was in love with.

Some years later on, Suzanne found Ronald, "the keeper." He was the only son in his family, but there was a cousin who also survived the Holocaust with him, and she called herself his "sister," a word Suzanne would say with contempt. This same cousin had been close to Ronald's daughter, Alexandra, for decades and evidently stepped in when Alexandra's mother died. She saw herself as a mother to Alexandra. Suzanne would have none of it.

I've known Holocaust survivors. What they went through is far beyond what any of us can imagine, regardless of books or movies. And if it were only the two of them left from their entire family, I can see why she thought of him as her "brother," and I imagine there were years when they clung together in sorrow, just trying to live beyond the horror and the terror. And by extension I get how she might feel as a mother to Alexandra. From what I could glean, Suzanne did her best to maneuver this woman out of the family, this "interloper" who pretended to be Ronald's sister and Alexandra's mother. And I imagine she used similar skills to maneuver Shannon out of Vernie's orbit.

Back to another recurring topic: her development.

> If you don't have credentials, nobody listens to you. It might have been selfish on my part to insist on schooling, but it's a horrible thing to be bright and possibly brilliant and not be able to live it.

The possibility of her not reaching her potential because of lack of education was one of the few topics she got agitated about, or at least as agitated as someone gets who speaks mostly in a monotone voice without much modulation.

Here's more from her voice:

> Later on, when I was teaching sociology and women's studies at the College of St. Catherine's, I would get angry at students who didn't know much and were satisfied. Sometimes I wanted to slap them upside the head. All I wanted to do was learn, and why didn't they want it, too? I taught sociology and women's studies.
>
> During that time I started a research project on children kidnapped by their parents, which was a replication of my stepdaughter's research. I got a huge grant and called her and said, "Look, it wasn't just Mom who likes your work. Other people like it and are financing it." [By *Mom*, Suzanne meant herself, though Alexandra was almost thirty years old when Suzanne married her father, so I doubt the name was ever used by Alexandra.] I was her rescuer in the family, because everyone always looked up to her older brother, the rabbi, and she got ignored. Alexandra initially rejected me, but I just let her be, and told Ronald to just be patient. Her mother had died and was, thus, a saint, which I never pretended to be. Later on, Alexandra and I became close, very close, through no help of Ronald's cousin [the one who called herself the sister], who tried to mother Alexandra, but which Alexandra did not want. So I finally told that cousin, "You want to be her mother? That job's already taken!"
>
> Now, you have to have some sense of people's feelings in this world, and the cousin made it worse. And Ronald sure wasn't close to Alexandra. And I know for a fact that the one person Alexandra is close to is *me*, because I didn't push her. And all the time she had to overcome her insecurities because of her brother, who ended

up marrying this woman who gave me sugar diabetes. I
don't trust people like this, all honeybun and stuff. I
think they got divorced.

And for me, the one thing I wanted before I die is to
have a happy marriage. I felt I had been gypped of that.
This is how I met Ronald. I was in the synagogue socializing in my usual way, which was with my back to the
wall and one foot nailed to the floor, when the rabbi
came along and said there was someone he wanted me
to meet and he took me over to Ronald, and I thought,
he's seeing two lonely souls. You know, I was afraid,
after all I'd gone through, and Ronald had had a bad
marriage since his first wife died. I saw he was afraid,
too, because that second wife had married him for his
money. I used to tell him, "I married you for your
money, too, but I'm still looking for it"

She laughed, like someone who loves hearing herself tell the
same joke over and over. She told me that one four times. Suzanne
also mentioned a couple of times how Ronald knew everything
about her—and loved her, anyway—but that there were lots of people in her current life who don't know anything about what she did,
and they'd be very surprised. She was glad she had a few people,
like Louisa and me—and that's it—whom she could be completely open with, she said.

The whole idea of her almost Don Draperesque quality of
changing her name and obfuscating her life details fascinated me,
and I wanted to know more, but I couldn't let Suzanne know how
much I already had learned. I found out later this is a common
technique journalists employ to get to the truth of a story. After
all, she was Elmira on marriage license #1, Suzi for #2, and
Suzanne for #3, #4, and #5. So I kept asking her about her name,
"Suzi," and when she changed it to Suzanne and what she had been
called in high school (she said Suzi), but I never could get her to
admit she had once been "Elmira." She did say once she hit thirty, it

was no more "Suzi" and only "Suzanne," and I didn't remind her she had identified herself to the sheriff as "Suzi," when she was forty-one.

We talked about David some more and she told me (as she had several times) that he'd had heart problems as a child and how much she worried about him back then. A few times she'd say, "You're just like David—going back over old times." I took that to mean both David and I were asking difficult questions that she did not necessarily want to revisit. Toward the end of that third visit, she said, "You know, David had a fancy to find himself a female physics professor as a girlfriend and I asked him, 'And what do you have to offer to her?' He sat around all the time and he wants what he wants. But I just felt I had to make that remark right then."

During the third visit Louisa was in her usual long skirt and blouse down to her wrists and almost up to her chin and talked to me about photos, since she'd casually mentioned previously that they had lots of old pictures of Vernie and his family. Shannon and I had talked about this and decided I should ask Louisa if she would either copy the photos or give them to me, if they didn't want them, so that my cousin Shannon ("Who's Shannon?" she asked) and I could enjoy the pictures. Louisa had eagerly agreed and promised to look for them in all their boxes still packed from the Alaska move. During that same visit Louisa looked at me with her bright eyes and red hair pulled back in the bun and told me she had found Vernie's wallet and police badge and my heart leapt. That would be something I would love to hold and I knew how meaningful it would be to Shannon. When Louisa mentioned to Suzanne what she'd found, and she was going to give the badge and wallet to me, Suzanne objected, "What does Dorothy need that stuff for?"

Louisa replied, "Because she's Vernie's family."

Suzanne replied, "Well, I'm his family, and I will keep them!"

And because Louisa couldn't even remember right then where she'd placed them, I didn't even get to look at the wallet or the badge. Louisa felt bad she couldn't find them. This was her nature, to be generous and cooperative.

Before I returned for the fourth visit at the end of April 2015, I thought I should let them know the writing project about my family and my uncle had morphed into one where Suzanne was a major character. Suzanne had been so open with me that last time, and I had attributed this change to her knowing I had a writing project in which she'd be a part. So, naturally, I deduced if she thought she was going to be more than a minor character, she'd really open up. Was I ever wrong!

Louisa responded by saying, "We have a lot to talk about when you get here."

I decided to go this time for two days (previous visits were all only one day) partly because I was led to believe that Alexandra (Ronald's daughter and Louisa's stepsister from the fifth marriage) would arrive the second day. The first day was a bust, with Suzanne's hospital bed needing repairs, but something still felt strange. I had no more than two minutes with Suzanne the entire long day. It felt like Suzanne was avoiding me. I just kept thinking about all the things I had left undone at home to come a day early. Phone calls I needed to make, writing deadlines, postponed meetings. Then Louisa sheepishly confessed she had "mixed up" the schedule and Alexandra wasn't arriving until after I had left. But I wondered if that was true. Maybe they didn't want me to meet Alexandra and risk me downloading all of my uncle's murder story from my mental hard drive.

On the second day I arrived from my hotel and actually got into Suzanne's bedroom and we chatted. Then I started asking her questions. She was evasive about everything and kept talking to her dog, instead of me. Suzanne would sit with perfect posture on her bed, legs under the chenille bedspread, while the brown-and-white Holstein would jump on the bed and land with his head on her leg or in her lap. Suzanne would cuddle him, and Holstein would rake his tongue all over Suzanne's face, and then she'd channel the dog's "thoughts" to me. After a couple of hours I saw the pattern. Whenever I asked a question she didn't want to talk about, she'd engage in a conversation with her dog, as if the dog was talking back. And I was meant to see this as cute. When she was describing the dumbness of her second husband, John Briggs (the Ph.D. insurance executive), and I asked how she coped, she said, "Holstein says Grandma's recovered from a lot of devastations. Grandma's so mean to us animals, but we put up with her." A few minutes later she got back on the "Vernie is cruel" wagon and went off on a side trip about whether Suzanne, herself, was cruel. "I could have. I could maybe have tried, but it wouldn't have worked. I can't be cruel to Holstein. Why would I want to?" she said as she petted him gently.

Somehow the topic of her first marriage came up. They lived with the in-laws, slept in twin beds, and Suzanne got fed up with the mother-in-law's Christian Science beliefs and told her husband, "Either your mother is right, or I am right, and I think she needs religion more than I do." Of course, we know she changed religions to Judaism not long after. So she divorced her first husband to "preserve my sanity," an interesting statement for someone who used lack of sanity to get off a murder charge. Regarding the sanity, she went on, "Maybe I didn't have it. Holstein says, 'Who knows what lurks in the minds of men? The Shadow knows.'"

Then she went in another direction, about how her family members had been so supportive when she went back to school and what it meant to her. And suddenly, "I think people didn't know what I was going through. I was not a complainer. I didn't complain about marriage or the person or what he did to me. I think they were shocked, because there hadn't been a litany of complaints against Vernie. Holstein thinks I would have been better off if I complained," she said, laughing. She didn't seem to have that lack-of-complaining problem anymore.

When I asked about her losing trust in men, she went off, talking about Ronald and how authentic he was, compared to other men who put on big fronts. Then she looked at her dog. "Holstein is helping so much right now, aren't you? I appreciate you, and not just for your kissy face." After which, Holstein licked all over Suzanne's face. And then she talked about how difficult life had been for her, and noted, "Holstein says, 'She didn't have *me* then. Now she's got a sweet dog to take care of her. And I'm going to get part of her lunch. Can't you tell?'" When I asked if she had considered divorcing Vernie, she said it would have been a smarter move on her part. "I suspect I probably did think of it. But all those sessions with the counselors confused me on what was in my head. Holstein says, 'But you had me.' She's licking her chops. She loves me. Just like some guys." And I'm wondering, how in the world did the counselors confuse her? She thought of divorcing Vernie, but she got confused and shot him instead?

At this point she made some jokes about Holstein and men liking her "protein bars," and then on to marrying Ronald and how scared she was. "But we got brave, didn't we, Holstein? Grandma took the plunge again," she said. "Ronald was really good," she continued, "except when I was mad at him," which made me wonder if she locked him out of the house or refused him sex, as she had done with Vernie. She returned to one of her most common topics, how smart she was. "The downside of being smart is that you leave other people in the dust," she proclaimed. "And then people think you're conceited. Holstein says, 'I absolutely don't understand why when Grandma would call somebody a dumb-ass, they wouldn't like her.' Holstein, you made that all up. You told a tale, Holstein."

Because I wanted to get a professional opinion, I had a therapist read through the transcripts of my interviews with Suzanne. The counselor noted how disjointed the conversations were, jumping here and there, with lots of non sequiturs. Was it age? Perhaps, but I also remember in the police report a couple of townspeople mentioning how Suzanne's speech could get incoherent.

One topic I was extremely interested in exploring was the marriage between Suzanne and my uncle. Having been unable the last couple of times to get any information about her wedding, and her claiming not to know *when* she got married, I thought to ask her *where*. If someone got dates mixed up, it seemed more likely they might remember a place. Who doesn't remember at least some approximation of where you got married? She said she didn't remember where. It's not like she had bad recall on her weddings.

During another conversation with me Suzanne had offhandedly mentioned the name of the minister—John Collins, from the Christ Presbyterian Church in Madison (which I confirmed later in the marriage license)—who had officiated at wedding number two to Briggs, in 1952. And what about her marriage to my uncle? When I pressed her, she said, yes, it was probably at her friend's house, in Madison. That was not true, I thought, because I'd been in contact with the State of Wisconsin Vital Records several times and had searched through them myself on one trip to Madison, taking the unwieldy black-covered books and looking up the index number in order to find marriage licenses in another oversized, dusty book on some high shelf in that one long room in the county office building. No way were she and my uncle married in Dane County, or anywhere in Wisconsin, for that matter.

I asked another way. Maybe they had flown off somewhere and got married? Was it possible they went to Florida, or the Caribbean, or wherever? But she said the only time she flew anywhere for something legal was for her second divorce, when she took a

plane to Mexico, a fact I was able to prove in my subsequent research through the Vital Records Department.

The second breakthrough was when I reminded her she'd told
me on the previous visit how cruel Vernie had been to her. Could
she give me some examples of his cruelty? She thought, and she
thought, and couldn't think of anything. Most married people I
know, happy or not, can rattle off all sorts of grievances about their
spouses. Then she said, "Oh, yes, there was one thing. He used to
go down in the basement and shoot off his gun, to scare me, because he wanted me to know he could come upstairs and kill me."
I wondered if this had really happened. Vernie kept guns and he
surely practiced with them, but previously I had only heard about
him taking David to the dump and using it as a shooting range.
But still, I wondered, this was the extent of how my uncle was
cruel, cruel, cruel to her?

Speaking of guns, during the third visit, I was slightly nervous
about my safety. After all, this was the house of the confessed
killer and I was prying into areas some people preferred to leave
undisturbed. I asked Louisa's husband, Bobby, are there any guns
in the house? "Oh, no," he replied with complete assurance, and I
never questioned his answer. They had lived for forty years in
Alaska, where you're given a gun about the same time you get
your first toothbrush. None of that crossed my mind, so I believed
him and was relieved. Even afterward, I never reflected on how
illogical Bobby's response was.

When I arrived a month later for the fourth visit, Louisa mentioned there'd been some local house break-ins because of the
high rates of painkiller drug addiction in the area. Bobby evidently did not remember what he had told me previously, and he
announced he had two guns in the house, because everyone—
and I mean *everyone*—in Alaska has guns, and he's still a good
Alaskan.

I tried to push ideas of firearms out of my mind on this fourth
visit; otherwise I would have been completely distracted.

* * *

Luckily, I did get several hours with Suzanne during my two days there. One thing I always came away with from those chats with Suzanne—during all four visits—was how pleasant, charming, and smart she was. I found myself forgetting what had happened so many years ago, or making excuses because she was such a cool person. Then I'd have to remind myself that she was the confessed killer who blew off half my uncle's head. At the very end of the fourth visit, something happened that snapped me out of my Suzanne-is-such-a-sweet-person stupor.

During breaks Louisa kept asking me if her mother and I had talked about my writing project that centered on Suzanne. "I mentioned it," I replied.

Louisa told me she had started writing about her mother's life, but hadn't gotten very far. I felt Louisa was struggling, doing the writing primarily because her mother expected it. It wasn't Louisa's real passion. Louisa had previously shown me some of her poetry, and she is a gifted writer. My breath was taken away when I read her words, and her paintings were phenomenally beautiful. But between the farm duties and taking care of her mother, she told me she didn't have the time for her art. What a waste of precious talent. And yet there was Suzanne, expecting Louisa to drop her own writing and painting to create *The Saga of Suzanne,* which I assumed would have had a similar tone to the article in the college newspaper, *The Wheel* (described on p. 163), listing all of her accomplishments, but conveniently neglecting the murder.

As I was ready to leave, Louisa came into Suzanne's bedroom and this was the exchange:

> LOUISA: Have you two come to some agreement?
> SUZANNE: About what?
> LOUISA: About the writing?
> SUZANNE: What's to agree?
> LOUISA: Who's going to write the story?

SUZANNE: There's nothing to discuss about it. You're my daughter and you are the one who has the right.

DOROTHY: She is your daughter and she is very talented.

SUZANNE: That's why I sent barrels of money, time after time, to Pratt in New York. They kept asking for more money and we'd send another barrel. [I remembered this was around the same time my cousin Shannon was forced to go to community college instead of university.]

DOROTHY: And it was worth it.

SUZANNE *(to Louisa)*: So you are the only one who has the right to my story. You're my daughter, whether you like it or not.

LOUISA *(putting her head down sheepishly)*: All right.

Then Suzanne looked at me with the eyes of a cold-blooded killer. I'd never seen that look from her, or from anyone else, for that matter.

I gathered up my things, as fast as I could, raced to my car, and sped down the road. As I drove to the airport, I was gulping for air, scarcely able to breathe. My stomach was tightening to the extent that it felt like steel wires being pulled taut to breaking. I could hardly stay inside my skin. I had looked into the eyes of evil and it was ugly beyond comprehension.

When I got to the airport, I discovered there was a problem with my ticket because I had changed the flight to leave earlier. I got extremely anxious from the possibility that I might have to stay in Chattanooga another night.

If they can't fix the ticket, I thought, *I will beg them. I will literally throw myself down on the cold tile floor. I'll tell them I just spent the day with my uncle's killer and* just have *to get out of town. Send me anywhere.*

After thirty-two minutes, which seemed like thirty-two hours, two young tech-savvy USAir guys came out to help. A half hour later, when I was getting completely desperate, they figured out what was wrong and smilingly issued me a ticket. If they weren't so much younger than me, I might have hugged them right there.

One thing I was grateful for: the clarity of who Suzanne was. For the previous dozen-plus hours of my interactions with her over the past fifteen months, I had felt some sense of confusion as she answered my questions how a reasonable and thoughtful person would. Maybe I had her figured wrong. Maybe she wasn't so bad.

But then I'd remember that she had either killed Vernie or been somehow involved in it. And she had evidently convinced at least three psychiatrists that she was someone who regretted losing herself for a moment to a psychotic break, but that she really was a nice person and ought not to spend much time in the hospital for something she would never do again, right?

The evil I saw in Suzanne's eyes that night was very intense. If Suzanne were younger and had access to a gun, I think she might have shot me, too. In her savage look and in her voice for those few minutes, I saw through everything. The idea of Suzanne losing control over who told her story, of the book not being written by someone whom she had molded into the acceptable way of thinking, well, that was just too much. She let down her guard completely for about two minutes. That was enough.

CHAPTER NINETEEN

Finding the Old Friends

I knew I had to locate anyone I could who had been involved, even tangentially, with the murder and with Vernie and Suzanne and their families. It took many months to find their former friends in Oregon, Wisconsin, or even people who were around in 1970 and who knew anything about what had happened. At first, I contacted the Oregon Area Historical Society, and those people were more than cooperative. They sent out e-mails to the membership list to see if anyone remembered the Stordocks or the murder, but nothing came back.

After I got the police reports in April 2015, I combed through them and discovered, despite generous redactions of names, that I was able to identify last names or full names of several of Vernie's and David's friends. No friends of Suzanne were listed, as everyone reported she kept to herself. When I sent those names to the society, I had visions of them locating some of these people for me, but no one turned up in their quests.

One person I really wanted to talk to was Joe Roznos, Vernie's best friend, according to the police reports. He had evidently moved to Arizona with his wife, who had died a few years ago, but none of the numbers I found worked. My next tactic, which I'd used before, was to look for their kids. Again I found nonworking numbers. Then I discovered one of his daughters had changed her name and that someone with that new name now worked as a supervisor at a car dealership in Chandler, Arizona, a business I remembered well from the multiple TV ads for their Tempe location, when I taught at Arizona State University back in the late '70s. I called the number and asked for Cynthia. When she got on the phone and I introduced myself, saying Vernie had been my uncle, she said, "How in the world did you find me?" And then, "Every time I think of Vernie, I think of fun." Turned out her eighty-six-year-old father lived with her, and I called a few times before I got him not resting.

Joe was happy to talk about Vernie, who had indeed been his best friend, someone he considered honest, full of integrity, and someone you could trust with your life. He missed Vernie every day and was heartbroken when he died, he said. There were only two options to what happened that night, Joe said. Either David loaded the gun and handed it to Suzanne, or he just fired it himself, because Suzanne knew nothing about guns. David was a skilled gunman, and Joe knew this from having gone deer hunting with him and Vernie at my uncle's cabin in northern Wisconsin. Joe thought Vernie and Suzanne got along fine, and never saw any indication of argument or conflict. Nor did he notice anything unusual in his relationship with David, as they seemed to get along as any father and teenage son would. And Vernie was always there when someone needed help.

I talked to the nearly ninety-year-old Howard Bjorklund, who had worked with Vernie at both the Beloit Police Department and the attorney general's office. "I give him an A-plus," he said on the phone in his deep and thoughtful voice, "for hard work, devotion, and intelligence." He said Vernie never, ever shirked any duties and was a joy to be around and to work with. "I credit my knowledge of the law to Vernie, because we'd ride in the patrol car in those early days and started talking and arguing about one law or another, with Vernie always bringing up complicated issues. Then we'd go to the station and look up the law and learn more. I loved being with him."

It took me a long time to get any working number on even one of David's friends, and I had little luck with David's girlfriend (as described in police reports), who had a last name of Lawson. Finally I managed to get phone numbers to David's three best friends in high school, John, Kip, and Kim. When I finally got John on the phone and asked him about a Lawson girl, he asked "Sherry?" But then he said he didn't know anything about her being David's girlfriend. Something was wrong, because during the investigation Lawson had told the police she and David had gone steady for the past four months. Surely, his friends would have known something about it.

John told me everyone in their circle of friends assumed David had shot his stepfather. "There's one thing about your mom shooting her husband," he said. "It's traumatic, but over time you learn to deal with it. You cope. But David never grieved in a normal process. He was completely out of whack emotionally after it happened, and he only seemed to get worse. Before the shooting we did a little alcohol and no drugs. But afterward, David started drinking more, and about a year later he got into drugs, and then got involved in motorcycle gangs. None of us ever asked him who pulled the trigger, because we just wanted to be there for him, whatever had happened. But we were all of the same mind: That he pulled the trigger that night to protect his mother from some abuse." I asked John if he had ever seen Vernie and Suzanne fight and he hadn't. I wanted to ask him where he got the idea that Suzanne was mistreated, but I was wary of alienating him. After we hung up, I looked through the old newspaper clippings. Sure enough, several of the 1970 through 1971 newspaper articles had recounted the allegation of the cigarette burn on Suzanne's back. One was on the front page of the *Capital Times*. Everyone in the Madison area must have read that account.

John saw David a few times after high school, but he didn't have a lot in common because of David's continual sinking into a destructive lifestyle. David bought an expensive house in Madison in the mid-1970s and John always wondered where a twenty-one-year-old like him would get the money. Then David sold the house a year later and left town. John felt bad that David didn't keep up with his Oregon, Wisconsin, friends after that. "We could have been such a support to him," John said wistfully. Two of them, Kip and Kim, were even closer to David, and he gave me their phone numbers.

Next I called Kip, who didn't seem surprised to hear from me, as everyone else had, and I realized John had alerted him, which was not unexpected. Kip said much the same thing about David and his downward spiral and how they all thought he killed his stepfather to protect his mother from abuse. When asked about Lawson, he couldn't even put a first name to her. "None of us had real girlfriends. We dated and fooled around, but nothing lasting. Certainly not four months. I would have known if David was involved like that."

He talked fondly about a few times that Vernie came home from work early and found the boys in their bathrobes hanging around the house. No scolding from Vernie, just some knowing smiles. He was no doubt realizing there's only one reason teenage boys are all in their robes on a weekday afternoon at someone else's house, even if the girls had already left.

Kip knew about Mrs. Freeman (Jocelyn) who had lived in the Oregon, Wisconsin, house while Suzanne was in the hospital. He told me he had visited Suzanne when she moved to Madison in the mid-1970s at her place on Regent Street, just off University Avenue. I asked if Danny was living there, and he said he didn't think so. This agreed with what the Gast brothers had told me, that Danny had stayed with Mrs. Freeman and hadn't lived with his mother anymore after Suzanne got out of the hospital.

Although the murder of my uncle, LaVerne Stordock, was officially a closed case, many puzzling questions remained. I launched my own investigation to find out what really happened. This is one of my favorite photos of Uncle Vernie. It was taken when he joined the Beloit, Wisconsin, Police Department in 1948. *Photo courtesy Beloit Police Department.*

Vernie, 8, with older brother
Donald Stordock, 13, in Beloit.

Vernie, age 11.

Vernie enlisted in the Navy on his seventeenth birthday in 1943 and was congratulated by Uncle Gil Stordock, a leader in Wisconsin's American Legion.

After serving in World War II, Vernie married his high school sweetheart, Jenylle Harriss. The young couple lived near Vernie's family.
From left: Jenylle, Vernie, Leone (my mother), and friend Lou, 1948.

Many of my happiest
childhood memories
stem from the hours
I spent with my
cousins in Grandma
Stordock's kitchen.
In this photo,
taken in 1954,
I am on the left.

Family gathering,
1955, in Grandma
Stordock's kitchen.
I am in center front;
Uncle Vernie is back left;
my mother is center right.

Vernie was recalled by the Navy during the Korean Conflict. Here he is at age 25, in 1951, with Navy service ribbons.

My cousin Shannon still treasures the time she spent with her dad.

Vernie loved his career in law enforcement. Here he is shown as a sergeant in the Beloit Police Department, 1956. *Photo courtesy Beloit Police Department.*

Vernie was proud of his squad car, Beloit, 1957.

Vernie's outstanding job performance led to his promotion to police captain. This photo, taken in 1962 at his mother's home, later ran on the front page of the Beloit News when his murder was reported in March 1970.

Vernie showed his creative side as a weekend deejay at WBEL in Beloit for several years.
Here he is on "The Gerry Shannon Show," in 1960.
The title was drawn from his middle name, Gerald, and his daughter's name, Shannon.

Vernie was trained in the use of weapons both in the Navy and in his work as a police officer. This photo shows him at target practice on a farm that belonged to his sister Leone (my mother), Waukesha, Wisconsin, 1967.

My step-father and mother, Reuben "Pete" and Leone Evert, in Waukesha, Wisconsin, around the time of the murder. *Photo by David Kipperman/O'Brien Photography Waukesha, Wisconsin.*

My sister, Janet Mittelsteadt, and her husband, Richard, in Waukesha, a few years after Suzanne became intensely jealous of Janet.

Vernie, Shannon, and Jenylle, 1957, during the happy time of their marriage.
Photo by Sharpe Studios, Beloit, Wisconsin.

Vernie, Shannon, and Jenylle, a year after the affair with Suzanne had begun and shortly before the marital breakup in 1963.

The house in Oregon, Wisconsin, where Vernie and Suzanne lived, and where his murder occurred. *Photo courtesy Michael Seeliger.*

This is the only family picture we have showing Vernie and Suzanne (*left*). It was taken in summer 1969, in Uncle Donald and Aunt Maxine's backyard in Waukesha. On the right, from the back: my step-father, Pete, Aunt Maxine, and Maxine's son, my cousin Richard. Seven months later Vernie was dead.

Suzanne's yearbook picture from the University of Wisconsin for her undergraduate graduation in 1974, four years after the murder.
Photo courtesy University of Wisconsin—Madison Archives.

Suzanne B. Stordock
Madison, Wisconsin
B.A., Correctional
Admin. & Sociology

Suzanne's son David, one year after the shooting, in a yearbook photo from Oregon High School.

DAVID BRIGGS
"Bricks"
Sex, drinking, and smoking aren't all that bad.

Suzanne's son Daniel, not long before his 1992 suicide.
Photo by Callen Harty.

These two pages show an artist's re-creations of 3-D crime scene images built by forensic expert Jason Kolowski of Forensic Insight LLC. The images were created from forensic and coroner's evidence, and laser measurements of the crime scene. The left page depicts the story Suzanne told to authorities. The right page is based on forensic data. All illustrations by Maggie Ivy.

Suzanne said she went to the gun rack, where she pulled down the top weapon, which was 6' 7" off the floor. She was 5' 3".

If Suzanne shot Vernie, the shooting had to take place as shown in this scene, with the rifle fired from hip height.

Same scenario, but from a different perspective.

Forensic evidence indicates David was the shooter, firing either on his knees or with his knees on the seat of a chair and gun resting over its back outside the bedroom, as Suzanne stood in the corner.

Same forensic perspective, this time from behind shooter.

Aerial drawing of the master bedroom and surrounding area, immediately after the murder.

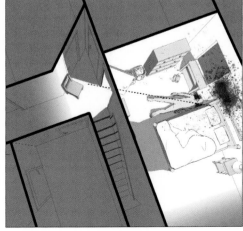

I returned to the house in 2015 and took this photo from where the shooter must have sat. The current owners' furniture is arranged differently from the furniture in 1970.

From outside the master bedroom I could see the same fancy staircase leading downstairs.

Sheriff Jack Leslie, whom Suzanne called at his home immediately after the murder. *Photo courtesy Wisconsin State Journal Archives.*

Psychiatrist Leigh Roberts was the first doctor called in for psychiatric evaluation of Suzanne and the first to give her a diagnosis of insanity. *Photo courtesy Wisconsin State Journal Archives.*

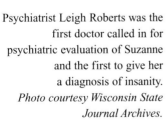

My uncle devoted his life to serving his country, his community, and his family.
Photo courtesy Eastlawn Cemetery, Beloit, Wisconsin.

Kip also talked about David's Madison house, how he lost money on it when it was sold. Just before David left Madison, they got together and David said he was going to use the money from the house and go to Florida and buy a boat. And that's the last they ever talked. "But I figured he was just trying one thing after another. 'Maybe I'll buy a house, maybe I'll sell the house and buy a boat,' and then later I heard he got a motorcycle. He was just too unstable to stay with anything for more than a few months." A later talk with another friend, Kim, supported what John and Kip had said, but Kim also noted, "Vern was a very fun-loving guy and was very understanding of teenage boys. He tolerated a great deal from us that other fathers would not have. He taught us how to hunt and survive in a cabin. He was a fine man. He really was. I was really saddened when he passed. It was a long time ago, but it stands out so clearly in my memory."

Kip talked about how all the friends assumed David had pulled the trigger and how carrying that burden had ruined his life, though Kip accompanied David for several years going to Beloit on the anniversaries of the death to visit Vernie's grave, until he lost touch with David. Kim also had vivid memories of my brother Johnny Ray, "who was quite a character," and told me how he learned the ranges of behaviors open to handicapped people. He remembered Johnny Ray, whose legs were as straight and thin as a mop handle, getting in his wheelchair and riding into his *Ironsides* van with hand controls. Or how my brother would challenge anyone to an arm wrestling match, and usually win. He also recalled my brother's obsession with Elvis Presley, and how the girls flocked around Johnny Ray, waiting for a smile or a touch.

By this time I had learned a lot about Vernie, Suzanne, and their life together. From the court documents and interviews I learned they owned a boat, plus a thirty-five-acre property in Winter, Wisconsin, within Sawyer County, where they often went on hunting trips, taking friends and Suzanne's family. They had bought the property in 1966 (after one of Suzanne's suicide "attempts") for $3,500.

I made a trip to the property during my research, accompanied by my friend Monte Hanson, who picked me up at the Minneapolis–St. Paul airport, and we drove almost four hours to an area much more remote than I had envisioned. On the way, we stopped to eat at the only place for a hundred miles, Burnett Dairy, which was packed. We still had a long way to go.

The biggest town nearby to tiny Winter, Wisconsin, was Spooner with 2,682 residents, but it is 49 miles from my uncle's place. As we got close to our destination, we went to the Village of Winter, hoping to get something to eat, but the only café had closed at 2 P.M. All that was open were two bars, located close to the four churches. No one was on the sidewalks, and I felt like a character in an episode of *Twilight Zone*. Winter has 302 residents and 165 properties for sale, so you can imagine the lack of economic activity.

Driving on narrow asphalt roads, we found my uncle's land, which was more like a deteriorating forest, with trees fallen in every direction and overgrown underbrush almost too dense to walk through. We wanted to see if there were any vestiges of life, so we entered the woods. Branches and bushes constantly scratched me, as I waited for hordes of ticks to bite me or poison ivy to afflict me. Was all of this worth Lyme disease or endless itching from a rash? At one point, Monte got so far from me on the property that he couldn't hear my shouts. I wondered, if we sank in the mud here, how long would it take someone to find us?

Then we came upon the cabin, which evidently was not the building my uncle had used, as Rachel Thompson (who works in the county assessor's office) had told me the original structure was gone. It was a small, probably modular, log cabin. We looked for evidence of a larger house there previously, but found nothing. How could my uncle. Suzanne, David, Danny, and various friends have all fit into a building that size? And they must have loved it, to drive the five-plus hours from Oregon on weekends.

In addition to new knowledge about the property and the boat, I had also learned about the "adopted" daughter, Jocelyn Brandon Freeman. Trying to figure out if I was the only who had been ignorant, I asked other members in my family. No one had ever heard about the boat, the cabin, or Jocelyn. And I, who had spent so many, many weekends at their house, never heard even the slightest hint about any of those three. It means they had to coach the kids before I came *not* to bring up those subjects. The things that their friends and Franklin talked about so casually and with such vigor ("Oh, we had such fun at that cabin," or "Mrs. Freeman was a wonderful person") had been cut off to Vernie's whole family. It was like we all lived behind some secret wall we'd never known existed.

CHAPTER TWENTY

A Trip to the Bountiful Oregon

I knew I had to go back to the mansion. I *wanted* to go back and see where the murder had occurred. After trying to get there for months, I arrived on Tuesday, May 12, 2015.

The house was majestic by any standard, and it stood out among the large, well-kept homes on the wide, clean streets, the newly mown lawns, the well-trimmed hedges, and the carefully planted flowers blooming reds, oranges, purples, and blues. As I drove down Main Street, I could see it up ahead, the outside painted in teal, cantaloupe, aqua, and dark salmon, quite different from the complete white it had been back when I had visited so many weekends in the late 1960s. The gables, the wraparound porch, the leaded glass, all added to its grandeur.

My first stop was the Oregon Area Historical Society. For a few months I'd been e-mailing two people, who'd been extremely helpful. When I got there, they had already gotten out newspaper articles and anything they had related to the Stordock case. Was I interested in high school yearbooks? Yes! But the only relevant ones they had were from 1966, where Louisa was shown as a senior, and from 1969, with David as a sophomore. Because I had found information that the girlfriend who had given David a sort-of alibi was named Lawson, I looked for her in the yearbooks. There was a Charlene Lawson listed as a junior in the 1969 book, and elsewhere I found the name of Sherri Lawson in a club, but with no picture, so I could not figure out if that Charlene and Sherri were the same person, but I assumed Sherri was probably the same Lawson from the police reports and the one I had discussed with David's friend, John. And despite weeks of searching and endless dead-end phone calls, I never did locate her. On a subsequent trip, I checked at the public library and found a couple of more yearbooks with pictures of David and Louisa. It was strangely comforting to see their faces as I had remembered them so long ago.

I had previously contacted the current owners of the mansion to get permission to come and view the house, to revisit the crime scene and to see if any old memories were unlocked. We had talked on the phone several times and the woman who lived there had a lot of questions about the murder, as she was fairly new to the house and had only heard bits and pieces from the neighbors. I parked my rental car on the street and walked to the back porch. I noticed the driveway was asphalt, but I was quite sure it had been gravel back in 1970.

Jan Bonsett-Veal answered the door and I saw a tall woman dressed in white slacks and a loose purple-and-black floral top, with wavy dark brown hair, parted on the left side. Her smile was warm and welcoming, and she led me into the kitchen, which had been completely remodeled. I thought I was in the wrong house. In my memory it was a rather crowded space with a kitchen table, cupboards, appliances squeezed in between an archway to the hallway, an entrance to the den and two doors: porch entrance and one leading to the back stairway. Now the kitchen was about 50 percent larger. A previous room had been knocked out to make way for a huge commercial stove and some cupboards, the whole thing done in contemporary style. It was very beautiful, but a contrast with the rest of the Queen Anne setting.

Whereas the kitchen seemed (and actually was) larger than before, the rest of the rooms seemed to have shrunk. What had happened to the huge living and dining rooms, which now were the size of those in many older homes? The staircase and its elaborately carved spindles were as magnificent as ever. We walked upstairs and I went to the doorway of the master bedroom. I noticed the bed was in a different place, but otherwise the room was quite recognizable. I could feel my chest tightening as I entered the room and could not stop my mind from imagining my uncle's dead body lying there.

I walked over to the wall and found the place where I thought the bullet had lodged itself. My fingers traced over the spot, which was below an oblong abstract painting. Then I looked straight to the doorway and saw right into the bedroom across the hall, the very place Franklin had said the chair was, with some pants over the back, the chair he believed David had used to aim the rifle. A minute later I found myself in that other doorway, looking straight onto the place where the bullet had been extracted. It *was* a straight line.

The rest of the rooms were only slightly familiar to me, as if I had only glimpses of them in my mind. Jan took me up to the huge attic, which her family used for living space. Then we went down to the den, the very room where my uncle's gun rack had protruded from the wall, and I tried to think how the frail Suzanne could have reached way up, six feet seven inches, to haul down a very heavy weapon.

I stayed for almost two hours, and if I hadn't felt I was starting to impose, I would have stayed all day. Some mysterious force was holding me there and I had to compel myself to leave. As we chatted, Jan gave me names of neighbors who had lived in Oregon for decades. After a number of calls in which people said they knew nothing, I talked to a previous owner of the mansion, Mrs. Alice Seeliger, who had lived there with her husband and children for more than twenty years, starting in 1977. We spoke for fifty minutes, and I felt instantly close to her from the warmth in her voice and her approachability. She told me that Louisa had stopped by one day and asked to see the house in 2000, and that Louisa said she'd used the attic for her art studio.

Right before I left the mansion that day in 2015, I asked to visit the basement, hoping there might be a stray bullet hole there as proof that Vernie had done some shooting practice. I was relieved when Jan said they'd done no work there, because that meant maybe nothing would be covered up. It was untouched from the time Suzanne had lived there, except the floor had been concreted.

It was dark and hard to find the lights after I opened the basement door. Going down the stairs was tricky. The wood planks were narrow, the light switches were all in unexpected places, and the architecture was more like one underground chamber or crypt leading into another, and it felt similar to being in Cave of the Mounds, just outside Madison. Rooms trailed off into other rooms, like some labyrinth, or one of those mazes where rats get lost. I examined the walls, which were made from those stones used back in the early 1900s, the kind farmers pulled out of their fields to make the land plowable. I didn't see any bullet holes.

As I was about to figure out how to get back upstairs and out of this quagmire, I saw a door leading to what originally would have been the root cellar, where the residents would store potatoes, carrots, and other root vegetables during the winter. The door was hammered sheet metal. In the upper center was a series of concentric squares painted in red, with hundreds of bullet holes surrounding the area. The owner of the house said no one had realized what those red shapes were for. Vernie had not gone down in the basement to randomly fire off guns in order to scare Suzanne. He had made his own shooting range, to make sure he maintained his marksman skills. In the kind of undercover work he did, you never knew when your firearm prowess meant the difference between life and death.

Now I confess that I fell in love with this story and was sadly disappointed to find out a year later from the Seeligers they had created this target for dart practice. Instead of bullet holes, the indentations were from the sharp tips of the darts. So not all my theories turn out to be true. That was a lesson for me.

Three other things Alice said to me in our first phone call were important in my research. One was that people would often stop by when Alice was outside in order to inform her that someone had been murdered in this house. This was in contrast to what people had told me on my brief visit to Oregon in 2006, when I talked to some neighbors who said no one had talked much about the killing. Secondly, Alice mentioned that people believed that David had killed Vernie (based on no particular evidence, just common belief), and the reason the cops never pursued the case very aggressively was because there had been abuse, and they didn't want to make this former cop look bad. Finally Alice told me she and her husband, Michael, had done some work on the kitchen around 1980 and had found a great deal of dried blood on the top of the patterned tin ceiling tiles. Because the kitchen was below a back bedroom on the other side of the house from the master, she and her husband had always wondered if the murder had taken place in that room and the body moved.

I considered that possibility as we talked, but then I told her the master bedroom had a bullet hole in the headboard and the wall, and there had been brains and tissue splattered over one side of the room. I should have asked her how they knew it was blood, but these were highly educated people, so presumably he would have been able to discern. Maybe there had been another, previous murder in that house, unreported, because it seemed they were the first owners to work on the kitchen. Was there some unknown crime? Louisa and the current owner had both reported to me strange noises and a presence that felt like the house was haunted.

* * *

The following day I rode around Madison, looking at all the houses that Suzanne had lived in. I was most interested in the house on Capital Avenue, because I knew there was a house where Vernie had taken my mother, stepfather, and me to visit Suzanne and her kids, early in their relationship. Once I saw the one-and-a-half-story white clapboard house, with a large bay window at the front, a driveway on the right, and the huge back, I knew this was the place where I'd been. In the back of my mind I remembered a large body of water down two blocks; and sure enough, as I drove in that direction, there was the beautiful and blue Lake Mendota peeking through some large trees. Going back and trying to remember streets and lakes from over forty years previous is slightly disorienting and incredibly fulfilling when you get it right.

Vernie was keen, back in 1963, for his family to meet the wonderful woman on whom he'd staked his future, though I only realized recently that Shannon did not know about Suzanne until a few months after this. I remember our visit to the Capital Avenue house as being awkward, though I was only fourteen and didn't really understand the dynamics of affairs and waiting for divorces. But I can only imagine how uncomfortable my parents must have been, as they both loved and adored Jenylle, Vernie's first wife. We all sat in Suzanne's wood-cabineted kitchen and had a meal, which was probably fried chicken and mashed potatoes. Then the kids/teenagers went outside to hang out in that big backyard, which had a huge, elaborate swing set, the kind I usually saw in playgrounds. None of my friends had ever had anything that grand in their own yards. That's the day I first met Louisa, David, and Danny, who were about fifteen, twelve, and three years old, but were really just a blur of nonadult human beings to me. I wasn't savvy enough to understand what these people would mean to me in the coming seven years, and ultimately the coming four decades. How could I have known back then the tragedy this group of people would bring to my entire family? Was there any way to see the emotional toll it would also take on each and every one of them—and us?

Suzanne and Irv Gast had bought the Capital Avenue house in 1961, and she got it in the divorce in November 1963. Because of comments Louisa made to me, as well as documentation in the Oregon, Wisconsin, newspaper, I've estimated Suzanne and the kids moved to Oregon between December 1963 and January 1964. When we visited the Capital Avenue house back in the early '60s, it was warm, if not hot, with no brown leaves. All this means late spring, probably May 1963, which would have put it before either of their divorces and not long after the Gast heirs meeting, where Suzanne and Irv's first wife duked it out.

After leaving that Madison house on that May 2015 afternoon, I spent three hours in an Italian café with Irv Gast's son Jim and his wife, Anne. Jim looked very much like someone who had gone back to school to get his doctorate in computer science: smart, well-spoken, and extremely personable. Anne had curly brown hair and a bubbly personality. She was easy to talk with, as was Jim. Initially I thought we'd meet for about an hour, and I forgot about my rental car and the parking meter, because when I went out to fill it after three hours, the car had been towed away Both Jim and I were eager to talk about parts of our childhood, some of which had been snatched away. In my case it was because of my uncle's murder, and in his case it was his immediate family. He'd barely ever seen his father and had never met his half-brother. "Do you have any pictures of Danny?" he asked.

Jim gave me copies of his parents' marriage license, and his and his brother's birth certificates. I noticed a keen interest in the parts of my research that related to when Vernie and Suzanne started their affair, which Jim believed did not end his parents' marriage, as they were likely already estranged.

* * *

The next day I returned to Oregon and drove through the charming downtown, with its 150-year-old restored brick municipal and business buildings, then headed to the bowling alley and its adjacent tavern. I walked in and stared at the room where my uncle had spent some of his last hours alive. I already knew that the bowling alley and bar were exactly the same, except for one small area, so I was able to really feel what the space had been like. The eight lanes looked very much like the kind I had bowled on decades ago.

About eight people populated the horseshoe-shaped bar, as the bartender and those drinking away their agitated emotions didn't—or perhaps couldn't—display any response when I told them I was there to see the last place my uncle was before his murder. They had as much reaction as the foaming beer exhibited in their glasses, and it felt as if I were talking to a room of mannequins. None of them seemed to care, or be curious in the least, about how or why such a violent episode had happened unusually close to the very location they currently occupied.

Then I stopped at the local Firefly Coffeehouse, encompassing two large areas filled with wooden tables, captain's chairs, overstuffed chairs, and couches. The place was bustling. I went up and talked to a few people, asking how long they'd lived in town, hoping to find some long-term residents. Nothing. All of them were either tourists or recent residents. Same responses at a nearby Mexican restaurant filled with bright-colored booths and plenty of tortilla chips on the tables. As I walked over to a number of groups and asked questions, I started to feel like a stalker, so I got in my car and headed west toward Mount Hope, where Elmira Brandon had spent her childhood.

At first, I thought the sparsely appearing white farmhouses and red barns, with the gently rolling green fields and occasional cows, were charming. But after more than an hour of one cornstalk after another, as the terrain became flatter and the periodic clumps were of houses was smaller and less frequent, I didn't know how much of this I could withstand. I got off one of the highway's scarce exits and started to turn around and go back to Madison. Thankfully, I forced myself to get back on the freeway, heading west. I felt I just *had to* experience how far it was from the Madison area to Mount Hope and then Boscobel, so I could get a sense of how difficult it was for Elmira and her family to get to Madison. And back when she was a young girl, there were only narrow two-lane highways and slower cars. If I couldn't stand driving even half the way to Mount Hope, how difficult must it have been for them back in the 1940s?

After another hour I almost came to the border of Wisconsin and Iowa, where stood Mount Hope, a small village of perhaps fifty mostly wooden ranch and one-and-a-half-story houses, flanked on one side by a large, active farmhouse, with barns and assorted buildings, all of which lay in the middle of vast croplands. I drove around the single main street—which felt more like a long drive-way around the homes—then got out of the car and imagined the smart and ambitious little girl who was going into high school in 1942 and realized how limited she would have felt here, considering she had even lived on a farm far outside this small enclave of people. Why wouldn't she want to go somewhere with more excitement, more intellectual and social challenge? The closest town was Patch Grove, population 168, so it would make sense to look for a bigger city.

It took me about thirty minutes to get to Boscobel, where Elmira had been sent away to board with a family, or so she had told me. Boscobel, with 2,400 people, must have seemed like a thriving metropolis to her. It had a real downtown, with restaurants, shops, and the stately Boscobel Hotel, built in 1863 and where the idea for the Gideon Bible started in 1898. It is also the "Wild Turkey Hunting Capital" of Wisconsin. The city has many neighborhoods, some with elegant homes. I went to the former high school, a Romanesque Revival brick building from 1898, which looked like a castle with a tall, gabled bell tower in the middle of a wraparound Gothic structure built from Wisconsin River bluffs limestone. After the construction of a new high school in 1984 at the edge of town, "the Rock School" became the elementary establishment.

Hoping to find some Boscobel high school yearbooks with information about and pictures of Elmira, I went to the public library, but had no luck. So I called the local historical society and was directed to call the Boscobel Hotel, where the woman told me not enough people had been interested and the society just fell apart.

Because I had to drive far north from Mount Hope to Boscobel, I took a different route back to Madison. Highway 14 was as isolated as the previous roads, but at least it had more trees and river bluffs, reducing the tedium of driving on monotonously flat roads. As I drove the endless miles, I tried to think how daunting it would have been for a high school girl back in 1945. How could she have found her way to Madison often enough to make friends with Carlotta Rhoades, whom she had often talked about? And was it in Madison that she allegedly got pregnant by a black man?

On the way back I passed through Spring Green, Wisconsin. When the exit sign appeared, I remembered a connection and considered getting off the highway. Suzanne's mother had died in 1980 and her obituary listed Suzanne as living in Spring Green, which had struck me as more than a little strange. Why not stop by there and just see if driving through town might give me some perspective? Spring Green's only apparent economic support was tourism for the town's Frank Lloyd Wright Taliesin summer home and the American Players Theatre. By the time Suzanne had lived there, she had gotten her bachelor's and master's degrees in sociology from the University of Wisconsin. I couldn't imagine how she might have earned a living in this place of 1,647 people, a town an hour from Madison and pretty much in the middle of nowhere. And why would she want to live there, anyway?

After all, she had fled small towns for city life most of her existence. Was she living with a man or what? That could be the only reason she would live there, as far as I could make out. Was she still Suzanne Stordock there (as the obituary listed her), or had she started using Suzanne Brandon? But how could I ever find out? If she never owned any property in Spring Green (which she hadn't—I'd already checked), it would be almost impossible to find traces of her.

After I got back to New York, I was doing research on Suzanne and Vernie's properties and wanted to get more information on their hunting cabin in northern Wisconsin, so I called the Sawyer County offices. I discovered Suzanne sold the land in 1987 for the same amount as they bought it in 1966—$3,500 (even though it was worth $60,000, according to the assessor's office) to a Fred Weir, who turned around that same day and resold it to Mary Klaus for $3,000. One thing the county clerk told me was that Fred Weir had lived in Spring Green. My head started to vibrate. Maybe that was the person Suzanne had lived with. But without any more to go on, it was not promising.

Searching for several months, I thought I'd never know what she was doing in Spring Green. Then a clue appeared almost by accident. During a phone call to one of Suzanne and Jocelyn's relatives, from Madison, I mentioned I was looking for people who remembered my uncle, and I got this answer:

"I saw your uncle quite a few times," this fortyish man said confidently, but I knew he hadn't been born until after the murder, so it threw me off. My mind was racing.

"We'd drive up to Spring Green to see Suzanne. Your uncle was a great guy."

"Spring Green?" My uncle never lived in Spring Green, and it took me a few seconds to catch on, and in my confusion I almost missed the next part: "He was the caretaker of a big hunting preserve."

"Do you remember his name?"

Unfortunately, he didn't. And yet I got more than I bargained for in that conversation. My intuition had been right. Suzanne went to Spring Green around 1978 (when she sold her house in Madison) to live with the caretaker. I wondered how many guns he kept in their house.

Fred Weir was the man she sold the hunting cabin to for a pittance. Was it some payoff? Suzanne was already married to Ronald by this time, so I doubted she and Fred were still involved. After I had dug through newspapers, I discovered Fred had a wife in a small town in Minnesota. Could this be the same man? Actually, it was. In the papers I also found names of village officials to contact, so I got on the phone and called about fifteen people. Eventually I found someone who had worked with Fred for about twenty years in Spring Green.

"Sure, I remember Fred. We both worked at the preserve for many years and then he bought some land and did farming farther out in the county." Did he remember a woman who lived with him by the name of Suzanne? "Yes, that does ring a bell. And Fred had a son who'd come around." Unfortunately, it wasn't until later I discovered Fred had no children of his own; otherwise I would have asked more about the son. It must have been Danny or David. Fred's coworker went on, "I also remember other girlfriends he had over the years. He sure liked to spend money. Was his wife disabled or something? She never came to Spring Green and he didn't go up there much, maybe twice a year." After I dug around some more and then got my daughter, Elizabeth, to help me with research, she found the house of Fred and his wife in tiny Trimont, Minnesota. Both Fred and his wife died around 2013, without any children as heirs. Their house was put up for sale and finally was bought in 2015, at which time all their papers and photos were taken to the local dump. Too late, again.

Nobody else I talked to in Spring Green had more than a cursory memory of Suzanne, but we already know from Oregon that she kept to herself. Then I tried to find out more about Mary Klaus, who married Tony Davidson a year after she got the property from Fred Weir. No one ever answered their phone, but I tracked down a relative, a close cousin, who said she had broken off contact with Mary Klaus years before, as all Mary did was try and manipulate money out of family members.

"Her mother died last year and she's been illegally spending money out of her mother's account and scheduled a hearing without telling her sister, who lives four hundred miles away. Nobody in the family wants anything to do with her."

When I talked about the northern Wisconsin property, the cousin quickly shot back, "None of us can figure out how she could have bought something like that. She's always in debt, with bill collectors chasing after her." When I explained about the transaction, she said, "Oh, Fred. You mean her sugar daddy. He was forty years older than her, but I guess she smelled his money."

If you subscribe to the theory about "birds of a feather," then the argument that Fred was a sweet-talking guy who used people, it's not much of a stretch to see one of his longtime compatriots (from about 1978 to at least 1987) Suzanne as someone who shared similar values. At last I had found evidence of her life in Spring Green.

One other question I need to answer in the same vein was about Jocelyn. Was she being used by Suzanne, or was she merely the lucky recipient of Suzanne's overflowing generosity?

CHAPTER TWENTY-ONE
Jocelyn Revisited

Finding out the truth about the "adopted" Jocelyn proved to be one of the most challenging parts of my research. I asked Suzanne and Louisa multiple times about Jocelyn, without letting on that I might know more about this daughter who had somehow been added into the family. When I would ask about Jocelyn, Suzanne would say, "I guess Louisa takes credit for introducing Jocelyn into our family, back when we lived near *her* family."

Louisa would always tell me about how she'd been out in the neighborhood when she'd found Jocelyn and was fascinated with her hair, so she brought her home to meet Suzanne. After some months I started to think how unusual such stories were. Thinking back to my neighborhood in Pewaukee, Wisconsin, where we lived from the time I was four until ten, finding friends was a different procedure, if you can call it that. If you asked any of my siblings about how we met Mary Collins or Nancy Stracka, we'd probably just shrug and say, "They were just there. Neighbors." What about where we lived before that, on Palmer Street in Milwaukee? I have no memory of any friends from back at that time, where I lived from age two to four, so there'd be no stories. My sister, on the other hand, who is four and a half years older, can recall quite a few friends, but how she met them is never part of her stories.

My cousin Donna encouraged me to find adoption records for Jocelyn, because Louisa and David had both told me Suzanne adopted Jocelyn as a grown woman, when Jocelyn was about thirty. Even if her childhood records were sealed, surely adult adoptions would not be so secret, my smart cousin reasoned. That made so much sense, but I found out that's not how adoption law works. Even adult adoption records are closed.

So when I was in Madison at the Vital Records Department, I looked through their files for any kind of birth record for February 11, 1945. Nothing. I did find Jocelyn's death certificate, which only listed Norman and Claudia Rhoades (who were both deceased by that time) as her parents. One of Jocelyn's children gave the information to go on the death certificate. In Jocelyn's obituary, which I had found on Madison.com, Suzanne was listed as her mother, and it went on to list Ronald Aaronson, David, Louisa Chappington and husband, and even showed that Jocelyn had been predeceased by brother Danny. It had Suzanne's MO all over it, the way she had to put all her family into it. There was no mention of Jocelyn being predeceased by her granddaughter, the child of Jocelyn's youngest son. Surely, this was a more important inclusion than David Briggs?

Then I called Jocelyn's adoptive brother Norman Rhoades Jr., then in his eighties and still living on Beld Street in Madison. He said he didn't know as much as Frank Rhoades did about Suzanne, as Norman was much younger. I knew Frank was ninety and wasn't sure if I should call. Norman said Frank was in assisted living and told me to call his children, but I could not locate a phone number for Frank or his children. Then I mentioned Jocelyn, who was Norman's adopted sister, and the probability that Suzanne was her real mother. "That's what I heard," Norman replied quietly. "That Suzanne was the birth mother. But I don't know the details of how it was arranged."

Norman's admission was powerful, but I needed more. So far, I hadn't been able to find Jocelyn's birth certificate. Adoption couldn't be an insurmountable obstacle; otherwise I would not have been able to find Daniel's birth certificate, which was altered when my uncle adopted him. The fact that I could not locate Jocelyn's must be because she was not born in Wisconsin. Then I remembered something very important. In the course of getting copies of marriage licenses of Suzanne's three marriages before Vernie, I noticed that on marriage licenses it lists the parents of each partner and where the bride and groom were born. Why hadn't I thought of this before?

I had come across information on Jocelyn's second marriage, to Roger Afterton in 1990, and if I sent away for that marriage license, I could perhaps find out some important information. After mailing that request to Dane County, I thought I would also try to get the license for her first marriage to William Freeman, with whom she'd had her three children. I couldn't find when they got married, but I did discover he was killed while on active army duty, in 1974. So she wasn't a widow when she moved into the Oregon house. Furthermore, her youngest child was born in 1971, and the newspaper listed Mr. and Mrs. Freeman as living in Oregon, Wisconsin. So they *all* lived there as a family, evidently.

When the envelope arrived from Wisconsin Vital Records, I was afraid to be too excited, as I would likely learn nothing new. Waiting a few minutes to open the letter, I calmed myself down; then I took out the 1990 license and immediately looked for "Parents of Bride (Jocelyn)": Suzanne Brandon and unknown father. Born in Illinois.

Was this the definitive answer? On the forms she filled out before the marriage, Jocelyn had not put down her adoptive parents, Norman and Claudia Rhoades, only Suzanne Brandon. One could argue that she was still in the blush of being adopted as an adult by Suzanne, but then why did Jocelyn say the father was "unknown"? Writing something like that would be terribly difficult, if not humiliating.

However, this new marriage license told me something I had

not known previously, that Jocelyn was born in Illinois. So I wrote away for her birth certificate, hoping any adoption would not get in the way. Two weeks later I got an envelope from the Illinois Department of Health, the certificate for the birth in Chicago of one "Jocelyn Brandon Stordock," which told me the adoption took place probably not long after the murder. Vernie was not listed, so it couldn't have been before, and Suzanne stopped using the last name "Stordock" a few years later, so it had to be sometime in the 1970s. Interestingly, there was not one single other place I could ever find the name "Jocelyn Brandon Stordock" listed in the newspaper, or in various obituaries or her death certificate. The birth certificate only listed Suzanne Brandon as her parent, and that Suzanne was sixteen at the time.

Next I wanted to talk to Jocelyn's children. It took me a couple of weeks to figure out how to be in contact. I tried many, many no-longer-in-service numbers, and her son seemed to be the only one who might have a working number listed. Finally I dialed and there was an answer, with a message saying the son and his wife had moved and had a new number. Could I finally be close? When I called the more recent number, I just got voice mail and didn't want to leave what would prove to be a confusing message to Marvyn. I'd just call back.

Five minutes later my phone rang and the caller ID had the Madison area code. It was Marvyn, wondering who had called. I introduced myself. He was, of course, a little confused at first, but talked about his mother and Suzanne, and how Suzanne had adopted Jocelyn as an adult. I asked some questions about his mother's birth and also the wedding to his father. The son stumbled around and kept saying, "I don't know."

After a few minutes I realized they didn't talk much about Jocelyn's history, and Jocelyn perhaps did not want to give away Suzanne's secret past. It was enough for her, evidently, to be able to tell her children that they were mother and daughter through adoption later on.

After repeated study of that Illinois birth certificate, I finally realized why Suzanne had adopted the adult Jocelyn, besides wanting free child care while in the mental hospital. Evidently, Norman and Claudia never legally adopted Jocelyn, so the birth certificate would have listed Suzanne as birth mother with no known father. But after the adult adoption, that original certificate would have been obliterated, and Suzanne could obfuscate Jocelyn's real parentage. But she could not stop me from digging deeper for the truth.

CHAPTER TWENTY-TWO
An Unexpected Call

Sometimes you get beautiful sunny weather on your day off, and sometimes one phone call can almost change your life.

On my list of things to do was to contact Jan, the current owner of the Oregon mansion, to ask her some follow-up questions about the property. I punched in her number, and after a couple of minutes, her voice changed from that of a polite raconteur of details to enthusiastic reporter of unexpected events. She energetically told me about a recent visitor to her home.

"My husband and I were sitting outside when a car zoomed into our driveway and out strolls a tall, Clint Eastwood–walking white man, with lots of gray hair, probably in his seventies, followed by a fortyish Chinese woman with a black blunt-cut hairdo. 'I came to see *my* house!' he announced, and we just sat there, not knowing what he meant," Jan Bonsett-Veal explained. "He introduced himself as Otis Wahlburger, who had bought the house from Suzanne back in the seventies, and pointed to his companion as 'my dance partner.' He lives in China and is back in the States for a couple more weeks and I told him about you, and he really wants to talk with you. He's a therapist and I think was Suzanne's counselor after the murder and that's how they met. But his story is really different from the one you told me."

This was more than intriguing. I had talked to all the owners except for the people who had bought it from Suzanne in 1973. Manna from heaven, I thought. Yes, there is a God.

Jan went on: "He gave me his business card, which is Chinese on one side and English on the other. It has his name and then says, 'Clever Monkey in China.' Underneath that is 'VIP English Teacher, Management Consultant, Nutritional Research.'"

Jan had no idea where he'd gone after leaving Oregon, but she gave me some phone numbers in the United States and China and e-mail addresses, one for the States and one for China. I called him three times over two days, but all I got was a voice saying the phone had not been set up with a mailbox. Then I tried e-mailing, first to the one evidently used in the United States and two days later the one in China, just in case.

On the third day my phone rang at 11:03 P.M. I recognized Otis Wahlburger's number, picked up the phone, and heard a deep, clear male voice. After making clear who I was and exchanging pleasantries, he related what Suzanne had told him about the night of the murder:

> She said her husband drank all the time, then he'd beat her up, would drink some more and beat her again. This went on for years and she suffered terrible abuse. Then one night he said he'd had enough and took a gun and went down to the basement to commit suicide. She heard the gunshot and ran down the stairs and saw he was still alive. Then she got mad that he had pretended to kill himself, and there was a struggle with the gun. It went off and killed him. But that's not the story Jan told me, I mean the one you told her.

I wanted to correct him and started to say something about court transcripts and newspaper articles, but he didn't seem interested. And, anyway, the important thing was learning what he had been told, and what his experience was with Suzanne:

> I had just finished graduate school in counseling and had taken all these psychology courses. Suzanne was studying psychology and criminology, so we had so much to talk about. She is really smart and such a nice person. And we both loved the house.

Otis had the same experience that Alice Seeliger had with various Oregon residents. They'd stop by and ask him if he knew someone was murdered there, and then they'd tell him they thought the son did it and the mother confessed to protect her son. While he was talking, I couldn't get his reported murder story out of my mind, so I said, "You mean she told you he was killed in the basement?"

> It seemed strange to me, because back then the basement had a dirt floor. We later cemented it. But the original furnace had huge pipes that ran across the floor, and when the furnace was replaced, the pipes were removed and there were just holes everywhere in the basement floor. Having a struggle down there didn't make sense.
>
> It wasn't just the basement that was a mess when we bought the house. The whole structure was in disrepair, and I'll tell you we worked so hard on it. I mean, I would drive thirty minutes to get home from work in Madison after a nine- or ten-hour day, then spend three to four hours on the house, plus ten to twelve hours on Saturdays and Sundays. We had six kids and I was earning one thousand dollars a month. Painting the outside of the house cost seven hundred dollars, not to mention all the damage the carpenter ants had done on the floors and walls that we had to pull out. The roof was leaking, so we put in a new roof. It was no easy job because of the high slant, so we had to use ropes up there.

But I understood how Suzanne wasn't able to manage, because she'd been in prison for five years, which I think was so unfair. Women who are abused like that don't deserve to do any time. As part of my graduate work in counseling, I visited a prison, and they took me to the wing where all the women who had murdered their husbands were. They were the kindest, most polite people, so artistic. You could never imagine them as killing anyone. When you think of murderers, you see slanty eyes and cruel faces and ominous stares. These women were so engaging, so charming. What an injustice.

I just listened. It wasn't my job to tell him how most murderers are not like the faces of criminals on the FBI's most wanted list. And after all the research I've done on sociopaths and psychopaths, I've discovered the one thing they do better than anyone else is to make everyone think how kind and thoughtful and caring they are. And I also learned how often they fool mental health professionals. Such as Otis Wahlburger.

I asked if he ever met Danny, her youngest son, and he said "no." Later on, I stated, "So, Suzanne was living alone in the house at the time you bought it," and he said she was. He would have noticed, because he and his wife looked over the house the day they happened to pass by it and saw the FOR SALE BY OWNER sign and also there were inspections done for the mortgage and so on, in addition to frequent conversations when Otis Wahlburger would stop by. I had heard from several sources that Danny didn't live with his mother after she got out of the hospital. Suzanne sold the house in May 1973, when Danny was twelve. And one of David's friends told me when Suzanne moved from Oregon to Regent Street in Madison, Danny was not living with her there, either.

Wahlburger went on with his praise:

Suzanne had so many insights into prisons, both from her own experience as a prisoner, and also from her studies. She told me how humiliated she'd been, because there she was an intelligent, "high-class" person who was under the subjugation of these low-class prison guards.

As he was talking, I thought how Suzanne described herself as eminently intelligent and under the control of people who had less intellectual competence. It was her explaining all over again how she was so smart that she left 98 percent of others in the dust.

I wondered what Suzanne considered "prison." She'd been in jail less than a day on March 1, 1970, before they moved her to the mental hospital for evaluation. Then, after a week in the hospital, she was transferred back to jail. Her bond was set on March 11 and she was out within a couple of days, so the maximum she spent behind bars was four to five days. She was in the mental hospital for eleven months and then was released because she was completely cured, but was still considered on parole until they gave a final judgment to set her free. Did she think her time in the hospital was prison? Or was she telling him those things to bolster her contention that she'd spent five years in prison and shouldn't be held responsible for a leaky roof? One of the problems with lying, besides the fact that it's morally wrong, is that when people get together and compare versions of the story, the stories often don't match.

Some months after my last interview with Suzanne, I went back to the coroner's reports and found out about an old friend of Danny's and was able to contact him. During the first few seconds on the telephone, I heard his loving voice and there was an instant connection; then we both shared stories and asked questions. I learned a great deal.

Within days we were Facebook friends. He told me later that

once he and I were connected, Suzanne, who was one of his Facebook friends, started commenting more on his posts. Not long after, I started noticing Suzanne showing up on my "suggested friends" list, even though we had only two connections in common. Many of my Facebook friends share one hundred or more common friends.

By accident I learned people show up on your suggested friends list because they have visited your page often. Did that mean Suzanne was looking to see what I was posting? She knew I was asking around, but she must have been awfully curious about exactly what I was finding. But even without knowing she was sort of stalking me on Facebook, I had made a rule for myself not to post anything related to my uncle's murder or the research I was doing. Later on, there'd be plenty of time. And then I suppose Suzanne got tired of lurking in the background. One day in late January 2016, I woke up and there was a Facebook friend request from none other than Suzanne. Should I accept?

After much internal agitation and several months, I finally accepted her as a friend. In one way it didn't matter, because I have nothing hidden. I use Facebook as more of a public site, so friends have no special viewing privileges, but there was the principle. After my book was accepted for publication, people asked me when I was going to post it online. My reply was "The confessed murderer is one of my FB friends, and I am not ready to disclose detailed information about the book to her."

CHAPTER TWENTY-THREE

Forensic Files—An Information System

I needed as much data as I could get. But after forty years, what is left? How do you find evidence that was recorded when Nixon was still president, when the Vietnam War was still raging? I had been trying to get the police forensic files on the case for five months with no results, so far, even though I had first requested them in December 2014.

I called the Dane County sheriff's office after a month and the woman said, "Oh, are you the one back East who made the request? We're working on it." This was the same response I got the next two times I called. Then in February, they told me "the lieutenant" was handling it, so I called her and left a message, thinking it would be another month before I had to call back again. She returned my call the next day.

The first thing Lieutenant Alicia Rauch told me was how she had initially thought I was calling the wrong office because the murder happened in the Village of Oregon, which should have done the investigation. But then she called Oregon herself and found out I had tried there first. Hesitating for a moment out of confusion, I finally said, "But Suzanne called the Dane County sheriff to report the murder." Now it was her turn to pause, after which she blurted out, "But why? That's not even our jurisdiction."

That was my first hint that Suzanne had taken control of the situation from the start. Our supposedly psychotic mental case had the clear thinking to look in her address book (or had she memorized it?) for the sheriff's home number and called him sometime around 2:15 A.M. Why wouldn't someone just look on the inside cover of the Oregon phone book and call the police, who were a one-minute drive away? Unless our psychotic wanted to make sure the investigation would be handled by the Dane County sheriff himself.

Then the lieutenant started asking me a lot of questions about whether Suzanne was still alive and whether I was in contact with her or her family. I started answering her openly, then wondered why she was asking. Would she find some way to deny me access to these files? At the end she said she'd work on it. It wasn't until many months later that I learned the real reason she asked so many questions, and it wasn't anything like I thought at the time.

Another month passed, so I called again. The lieutenant had the files, the clerk told me, so I called her again. Two days later I got an e-mail from the Dane County sheriff telling me how much I owed for the copying, so I paid immediately online and called the next day to confirm. Oh, they'd have these out in a few days, I was told. Weeks later I called. Oh, it is so many pages, they said, so it's taking a long time. I started to wonder if I'd ever get anything, or if they were just stalling and hoping I'd give up.

Just when I *was* wondering if the best strategy was to move on, a letter arrived in mid-April 2015 from the Dane County Sheriff's Office. It wasn't thick enough to be the forensic files. Maybe they were telling me I'd never be able to read those reports. With shaking hands I opened the envelope.

CHAPTER TWENTY-FOUR
Forensic Files and Ethical Matters

Our justice system sometimes seems like it is weighted in favor of the accused. The Fourth Amendment to the U.S. Constitution protects against unreasonable search and seizure, the Fifth Amendment allows refusal to answer questions that might be self-incriminating, the Sixth gives the right to a speedy trial and trial by jury, while the Eighth prohibits excessive bail. Ergo, four of the ten amendments known as the Bill of Rights are protection for those accused of crimes.

These are based partly on the Magna Carta, where England's King John was pressured in 1215 by defiant and rebellious barons to protect subjects against royal abuses of power. Our Founding Fathers had seen enough abuses of royal power to want to prevent that in the new system. And because that abuse had been so egregious, the Bill of Rights was an attempt to balance the power and give the accused some rights under the law.

It wasn't until the 1970s, when the consciousness changed about victims' rights, and the tide was turned with a 1973 Supreme Court decision that said an unmarried mother who was not paid child support had no legal standing to pursue a case. However, the Supreme Court went on to encourage Congress to "enact statutes creating legal rights" for victims. A final report on the President's Task

Force on the Victims of Crime was released in 1982. That same year the federal government passed laws protecting victims, and since then thirty-three states have legislated victim's rights statutes.

Even the idea of wrongful-death suits wasn't popularized until the 1980s and later. O. J. Simpson was declared *not* guilty of murder by a jury in 1995, but in 1997 a different jury found Simpson liable and ordered him to pay $33.5 million to the families of Nicole Brown Simpson and Ronald Goldman. Standards in civil trial wrongful-death suits are less stringent than in murder cases. Shannon would have been the only one to have any legal standing to file such a suit. However, the first inkling of any legislation in Wisconsin was 1971 and it wasn't until the 1980s, probably in tandem with the victim's rights movement, that there was any real attention paid to such legal claims.

An important piece of this legislation was put in place in 1988: *A person who "feloniously and intentionally" kills his or her spouse is not a surviving spouse for purposes of sub. (2) and is treated as having predeceased the decedent. Steinbarth v. Johannes, 144 Wis. 2d 159, 423 N.W.2d 540 (1988).* In Wisconsin, as in many other states, the statute of limitations in wrongful-death suits is three years.

It was too late for us, because the case took place back in 1970 and it took more than ten years to have any meaningful victim's rights laws, but not too late for me now to at least be allowed to get information, as one of the victims of the murder. Before my uncle's death there were three surviving children of my grandmother, Dorothy Stordock. The oldest of the original five, Katherine, had died of rheumatic fever at age fifteen, and then the diabetic Amos died of insulin shock in 1967, just one month short of age forty-eight. Grandpa Oscar Stordock died one year later. Add to that my brother Raymond, dying at age twenty in 1962, and you've got a lot of deaths in a few years. Even before Vernie's murder, we'd had three deaths in six years, but we were still functioning, talking on the phone, visiting one another, and somehow bearing the grief.

Then Vernie got murdered, brutally, and my grandmother was denied not only her son, but the chance to see him in an open casket. At that point my grandmother had two living children left, out of the original five. Donald had retired from the army and moved to Waukesha, to be close to his sister, my mother. Grandma soon followed, leaving her Beloit home. Our big family gatherings were not big anymore and were not as often. Our family world had shrunk and everyone bore wounds, before—and more since the murder.

A few years after the murder, Donald and my mother died within days of each other; both of cancer. On April 7, 1977, Donald finally succumbed. Two days after his funeral, my mother died on April 12, which sadly also happened to be the day after my stepfather's birthday. He died three years later. The priest at the funeral said the light in my stepfather's life went out when my mother passed.

I spent years wondering how it could be that Donald and my mother died so close to one another and with the same illness. I've read articles about how traumatic events can increase cancer risk five years later. Is that what happened here?

What makes sense to me is that Vernie's death essentially took out the entire remaining generation in the Stordock family: not only Vernie, but also his two remaining siblings. And then the death of my stepfather, who couldn't really live without my mother. We had no elder Stordocks, other than my grandma, to call on for advice, for help, for companionship.

Jenylle remarried (a happy union that lasted until her husband's death many years later) and moved to Los Angeles. Maxine remarried and moved to Florida. Grandma was left alone in Waukesha, with assorted grandchildren and great-grandchildren, but that's not the same. And I can tell you it's not the same for those in my generation. I saw my cousins, plus the aunts, periodically, and my grandmother more often, but family gatherings were no more. Where would we have them? In Grandma's five-hundred-square-foot apartment in the assisted-living facility? The loss was highlighted for me in 2015 when my ailing friend Philip asked me to take him to the hospital, and the intake nurse was getting information. Philip said his birthday was February 20, 1926. I just looked at him as my heart broke apart one more time. My uncle was born February 25, 1926, and he could be still alive, and he would be the exact age as Philip, with probably the same gray hair and wrinkles, but a determined and indomitable spirit.

I had pushed all the grief inside for many years and only now really see what I lost, what we all lost. And then to have the confessed killer spend only eleven months in a mental hospital, and after she was released, she went on to receive Vernie's life insurance and all his assets—that is a lot to bear. Where were our rights as the victims of this tragedy?

When I ordered the police reports and had such difficulty getting them (the court documents were much easier), I couldn't understand what was going on. Sure, it *was* a long time ago, but they did have the records, or so I assumed. I ordered them in December 2014 and finally got them in April 2015, after numerous phone calls, even talking several times to the lieutenant who was in charge of records. When some of the records finally arrived, they came with the letter from that same lieutenant, with excerpts below. And this is long after the victim's rights movement had taken hold:

> As custodian of records for the Sheriff's Office, I must
> balance competing interests when determining whether
> or not to release a record in my custody. . . . I have deter-
> mined that the public interests favoring non-disclosure

substantially outweigh the public interest in disclosure of some information. Therefore . . . certain information has been redacted from this report.

She went on to give the exclusions allowed by law: anything medical, which just about covers all things having to do with my uncle's body and his condition. Names of juveniles were redacted, which is understandable, and also anything having to do with motor-vehicle information, which I assumed meant license plate numbers. Then she said I needed to get the coroner's report directly from that office, which I did, and it came immediately. And I also tried to get my uncle's FBI file, which somehow disappeared during the few weeks I was trying to retrieve it. They were going to send it, and then *poof,* it had been destroyed. I even appealed that ruling, but was turned down. No report exists anymore, they said. I tried to get Suzanne's, but she was still alive, and the FBI wanted to know why her right to privacy was less important than my desire to know. I thought I was asking under the Freedom of Information Act, but it did not feel like information was free.

Anyway, I thought I might as well try and get my own FBI file. When I was in college at the University of Wisconsin, I was in one protest after another, as I was also in Milwaukee the year I dropped out. My uncle, who worked undercover in Milwaukee, told me the organization I frequented was a Communist front, which I discovered years later was correct. Photographers were always there, taking pictures. And I had roommates who were so into drugs that narcotics cops would sit outside our house 24/7. All these years I had wanted to see what was in my FBI file. After my request they wrote me a formal letter that there was no file on me. I was quite disappointed, but not as disappointed as I was to be restricted from receiving some information in the police report.

In that same letter the lieutenant used victim's rights (does she mean my uncle Vernie as the victim?) to tell me I cannot see or read anything of a graphic nature of the crime, to allow for privacy of the victim. Are we family members not also victims, and aren't we now allowed to finally know what happened? All I can see is that this censorship protects, mainly, the murderer.

What about the rights of my family? Does anybody care? Do the confessed murderer or her family members feel any twinge or regret for the killing?

During my four visits with Suzanne and family, no one ever said anything like they were sorry, not even sorry that the death had happened, much less that one of them had done it. David got close to saying something similar, but not quite.

At first, I was hurt and angry that no one would even show a hint of remorse, but then over time I learned to accept it. They would never come to that place. Suzanne justified what she had done because Vernie was so cruel, and Louisa thought of Vernie as a monster, so I guess it was some kind of relief for her, as well, when he died. I've also learned to see Louisa's point of view. She *had* to believe her mother's story; otherwise her whole emotional world would collapse. Louisa and David both found God and Jesus as a healing balm for their psyches, and I could see how hard they had tried to overcome the chaos that was their lives.

Even though I thought I was beyond expecting penitence from them, I did feel pain again in 2015 when Louisa and I were texting. She wished me Happy Resurrection Day, which is the way, I assume, Messianic Jews refer to what Christians call Easter. Another text that day, April 5, also said it was a difficult day because even though they had a lovely Seder, it was also Danny's *yahrzeit*, the remembrance of when he passed, but they said Kaddish and Sabbath prayers and moved on. I felt for them.

Even though I hadn't seen Danny for decades, I missed him, too. But I wondered if they had done *yahrzeit* on March 1 for my

Uncle Vernie. Of course I knew they did not, because I assume they only did it for loved ones whose death brought sadness to them.

At the same time I was fighting my own ethical and moral battles. When I started out, I just wanted answers, wanted to find out for Shannon, and for me, what had actually happened that night. But as time went on and I got close to David, and then developed a relationship with Louisa and her husband after David died, I started to feel guilty. I felt genuine love and care for them, but I also wanted answers to questions too long buried. How could I possibly claim any moral high ground? Sometimes it would get so bad, I'd hyperventilate. I talked to several friends who'd calm me down, telling me I was doing this for justice, for my uncle, for my cousin, and for the rest of the family. But was I just fooling myself with these excuses? All my life I've tried to be honest and fair, but how could I claim I was being so now?

Then I remembered my uncle Vernie had worked undercover most of his career, starting back in the navy in Japan during the Korean Conflict and later doing undercover work with the Mafia in Milwaukee, on a prostitution sting in Hurley, Wisconsin, and many other assignments I didn't know about.

What I was doing with Suzanne and family was undercover work. It helped me to understand what he went through. Did he feel guilt when he'd develop a relationship and then later testify against that person? Or was he more able to be detached? But how could I use Louisa's kind heart and loving nature to get information out of her? On the other hand, she did know I was a writer and that I was writing about the murder.

CHAPTER TWENTY-FIVE
Police Reports

A few days after I got the letter about victim's rights and redactions, a thick envelope arrived from the Dane County Sheriff's
Office. I didn't open it for a few days, because I thought the forensic pictures would be in there and they would scare me, so I
waited until a friend came over. No pictures, unfortunately—but,
oh, the other things that were there!

At first, I found it overwhelming to read the police files, which
were in the old Courier font of typewriters and obviously had
been copied several times over, indicated by all the stray marks
and illegible type on some lines. The files were a string of short
reports in an almost chronological order, with a lot of overlapping
and sometimes contradicting information. Even after reading
them six times, I was still overwhelmed.

It was causing me a great deal of confusion and anxiety until I
figured out a way to make sense of the 121 pages. After reading
the reports for the seventh time, I categorized and then indexed
the information, line by line, ultimately putting all the details on
205 color-coded note cards. Then I sorted the cards by topic and
wrote down the data in a narrative form, which made it more
readable than the raw police files.

The police conducted a pretty thorough investigation, interviewing Suzanne, David (not much, though), all their neighbors

and friends in Oregon, including any persons who were in the bowling alley with them that night, just before the murder, as well as talking to Suzanne's parents and a few other relatives. Almost everyone was asked about the nature of the relationship between Vernie and Suzanne. But why they didn't interview any of Vernie's family is a puzzle to me. My grandma, mother, or uncle could have provided a lot of information about dramatic incidents between Vernie and Suzanne and given some insight into her unpredictable and punitive behavior. Here is a short summary of the police and coroner's reports:

1. The first call Suzanne made after the murder was to the home of the Dane County sheriff Vern Leslie, at 2:17 A.M., saying, "This is Suzi. I just shot Vern." She then hung up and immediately called the sheriff's office. "My husband has been shot and we need help right away." Patrol car was dispatched at 2:20 A.M.

2. Vernie was sitting up, on the side of the bed when he was shot. With the coroner's report, I saw that Vernie was not only sitting up, but that his head was turned away, looking toward what was the corner of the room, where two dressers—and nothing else—stood, on each side of the corner. There was no sign of struggle in the room.

3. The killer fired the gun from some feet away, at least in the doorway, if not farther away, and it was held at hip height. This agrees with Franklin's theory that the gun was resting on the back of a chair in the doorway to the other bedroom.

4. Though both Suzanne's and David's fingerprints were on the gun, and Suzanne had blood splatters on her person, nothing was written whether David had any splatters. And when I had asked David during that last time I talked to him, he told me only his mother had blood splatters. That put her in the room. Not to mention the small piece of brain that was removed from Suzanne's

hair at the police station. The skull exploded to the right, away from the shooter. In order to get hit by blood splatters and brain fragments, one would have had to be closer to Vernie and also either in front of or to his right side. The shooter was relatively far to the left.

5. The gun was left on the floor, close to the body, as seen from the crime seen diagram (Figure 2). In the upper left are laundry baskets, from which brain tissue was taken. On either side of the bed are electric blanket controls. Both were on. Vernie was getting ready for bed and had turned his on. It was, after all, a freezing Wisconsin March night. Suzanne's was also turned on. Since she had not gotten in bed yet, we could assume he had turned hers on to get the bed ready for her. Also important is #17, telephone on the floor. Was Vernie reaching for this when he was shot? He was leaning toward it. And also, he was looking toward the corner, which only had two dressers, at a right angle, almost touching. Item #15 was originally redacted from the descriptions, but I had surmised from reading the rest of the report that #15 was the attaché case filled with drugs. What I didn't know until I got the second copy of the police report,[2] was there were pieces of bone and flesh on the top of the briefcase. Because the case was so far outside the area where the skull and brains had splattered, it seemed clear the case had been moved after the murder. Also redacted was #11, and I found out later it was a moist substance on the "private parts" of Vernie's body.

6. In the photo spread there are more explicit 3-D crime scene diagrams based on the forensic evidence and originally designed by Dr. Jason Kolowski of Forensic Insight LLC.

---

2. I hired researcher Gregory Smith late in the process, and he was able to get the police reports with fewer redactions.

Crime Scene Diagram

SUPPLEMENTARY REPORT

Case No. 36189   Report By. Klein   Date 3-1-70

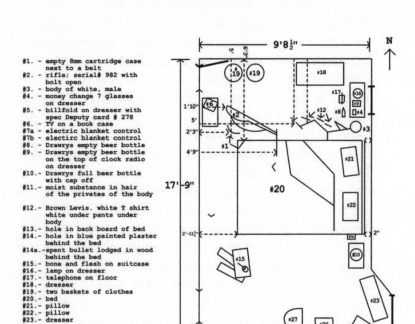

#1. - empty 8mm cartridge case next to a belt
#2. - rifle; serial# 982 with bolt open
#3. - body of white, male
#4. - money change 7 glasses on dresser
#5. - billfold on dresser with spec Deputy card # 278
#6. - TV on a book case
#7a - electric blanket control
#7b - electirc blanket control
#8. - Drawrys empty beer bottle
#9. - Drawrys empty beer bottle on the top of clock radio on dresser
#10.- Drawrys full beer bottle with cap off
#11.- moist substance in hair of the privates of the body
#12.- Brown Levis. white T shirt white pants under body
#13.- hole in back board of bed
#14.- hole in blue painted plaster behind the bed
#14a.-spent bullet lodged in wood behind the bed
#15.- bone and flesh on suitcase
#16.- lamp on dresser
#17.- telephone on floor
#18.- dresser
#19.- two baskets of clothes
#20.- bed
#21.- pillow
#22.- pillow
#23.- dresser
#24.- dresser
#25.- hair dryer
#26.- chair
#27.- rocking chair

Figure 2. (Re-creation of police sketch by Maxim Zhelev)

7. When the police arrived, Suzanne was very calm, but gave several hand gestures and facial expressions to show how upset David was, and indicated that they should be careful when they told David that Vernie was dead. At one point she just shrugged to the police, referring to David's reactions. David, on the other hand, was crying and wailing and biting his hands to keep from further crying. He was very nervous and chain-smoked the whole time. The coroner's report, however, included Suzanne breaking down and crying for a few minutes in front of a detective.

8. Suzanne made a number of phone calls before the police arrived, and also after they came, to tell people, with the police officers' permission, "I shot Vern." The report says her first call was to the home of Dane County's sheriff, Sheriff Leslie, which she did before they arrived. After they were there, she called a sister-in-law in Waukesha, a brother-in-law in Pewaukee, her daughter in New York, her brother, her second husband, and perhaps others. When she would make these calls and tell the person what she had done, David would leave the room, saying he couldn't listen. Later on, officers reported that they received returning calls from Suzanne's daughter, Louisa, and from brother-in-law Pete Evert, my step-father. When I read this, Pete's face appeared before me with its kind expression. He was a like a rock and provided a home for his stepchildren and treated us like his own.

9. Though they lived in Oregon, Wisconsin, which had its own police department, Suzanne chose to call the sheriff at his home in the middle of the night, about which she later bragged to me. She reached out to another jurisdiction when the Oregon Police were a one-minute drive away, and Sheriff Leslie was on Harbor Court in Madison, about twenty-five minutes from Suzanne's home.

10. Regarding her calling her attorney, she made some comment that one of the officers overheard: "Well, at least we can afford it now." Does not seem to me the comment of someone in psychosis.

11. The rifle used in the shooting came from the downstairs gun rack. David was able to show the detectives where the ammunition was kept. It's not clear if the officers even asked Suzanne about the ammunition. David testified at the hearing that he wasn't sure where the ammu-

nition was kept. Later in that testimony he said he did *not* know where the ammunition was kept. The district attorney did not seem bothered by these inconsistencies.

12. When detectives came back with a search warrant to look at the scene more carefully, they looked in the den cabinet and found an 8mm ammunition clip that held twelve shells. Only one cartridge was missing. And there was no evidence that anyone had been rooting through the ammunition drawers. Nothing was out of place, and only that one specific bullet was gone. Why would someone planning to kill another person only take one bullet? And especially if you were not familiar with guns, how would you know which ammo goes with which weapon, and then why only take one? What would be the chance you would hit your target the first time? Was that confidence or something else?

13. The rifle was found on the floor with the shell ejected. David testified that he first came into the room, saw the body, then went downstairs, after which his mother said something about a gun, so he ran upstairs, picked up the weapon, and ejected the shell.

14. The gun used came from the top shelf of the rack, as you can see from the police diagram (Figure 3). That top shelf was six feet seven inches from the floor, and in front of it was a cabinet protruding twenty-one inches from the wall. Franklin said when he went there the next day, there was no sign of any furniture having been moved to reach that uppermost gun. He and David were the same height—about five feet nine inches—and Franklin could barely reach the gun. Suzanne was six inches shorter and more slight, making it impossible to maneuver a heavy rifle off that high place. Below that weapon were three other shotguns on lower racks. Also, in the corner, lying against the wall, were two more weapons. Why would someone who has no knowledge

of guns choose the converted military-grade 8mm
Mauser, sometimes referred to as a "sniper's rifle,"
probably the deadliest weapon in the house, which also
happened to be the most inconvenient to reach and
the most complicated to operate?

Gun Rack Diagram

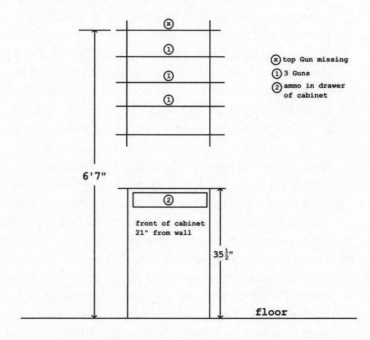

SUPPLEMENTARY REPORT

Case No. _____36189_____ Report By. _____Larson_____ Date _____3-1-70_____

RE: Death (Stordok)

Gun rack and cabinet located on first floor in the den.

ⓧ top Gun missing
① 3 Guns
② ammo in drawer
  of cabinet

6'7"

②

front of cabinet
21" from wall

35½"

floor

Figure 3. Gun rack and cabinet located on first floor in the
den (re-creation by Maxim Zhelev).

15. Detectives found an attaché case in the home that was filled with numerous vials and bottles of pills, including barbiturates, heroin, marijuana, uppers and downers, and many more. What was that about? The inventory of drugs was so long it took two pages. Did Vernie really need all of those for his work?

16. While he was still in the home, a detective asked Suzanne if David was involved in the shooting, and Suzanne replied that she did not know, but that she didn't think she should say any more to him at that time. Aren't such remarks from a person who understands what is going on?

17. One of the officers noted a subsequent phone call from a neighbor, David Dolan, who reported a very suspicious phone call at 1:30 A.M. to his nearby home. Someone answered and was asked if this man, David Dolan, was home. When told he was not, the man hung up and kept the line engaged for the following twelve hours. Back in those days, if someone called you and did not hang up when you did, there would be no dial tone, until the caller hung up. Therefore, someone with bad intentions could keep you from calling out on your phone. Fortunately, the phone company fixed that glitch some years later. There had been speculation in my family that Vernie's murder was a "hit," because he was involved with some high-profile cases concerning the mob and doctors losing licenses, and there were a number of unsavory characters who might be relieved if he died.

18. David and Suzanne were taken to the sheriff's office and read their rights, and they signed away their right to be silent. Then they were interrogated, but Suzanne was not talking, though David did give his version of how his mother woke him up after the shooting. Both their fingerprints were on the gun, but evidently only Suzanne had blood splatters.

19. Suzanne was booked on first-degree murder charges and taken to the women's jail, with constant suicide watch. Here's where my mind went off. If she actually did kill Vernie, and then wanted to kill herself, why couldn't she have just skipped shooting Vernie? When I read this, I thought about the fact that murder-suicide can seem like a common occurrence, but it amounts to only about five percent of homicides. Ninety percent of perpetrators who murder and then commit suicide are male. Therefore, women killing their partner and then themselves amount to one-half of one percent of all homicides.

20. Suzanne's family physician, a GP, showed up at the police station and said Suzanne needed psychiatric evaluation. The doctor made arrangements with the hospital. At the final hearing, January 1971, the prosecutor gave this as perhaps the most compelling reason to grant the insanity plea, i.e., that the DA had allowed Suzanne to be taken for psychiatric evaluation before she was arraigned.

21. It took several readings of the police report for me to get clear on the details about when she was transported from the jail to the hospital. In the court transcript of the final hearing, Mussallem said it was at 6:30 P.M. on Sunday, which would have given the doctors very little time to evaluate her before the arraignment the next morning. But the way the police reports describe it, she might not have left until around 8:00 A.M. on Monday, which meant by the time they got her from the jail to the vehicle and drove thirty minutes through rush-hour traffic and then got her checked in, she might have been in her room by 9:30 A.M. and would have had to turn around and go straight back for the hearing, which was 11:40 A.M. on Monday. But even if she did go the night before, it's likely by the time they cleared her out of the jail, making sure they followed security protocol, with a ma-

tron in tow and with Policewoman Ann Edwardson and
Lieutenant Kisow accompanying Suzanne, they probably
would not have gotten to the hospital before 7:30 or 8:00
P.M. The earliest any doctor could have met with her
would have been maybe 8:30 or 9:00 P.M., which is
about the time they get people ready for bed. Then she
would have been up in the morning, getting dressed and
prepared, always with the suicide-watch matron observing, breakfasting, and maybe ready to see a doctor at
9:00 A.M. Then, in order to get to the courthouse with
enough time for Lieutenant Kisow to take Suzanne to the
interview room next to the women's jail quarters and
read her the warrant, and then be on time for the arraignment, they would have had to leave the hospital by 10:00
A.M. When did they have time to have any meaningful
sessions with her that would make it so vitally important
she get to the hospital before the arraignment? And why
wasn't any time listed in the reports for that transfer,
which turned out to be extremely important in granting
the insanity plea? In the same report that talked about the
transfer, Lieutenant Kisow wrote that he had been
informed by the pathologist at 10:30 A.M. on Sunday that
the cause of death was homicide. Why wasn't there such
specificity on when she was moved to the hospital? My
assumption is that no one thought the time of her move
was very important. How could any police officer imagine such a piece of information would be crucial in the
difference between mandatory life in prison and spending eleven months in a mental institution?

22. And who, by the way, decided she should go for psychiatric evaluation on Sunday night? It was her GP, Dr.
Walter Washburn, who somehow magically appeared
in the jail and examined Suzanne. In his expert, non-
psychiatric-trained mind, she *must* go to the mental hospital. On his own volition he called in Dr. Leigh Roberts,

a psychiatrist with privileges at the mental hospital. No one ever questioned Dr. Washburn's judgment in this capital case of what was essentially a cop killing. Seven months later, in October 1970, he wrote a letter to Suzanne's lawyer Jack van Metre, regarding his examination of her on March 1, saying he had been summoned to the jail by Kenneth Orchard, Suzanne's longtime attorney, who had signed off on her divorces, wills, name changes, and real estate transactions. In my imagination I can hear what Orchard likely said to the congenial and well-liked physician, who, by all accounts, was seen as a caring, thoughtful, and hardworking doctor, the kind of man who someone with an agenda could probably manipulate. Here's some of what Orchard might have said: *Suzanne is in bad shape. You know how fragile she is psychologically. Her husband burned her with a cigarette and she just lost it, went into a trance or something. I need you to come down here and look at the burn and to help me get her in for mental evaluation immediately. You know how suicidal she is, and I just don't trust the jail to take proper precautions.*

23. The GP also noted (and later wrote in that letter to Jack van Metre) that Suzanne had one cigarette burn above the right scapula, a position that seemed more likely to me to be self-inflicted. Suzanne told the doctor that Vernie burned her when she tried to hug him, but she told me several times that they were dancing and she felt something like an ice cube on her back. By the time of the final hearing, this one cigarette burn had become three to five burns.

24. In the later, less-redacted police report, it described Suzanne's lawyer at the police station pointing out some small scars on her back, which he claimed were previous cigarette burns, but there was no other evidence of those scars being burns.

25. In the police reports and subsequent interviews of the police officers six months later, all of them reported Suzanne to be calm, polite, cooperative, in charge of her faculties, and sane. During the final hearing when the ADA summarized the statements from the police, he said they all described Suzanne as being in a trancelike state. I found nothing in the police reports to back up Mussallem's assertion.

26. All the neighbors thought Vernie and Suzanne got along pretty well, were quite compatible, but that he was more outgoing. A couple of people mentioned she would act strange, often not making any sense, when she drank, and that she had a "nervous" personality. Another neighbor, who babysat for Danny, said Suzanne almost never went to the house, instead sending Danny over and then calling to have him walk back home. She just kept to herself, the woman said. She was intelligent and had a many-sided personality, she said. What does that mean? I thought. If someone says you have a many-sided personality, I think of it as a kinder way of stating you are complicated with a darker, meaner self that appears now and then.

27. None of the neighbors said they heard the blasting sound of a converted military weapon around 2:15 A.M. on a quiet Sunday. Seems improbable but certainly possible.

28. People who had been in the bowling alley and bar that night said that the couple was getting along well, looked like they were having fun. At one point Suzanne even sat on Vernie's lap. No mention of any quarrels or Suzanne screaming out because Vernie was burning her back.

29. Several people in the bar said Vernie was more subdued and quiet that night.

30. One man overheard Vernie tell Suzanne he wanted to go home, but she preferred staying. He said he was going to see his daughter the next day, which Suzanne was not

happy about, and she said pointedly, "Is there something I should know about?" So Vernie left alone.

31. A little later on, Suzanne wanted to go home, but she said she was inebriated, that she was afraid to drive their brand-new car, for fear she'd dent it. Some neighbors drove her, and they picked up Vernie on the way, as he had been walking back to get the car. Vernie invited the neighbors in. Everyone was having a lovely time. No hint of anything negative between Vernie and Suzanne. The neighbors left around 1:20 A.M. (The neighbors were Mr. and Mrs. Donald and Arlene Ace.)

32. Many friends and neighbors said they had never seen Suzanne hold a weapon or talk about using one, but they knew David had been taught by Vernie about guns. A number of them had been on hunting trips and had seen David's facility with guns and Suzanne's lack thereof.

33. David's girlfriend said they had known each other for five years and had gone steady since November. David was dropped off at her house around 11:45 P.M. and he stayed there until 1:30 A.M., when she drove him home. She didn't get out of the car. David had to knock on the door and was let in by his dad (in court testimony a few months later, David said his mother had let him in that night). He told her on the phone later that his dad thought he was already in bed, so the door was locked. They talked on the phone until 2:00 A.M. She noticed the 2:00 A.M. signal on the radio went off right after she hung up. She always thought the family got along well, though she knew his parents drank heavily. David was very against drugs, though, and told her that if she ever tried marijuana, he would break up with her. (David had testified that he went to bed at 1:30, then called his girlfriend at 1:35 A.M. His mother came into the room at 2:05 or 2:10 A.M., though he had heard them arguing earlier.)

34. Shortly after the murder, Suzanne's parents had gone to their local Grant County DA (James Halferty) to report that Suzi had threatened to kill her husband Vernie. Later the parents retracted that statement and said that DA Halferty had gotten confused.

35. Suzanne's parents, Mr. and Mrs. Robert Brandon, said she was born Elmira but had changed her name legally after leaving home at age seventeen. The mother said Suzi has lived her life in a very selfish way, never thinking of anyone else. For example, her parents had been very sick and sometimes hospitalized, with Suzi never expressed any concern. And with her four marriages and three divorces, she had created much emotional havoc. Mrs. Brandon talked about Suzi's very bad temper, at times smashing all the dishes in their home for no real reason. Her mother discussed Suzanne's extreme jealousy. She said her daughter was heavily into drugs, sometimes answering the phone with a slurred voice and incoherrent speech, which surprised her, considering Vernie's work in drug investigation at the Wisconsin State Medical Examiner's Board. She felt that Vernie had a good relationship with the sons, who were both still living at home.

36. Mr. Brandon said Suzi's brother Bob had given two versions of the murder. In one, David had heard the shot and gone running to his parents' bedroom; in the second version David was asleep and Suzanne woke him up, knocking on the door, saying she had shot Vernie.

37. Both parents had no knowledge of Vernie ever being involved with other women, but Suzanne showed up at her parents' place in Boscobel in October 1969 with a boyfriend, and she told her parents that Vernie approved of this relationship. This one caught my attention. My uncle was a decent guy, honest, but I don't think anyone would label him particularly "liberal." He was a regular

churchgoing Lutheran, someone who'd lived all his life in smaller towns and cities. Back in 1969, when it was still shameful to "live in sin" before you were married, how am I supposed to believe that an upstanding law enforcement officer would take kindly to his wife having an affair?

38. Out of nowhere the two parents blurted out that Suzanne had no knowledge of guns and they don't see how she could have shot anyone.

39. Mrs. Brandon was very concerned that Suzi had gotten the court to set her bond low enough that her two living brothers would try and raise money for it. She felt this would be divisive to the family and create more chaos.

40. By order of ADA Mussallem the police officers who had been on the scene the night of the murder were interviewed by detectives to get more information about Suzanne and her state of mind. Sheriff Leslie said she was ordinary, though a little disheveled that night when she got to the jail, and he knew of nothing ill between her and Vernie. The other six officers all said she was polite, calm, rational, cooperative, in charge of her faculties, and sane. This contrasts with Mussallem's arguments at the final hearing, when he said interviews with the police officers indicated that Suzanne had been acting strangely and in a trancelike state.

41. Six months later the detectives were instructed by Mussallem to reinterview the people from the bar, neighbors, and some others to find out the nature of Vernie and Suzanne's relationship and anything unusual that night. They all said the same thing they had in March, that she was in charge of her faculties and sane. None of them knew of any conflicts between the two and that night seemed like any other night, as far as Suzanne was concerned. Some of the newer interviewees said they didn't know the Stordocks well enough to comment. I

wondered again why no one on my uncle's side of the family was ever interviewed, either in March or in September.

42. Police reports indicate Suzanne was going after an insanity plea. She claimed later on that she had a psychotic break. How does someone who has lost touch with reality, and has no knowledge of guns, get a heavy military weapon off a rack way too high to reach, forage through all the various ammunitions and know which one to use, and then load it, haul it upstairs, and shoot it from hip height and hit the target perfectly? And then afterwards has the mental capacity to ask for an insanity plea, in the police station, just hours after the murder?

43. Also included was a letter, dated March 6, 1970 to Sheriff Leslie from John Edgar Hoover (signed) confirming receipt of evidence in the Stordock murder case, with Suzanne Stordock as suspect. Hoover said the "examination is being made with the understanding that the evidence is connected with an official investigation. . . . Authorization cannot be granted for the use of the laboratory report in connection with a civil proceeding." I've been told by someone close to the case that this was the first time in Wisconsin that any pre-DNA evidence was sent to the FBI. I tried for almost three years to locate the report from the FBI. My research associate, Gregory Smith, was told those files were destroyed, which he said was highly unusual. His theory was the sheriff had suppressed evidence.

August 2015 brought two developments. I heard through the grapevine there was one police officer still alive who had been at the crime scene the night of the murder. A few days later I got a call from a detective at the Dane County Sheriff's Office, who had just been assigned to answer any questions. Was it because of a recent request I made for police photos (which I was told they no longer had), or was it their realization that I was very determined and so they started paying more attention? It did not matter. I was just grateful to have a person I could call on. This was my first inkling of how cooperative the Dane County Sheriff's Office had been already and would continue to be on this case, which was a pleasant surprise to me. Detective Tim Blanke and I talked for about an hour that first time.

"Since you asked for those records, a number of us have read the reports and we can't figure out how that one got away," he said soberly. So it wasn't just me acting out of age-old family pain, I thought. "We've had a lot of conversations about that case," he continued, and then paused. "The only thing that makes sense to me is that the murder took place in March 1970, with the case dragging on until January 1971. One catastrophic event during that time period was the bombing of Sterling Hall."

I clearly remembered the bombing he mentioned, because I had been a student on campus, but happened to be away that weekend. An underground, radical antiwar group set off explosives to destroy the Army-Math Research Center (AMRC), which was housed in Sterling. One graduate student died, plus years and years of faculty members' research efforts were destroyed. The only damage the AMRC suffered architecturally was that the floor to their coffee room collapsed. This event basically ended the protest movement in Madison, because it seemed all of us suddenly realized this was serious business.

"I think the gravity of having to deal with the aftermath of the bombing probably caused them to give up on some of the other cases," he explained. After we hung up, I did some research. Blanke's theory would make sense if the timing had been different. Suzanne's charge was dropped from first-degree murder to first-degree manslaughter and turned over to an inexperienced ADA in late July. The bombing was August 24. I could accept that they might have been unable to process previous cases to the full extent of the law, but Suzanne was essentially handed her insanity plea one month before the bombing.

During our conversation I asked Detective Blanke about the identity of the officer still alive. Kenneth Pledger had since retired and was still living in Oregon, Wisconsin, after all these years. I called him. It took him a few minutes to recall the case I was asking about, to get his full memory back about one of the thousands of cases he investigated in his long career.

"There was a lot of strange things about that case. It made more sense to me that David was the shooter. For one thing the gun was David's gun. He used it when they went deer hunting," he said. "My understanding was that Suzanne didn't know much about guns, and that was certainly the most complicated gun in the house, because it was bolt action. Secondly, it was on the top rack, very difficult to reach, and she'd have had to get up on something to pick that gun off the rack. There was no evidence of furniture having been moved. And then there was a drawer with ammunition, which had several kinds of ammo. But whoever took the one bullet out of the ammunition box had to know which type to take, had to have some knowledge with that particular firearm, because it wasn't like the ammunition was all tore apart like somebody looking for which bullet to use."

Pledger was more animated by this time, as I could feel his thoughts becoming clearer about that incident forty-five years ago. "So many strange things. If she was the shooter and was standing in the doorway, how in the world did she get brain tissue and bone fragments in her hair? It's just not possible under the laws of physics." He was stating what I had been thinking ever since I'd read the police reports.

The retired officer continued to speak. "We measured how the bullet traveled and it had been held at hip distance from some feet away. There's no way when you're dealing with a rifle, well, you can't just point and shoot somebody in the temple, unless your gun is right next to him, which would have left splattering on the gun. And there was no blood on that weapon. And if a person is inexperienced with firearms, they just can't hold it up and . . . it was not logical that she fired the gun." Listening to him was strangely hypnotic for me, perhaps because he was speaking so plainly and without any agenda.

I asked him where he thought Suzanne was at the time of the shooting and he said in the room, next to Vern. She had to have been, because of the brain tissue in her hair. Pledger had some theory about them doing sexual acts using lighted cigarettes and then David bursting in on them, thinking his mom was being abused. I don't know if that's true, but I wonder if she was that close to Vernie how David could have been certain his mother wouldn't have gotten hurt, too. Then he talked more about Suzanne and David that night.

"When we got there, Suzanne was right there at the door. I tried to talk to David, but she kept holding her hands up to me like [a] *'Don't. Don't. He's going to explode'* kind of thing. She did her best to keep me from talking to him. Like she didn't want me to get his story."

I found this narrative fascinating. Having read the police report numerous times, I knew about her holding her hands up regarding David, but I had always thought she was protecting him. Here this man who'd been at the scene was telling me she was preventing the police from questioning David, by exaggerating his mental fragility. It was another case of Suzanne using illness as an excuse. Pledger went on, "I had my own thoughts about things. She apparently contacted the sheriff, in his home, before she called the ambulance.

"I thought there was some kind of a deal between her and the sheriff, because I knew they were *at least* casual friends, and that case did not proceed as it should have. In her interaction with the sheriff she said she pulled the trigger, but I never believed it. Not long after that, I heard she was on kind of a leave from prison and was let loose on weekends or something."

Was there some kind of agreement between Sheriff Leslie and Suzanne? I really believe this brilliant Mensa woman, who loved to outsmart people, *had to* know someone had her back before she got involved in committing a murder. My cousin Donna is convinced Suzanne was having an affair with an important man, who would do anything to keep Suzanne quiet. Was that the sort of thing Pledger was hinting at?

CHAPTER TWENTY-SIX

From the Doctor and Psychiatrists

When I first got the court documents, I was very disappointed that there were no letters from the psychiatrists. How would I ever know what the diagnosis was, other than what was reported in the transcripts, which was chronic paranoid schizophrenia? Then I hoped maybe something would be in the police files, but I was told such information was "confidential."

A few months later I went to Madison and looked through the microfiches myself. I stumbled upon three letters from court physicians, dated September through October 1970, which had been somewhere deep in those files. I copied them. Unfortunately, these were not all the letters, and I was especially wanting to read the one from the psychiatrist who did not believe Suzanne was insane, but that letter had disappeared. The family GP, Dr. Washburn, wrote:

> On March 1, 1970, I was asked to go to Dane County Jail by Mr. Kenneth Orchard to examine Mrs. Suzanne Stordock. Several hours prior to my examination she had shot and killed her husband and was being confined in the jail pending further procedures.
>
> When I first saw Mrs. Stordock I was impressed by the apathetic manner which she presented with almost

complete loss of affect. She indicated at this time that
she was psychologically numbed by the experience and
kept repeating that when considering problems of concern, she would consider asking her husband, LaVerne
for help, but then would realize that he was dead and not
available. I was somewhat taken aback by the inappro-
priate manner in which she approached the problem of
this tragic incident and felt that she was mentally ill and
in need of psychotherapeutic care immediately. It was at
this time that I elected to call Doctor Leigh Roberts, of
University Hospital's Psychiatric Department, a man of
extremely high competence and one in whom I have
great confidence.

   Examination of Mrs. Stordock at this time revealed a
½ cm circular burn over her right scapular area judged to
be between a first and second degree burn in severity. It
was not blistered or weeping. She indicated that prior to
the shooting while trying to embrace her husband that he
had purposely burned her back with a lighted cigarette.
No treatment was rendered to this burn as it was felt that
open air care would be of most benefit.

   I have been Mrs. Stordock's physician for
approximately ten years during which time she has been
seen several times for emotional difficulties. My partner,
Dr. Edward Kolner, cared for her in August of 1966, at
which time she attempted suicide which was almost successful following the ingestion of six to eight hundred
milligrams of Seconal. She was also seen at this time by
Dr. Stanley Miezio, who treated her following discharge
from Madison General Hospital for a psychoneurotic
depressive reaction.

   Dr. Washburn, who evidently had no psychiatric training, felt
competent to determine what "loss of affect" means. And remember her alleged suicide attempt in August 1966 was shortly before

the court hearing when Vernie asked to end child support. During those months Suzanne also announced to everyone that Vernie would not get sex unless he did what she wanted.

Next we have more information from one of the court-appointed psychiatrists:

> The period of her hospitalization was March 23, 1970 to June 13, 1970. Because of the history of previous serious depressive reaction with suicide attempt—August 1966—the recent death of her husband, the presence of anorexia and insomnia and the findings of marked emotional liability and depression poorly defended by intellectualization and hypomanic intensity of affective behavior, hospitalization seemed indeed appropriate and essential.
>
> I met with her daily for a supportive and reality oriented psychotherapy. Throughout the larger period of her somewhat lengthy hospitalization, a process of mourning the loss of her husband was prominent. She spent much time ruminatively preoccupied with the events surrounding her husband's death; partial amnesia was present initially but many memories returned as time passed, occasionally with abreactive emotional tone.
>
> The use of psychotropic medication—Sinaquen 25 mg i.d.—seemed useful to mediate her insomnia and anorexia. Ultimately her depression was controlled and her sense of self-esteem and hope for the future bolstered sufficiently to permit discharge to out-patient care.
>
> Mrs. Stordock's reactive depression has seemed to be a product of decompensation of a longstanding character and neurological reaction to the events surrounding her husband's death. Signs of gross thought disorder or regressive thought and behavior of a schizophrenic nature were *not seen* [emphasis mine] during her stay at

Madison General Hospital. Occasionally unusual suspiciousness was present and her associations were replete with suggestions of feelings of inadequacy and inferiority, but with these exceptions, paranoia was not seen.

In my judgment she suffers from a mixture of neurotic and characterological problems; her level of ego strength permits a generally adequate level of social function but allows little room for regression so that under unusually stressful circumstances mental disease of psychotic proportions may result. I believe that Mrs. Stordock suffered such a transient psychotic state the evening of February 28, 1970 and thus lacked substantial capacity either to appreciate the wrongfulness of her conduct or conform her conduct to the requirement of the law.

Anorexia and insomnia? Could that be from the drug use her mother indicated in the police reports? This reminded me again of all the drugs they found in the attaché case in the bedroom the night of the murder, after the execution of a search warrant. Though my uncle worked for the medical examiner's board and did drug tests, why did he bring the case home and have it out in plain sight? Inventory of the leather attaché case showed Demerol, pot pipes, a roach clip, syringes, amphetamines, codeine, marijuana and morning glory seeds, cocaine, heroin, spoon, one surgical hose, hashish, one bottle white powder, one can of nutmeg (four teaspoons gives hallucinations), phenobarbital, LSD, and lots of capsules and pills, plus one vial of something that was redacted. There was also one bottle of 144 red and black capsules. (Could those be the infamous Black Beauty uppers and Red Devil Seconal downers?) Where was Suzanne getting drugs to be so intoxicated that she slurred her words and did not recognize her mother's voice on the phone? Was it from the stash in the attaché case? And reading in the letter how he described her condition and her psychological state, I cannot see how Dr. Gerald L. Clinton, one of the psychiatrists assigned to the case, arrived at the conclusion she had a psychotic breakdown. But then, I'm not a psychiatrist.

Finally we have a report from a psychiatrist that gives more detail about Suzanne's background and family (italics are my choice):

Mrs. Suzanne Stordock has been seen extensively for psychiatric evaluation above March 1, 1970. She was hospitalized on the University of Wisconsin Hospitals Psychiatric Inpatient Services on March 1, 1970, the date of an alleged gunshot killing of her husband and remained on that service until March 6. I subsequently saw her on multiple occasions during the next month on the Psychiatric Service at Madison General Hospital. The record of family psychiatric interviews at University Hospitals Psychiatry Clinic in 1967 was reviewed as well as an interview conducted with her daughter, Louisa Briggs, on March 4, 1970. She was also referred for psychological testing to Dr. David Rice, a Clinical Psychologist on the University of Wisconsin faculty, whose findings are contained within my report.

Mrs. Stordock is a 41-year-old, four times married, thrice divorced, mother of three children. She is an office worker, Jewish by religious conversion, lady who was reared in rural Wisconsin as the eldest of 3 children. The family home was very insecure with her parents fighting, threatening each other and ultimately obtaining a divorce. Her mother subsequently experienced serious mental illness on several occasions leading to institutional treatment while maintaining a hostile dependent guilt inducing depressed response in Mrs. Stordock. The relationship with each of the first three husbands resulted in a child, but also sufficient problems that in each instance a divorce followed. *Her relationship with her own daughter, Louisa, has tended to parallel that with*

*her mother, with poor communication, frequent mis-
understanding, acting out, and neurotic dependency. She
has tended to dominate members of her family, has had
neurotic attachments and alliances with family members
bidding one against another, tying together the family by
means of crises, and at times, threats of suicide.*

Mental states examinations reveal a tense,
preoccupied but cooperative woman, with at least average intelligence. There was no indication of any organic
brain difficulty. She is well-oriented and able to perform
intellectual tasks without difficulty. Her external facade
is that of an hysterical type of personality with one of de-
nial and suppression of prominent defense mechanisms.
She also is quite suspicious of others, particularly males,
and *tends to project her own ideas onto them.* She is not
secure of her femininity and is very dependent upon
other persons for their positive opinion of her. She tends
to overreact to the ideas and feelings of others and *is
quite capable of acting very impulsively without consideration of possible harmful consequences.* She has not
been able to develop close sustained relationships due to
this lack of trust and poorly communicates intimate emotions. In the face of stress, particularly from males who
may be viewed as threatening, she is capable of losing
contact with reality.

My diagnosis is schizophrenic reaction, chronic paranoid type. It is my opinion that as of the time of the alleged events she was unable to appreciate the criminality
of her conduct and unable to conform her conduct in the
law. As of the time of my examination it is my opinion
that she is able to understand the nature of charges
against her and to participate in her own defense.

The italicized sections are the most telling. She had neurotic
relationships and pitted one family member against another, con-

trolled the others through crises and threats of suicide, and could be dangerously impulsive. Do neuroses and impulsivity add up to the kind of mental illness that gets away with murder?

On July 31, 1970 (seven months before the final hearing), the case was turned over from DA Boll to the twenty-seven-year-old Victor Mussallem. It took me ten months of digging to uncover some fascinating aspects of his behavior in this case. During my second visit to the Madison Clerk of Courts Records Department, and after an exchange of probably thirty e-mails with the person helping me do the searches, I was knee-deep in microfiche pages when I discovered (by rereading every motion and set of voluminous invoices sent to the court) that Mussallem was not happy with the diagnosis of Dr. Joseph B. Brown, the state's main psychiatrist.

Dr. Brown said Suzanne was not legally insane because she exhibited *not one* single characteristic of insanity or psychosis. So Mussallem sent Suzanne back to see Brown, for three hours in September, and then in October, for more testing and evaluation. Afterward, Mussallem himself spent a total of 9.25 hours in conference with Dr. Brown during the course of those two months. I saw no evidence of him conferring with the other psychiatrists. Could there have been any other reason than to try and convince Brown how wrong he was? Or to try and win him over to Mussallem's side? We know Mussallem was corruptible, because he was disbarred later on, and perhaps he thought Brown had a price, too. His frustration at not reaching this goal might be one reason he spent half of the twenty minutes of the final hearing discrediting Brown's evaluation.

If we jump ahead from the hearing in January 1971 to Suzanne's release from the state mental hospital eleven months later, we can see more medical evaluations, if you can call them that. On November 30, 1971, the superintendent of the hospital, who was also her legal guardian, Dr. Darold Treffert, adjudged Suzanne

well enough to be paroled. She never returned to the mental institution and one year later, on December 7, 1972, Dr. Treffert swore
she had now "fully recovered her mental health," though I could
find no reports about her progress. I've had several mental health
professionals react with shock at how quickly she was released
from the mental institution and subsequently completely healed.
It's just not reasonable, they all said. No one ever, and they meant
ever, gets healed from schizophrenia.

One could get confused reading the prior materials. And since
I am not a mental health professional, I sought analysis from
competent professionals. I consulted one psychiatrist (Dr. Laura
d'Angelo), a nurse practitioner (Rose Presser) who works in behavioral health (in addition to my psych nurse cousin), another
Ph.D. psychologist (Robert Kinney), and a licensed therapist
(Marlene Kramer), none of whom had any connection with and
very little pre-knowledge of the case. Below is a summary of
what they told me.

I asked Dr. Laura d'Angelo, who is slim and attractive, with
salt-and-pepper hair and dresses in business casual clothes suitable for the Florida climate where she lives, to look at the doctors'
letters, which included those of GP Washburn and two psychiatrists assigned to the case (Clinton and Roberts) who determined
some kind of psychosis in Suzanne. Dr. d'Angelo asked if there'd
been any history of hearing voices or psychotic breakdowns prior
to the murder episode, and I said not as far as I could determine.
"Schizophrenia is not a disorder that suddenly appears in the 40s.
It typically manifests itself in the late teens or early 20s. And
there is no 'cure' for schizophrenia. It is a condition that is managed throughout a person's life."

Presser, who reminded me of a slightly younger Meryl Streep,
similarly explained the diagnosis of *chronic* schizophrenia is very
suspect, because Suzanne had no symptoms of hearing voices and
breaks with reality previously, and these behaviors usually begin

in the teens. Getting completely cured is out of the question. Such a condition can only be managed for the rest of the patient's life, through medication.

The refined Kramer, who sat with perfect posture and a sense of deep intelligence, and always looked as if she could have become a model some decades ago, said Suzanne was mindless about her personal life, i.e., five husbands and three children. Despite her impulsivity she managed to go back to school and finish her undergraduate, as well as master's, doctorate, and law degrees. And her majors and research generally had to do with criminal justice or abused women.

I thought about Suzanne's degrees. Her Ph.D. dissertation was sloppy, and that seemed consistent with impulsivity. Any writer knows how tedious and mind-numbing rewriting and copyediting can be, each requiring skills of focus and patience, which are opposites of impetuousness. And what about all her research centering on women in prison? Wasn't that just a little narcissistic? Plus her not securing any meaningful employment after all those degrees also suggested impulsivity. Working as a junior associate in a law firm requires long, grueling hours under the strict control of partners who looks down on associates; while becoming a full-time academic means overwhelming teaching prep in the first years and a solid plan for research and publication, most projects taking years before they see publication in a journal article. The Suzanne I knew would not like those kinds of jobs.

My attention went back to Kramer, who was talking about the letters from the psychiatrist referring to loss of affect and Suzanne's apathetic manner. She said these behaviors didn't have anything to do with the murder. And even if she had murdered my uncle, Suzanne could still be talking about the loss of her husband. Then she switched topics and said that Suzanne's converting to Judaism would have been to gain money, because she knew which side of her bread was buttered. And Kramer spoke about the matter of Suzanne's invalidism, which gave her a great deal of power and she could be "the Command Control." All she had to do was express a need and people jumped to fill those needs. It was a power mechanism, and it was likely something she used to maintain control.

Presser, the behavioral nurse practitioner, noted that none of the psychiatrists observed any psychotic or schizophrenic behaviors, and said so in the letters. So they were basing their diagnoses on what *Suzanne reported* to them about her psychotic state. She went on and said that she assumed if someone had been convicted because of mental instability, it would show a long-standing pattern, not just a brief psychotic episode. Dr. Clinton's letter said Suzanne suffered a transient psychotic state and lacked capacity. How could a person go in and out of capacity, in a convenient time frame? Presser asked. It can be true, she continued that a person may be judged to lack capacity and at a later date return to capacity, but again it is usually months of incapacity. Not on such a convenient time line. As far as the letter from Dr. Leigh Roberts, Presser couldn't imagine how he could say she was psychotic when he had never seen her behaving thus. How could she have a *chronic* condition when no one ever saw her with the condition? Getting "cured" after eleven months did not fit the diagnosis. In Washburn's letter he mentioned when he saw her hours after the murder she indicated to him that she was psychologically numb, which was a very self-insightful statement to make. Presser didn't think that was something a psychotic person would say.

Psychiatrist Dr. d'Angelo read the doctors' letters, including Dr. Clinton's, which described Suzanne's transient psychotic state. There was no evidence she had psychosis before the crime, and, in fact, the doctor said he saw no evidence of schizophrenia during her stay in the hospital. Dr. Washburn had said he thought Suzanne was mentally ill. However, according to Dr. d'Angelo, that is a very nonspecific term. In the court transcripts, Assistant DA Mussallem said the diagnosis was schizophrenia, but d'Angelo was unable to understand how they arrived at that from reading the doctors' letters.

In Clinton's letter it said she was treated for depression after the alleged suicide attempt in 1966. Another mental health expert, Dr. Robert Kinney, said some people behave in such a way as to mimic mental illness. It's called "malingering" and they are going after what mental health professionals call "secondary gain," which means they expect some reward after the suicide attempt. The general practitioner had written that Suzanne had no affect: no sadness, no happiness. Kinney believed she was feigning a psychological state, which evidently fooled Washburn. Then Roberts said he had given her an extensive psychological evaluation in the hospital. She noted Suzanne's parents fighting and Dr. Kinney commented, "Who doesn't have that?"

Regarding Clinton's observations that Suzanne tied together her family through crises and threats of suicide, Dr. Kinney casually said, "That's what they do. They are very manipulative and always have to be center stage, with drama and chaos at all times. They don't want others to be happy, either."

Kinney said none of the letters indicated any organic problems. Suzanne was not demented, nor intellectually deficient. The letters further described her with a hysterical personality, suspicious of others—especially men—and quite capable of acting impulsively without consideration of harmful consequences. d'Angelo said this was more akin to personality disorder, which Kramer had also noted, or more like mixed personality types. The fact the psychiatrists said she was not able to develop personal relationships didn't prove anything, these experts said. There could be countless reasons for that. It could be character flaws, which are not really understood much in psychiatry. Kinney also said, "The diagnosis of schizophrenic reaction, chronic paranoid type, means nothing, All schizophrenia is chronic."

Kinney told me the psychiatrist was essentially saying that Suzanne was crazy at the time of the murder and didn't understand, but now she did understand, so Suzanne could stand trial. He stated, "This is gobbledygook. That's my professional assessment." He went on: "I find the letters useless, because they don't tell me anything. Nothing substantiates chronic schizophrenia. But for a person who is not a mental health professional, a lawyer or judge, they value what an MD puts in writing. But these letters get an F. They are just terrible. No professionalism. Nothing systemic, nothing consistent. Bad, bad, bad." None of the mental health experts I consulted felt the letters really led to the diagnosis Mussallem used in the final hearing.

"These letters don't make sense," noted Kinney. "They are embarrassing to my profession."

CHAPTER TWENTY-SEVEN
Is She a Psychopath?

My cousin Donna, the psych nurse, was convinced Suzanne was a sociopath. Since I first talked to her about it, I've done extensive research, searched through databases of scholarly articles, read seven books on the topic, and talked to a number of mental health professionals. The recognized leader in the field, Dr. Robert Hare, who has done considerable research on psychopaths, both in prisons and in everyday life, distinguishes between sociopaths and psychopaths, but all mental health professionals do not necessarily distinguish between those two terms. So as to not confuse the reader, I will not differentiate between them, either. Hare, however, is generally understood to be the intellectual giant in the field of psychopathy.

According to recent research and thinking, psychopaths are born with a brain malfunction that is analogous to being color blind, only in this case they are born without a conscience. In fact, the name of Hare's seminal book is *Without Conscience*. One school of thought says these people are born with a tendency toward psychopathy and then their childhood reinforces such a condition, much like how babies can be born with a predisposition toward diabetes, but then the kind of diet determines whether they actually become diabetic.

Psychopaths, according to Hare and others, are the ultimate con men (or women). Psychopaths definitely know right from wrong, but don't feel any sense of "should" in the sense of doing the right thing. Also lacking empathy, they mimic others to know how to pretend to feel and to impersonate sympathy, all in the service of gaining control, seeking admiration, or looking for material rewards. People are the means to an end, and psychopaths have no sense of remorse or any idea that their victims might have suffered. In fact, they despise their victims and find ways to blame them for the violence or misfortune that they, the psychopaths, have caused. The only kinds of "happy" feelings for them are ones of dominance, control, and outsmarting everyone else. Because they feel an extreme superiority to others, they assume no one could figure out what really happened.

Kramer said that profound narcissists and psychopaths have a very difficult time being alone, because they are emotionally shallow, have no inner life, and cannot have real feelings. They need another person (or people) to be able to give them some focus, to project all their negativity onto. She said someone like Suzanne would need another person to hold the feelings she cannot feel. And this emotional projection is often sadistic because these types of people have feelings that are often negative and they *expect* the other person to keep those horrendous emotions.

This emotional shallowness and self-centeredness is one reason it is so difficult for narcissists and psychopaths to change, because their only point of reference is themselves. So it made sense to Kramer that Suzanne would move in with her children after her fifth husband, Ronald, died and then basically blackmail them emotionally to leave their lives and adult children in Alaska and move to Tennessee, where Suzanne insisted they all go. She needed all of them around her. And what better way to keep them forcibly close than to become an invalid?

I asked whether Suzanne's involving David in Vernie's murder was an example of how (as one of her psychiatrists stated) she used family crises to tie family members together. Kramer agreed. Suzanne had to be manipulating David his whole life in order for him to be available to commit the crime for her. He had been shaped from babyhood to have his mother's needs, no matter how bizarre they might seem to others, as a primal purpose in his life. Suzanne would always claim victimhood and how she had been done wrong, and enlisting her children to help her would make David more likely to keep following her commands.

Researchers agree that psychopaths make up about 1 percent of the population, but 20 percent of the prison population (and 10 percent of CEOs). However, those 20 percent are the cause of 50 percent of violent crime.

In Hare's book he shares the checklist of psychopaths that was first developed after years of working in prisons and being conned many times. Even as a Ph.D. psychologist studying psychopaths, he was fooled enough times that he realized he wanted to study them more deeply.

After reading all the books by Hare and others, I decided to fly to Portland, or to become certified in the only instrument that measures psychopaths. I sat in a large meeting room of the Portland Art Museum with fifty-nine psychologists, forensic attorneys, prison therapists, district attorneys, and other lawyers, many of whom worked with prisons or as expert witnesses in trials. An unusual number of them worked with sex offenders. Our homework had been to read 450 pages of dense academic articles by Hare and others. Some articles had thirty pages of references at the end.

Dr. Hare, who looks like a thoughtful, bearded Richard Dreyfuss in glasses, taught us theory for half a day. Then he introduced his copresenter Dr. Matt Logan, former Royal Canadian Mounted Policeman and crime investigator, who was tall and completely bald and had more of a hard edge than the grandfatherly Hare. Logan gave us a thorough background on the Psychopathy Check-list-revised (PCL-R) and then presented many videos of criminals we had to evaluate and score, in groups. At the end we were all tested on scoring the inventory, which is best used when reports from law enforcement or prison officials, court records, and extensive interviews of four to six hours are also available. It is *not* a self-report test, because psychopaths would figure out how to get the result they need. Instead, the assessor uses the tools of reading reports and asking questions, always remembering that two of the traits of psychopaths are charm and pathological lying.

The checklist has twenty items, which are to be scored 0, 1, or 2. If 0, it means that particular characteristic does not at all apply in this case, while a 1 means somewhat applies, and a 2 is highly indicative. Maximum score is 40, with a range of 26 to 30 or more indicating a psychopath.

I'm not a psychologist, but I have a doctorate in organizational behavior/managerial psychology, a field I taught full-time for more than twenty-five years, during which time I did a lot of original research in related areas. In addition, I have consulted with one psychiatrist, two psych nurses, and two trained counselors in the writing of this book about items on the checklist. Finally, keep in mind, I have known Suzanne for almost fifty years (though not continuously) and have seen her in a number of situations, as well as having interviewed her for a total of fourteen hours for this book. Here's my assessment of Suzanne, remembering I am now certified to use this instrument.

1. *Glibness/superficial charm.* Upon first meeting Suzanne, or even if she is known to you for a length of time, she can be charming and full of witty retorts, especially if she wants to be seen favorably. If she is crossed or feels jealous, that can change in a microsecond. But though she is charming, she's not the best I've seen. **I give her a 1.**

2. *Egocentric/grandiose sense of self-worth.* Her needs
were always more important than those of others,
whether it was her children, who got little attention, or
her husbands, whom she casually discarded, after getting
their assets. In addition, she saw herself as smarter than
98 percent of people and was smug when she talked
about Mensa, all her degrees, and how husbands and
other people bored her. When she talked about people
she hadn't seen for a while, she thought they all admired
her and wanted to come running to see her in Tennessee,
even though I had talked to some of them, who barely
even remembered who she was. Then there's the matter
of her doctoral dissertation, which Suzanne's daughter
lovingly gave me. (I got David's copy, which I treasure
because it belonged to him.) My academic career had me
reading lots of dissertations and serving on many doctoral committees. As a stand-alone research document,
it's only so-so. The research was more elementary than
I'd expected from the sociology department of the University of Minnesota, but then she had a male advisor
some years older than she, and I know how she could influence men. It wasn't until recently that I looked at the
dedication and acknowledgments. Generally for dissertations (or books), the dedication is to one person, or
maybe two or three children, and you see one or two
lines of text. Suzanne, though, dedicated her dissertation
to twenty-five people, including a sister who died at birth
fifty years ago and her great-granddaughter, and then
through to the illegitimate birth of Jocelyn. It took fifteen
lines. And then I saw the acknowledgments. Normally,
people start with their advisor and committee and give
others who helped in the actual work, then list the names
of a few family members who were supportive and also
some friends. Then came her acknowledgments, which
she started by saying she wanted to recognize her entire

family, who were supportive during her educational
years, allowing her to finish several academic degrees,
during a time of her own personal growth. She went on:

I, and all of my accomplishments, are merely part of the
continuity of generations—from my parents, through
me, on to my great-grandchildren and others to follow.
Life (and academic pursuits) has more meaning when
shared with loving and supportive friends. I have been
particularly blessed in this area. Each of you knows who
you are [most people would list names] and how much
you mean to me in all of life as well as during the academic adventure.

This illustrates some of grandiosity. **I give her a 1.**

3. *Pathological lying.* Her story of the murder just does not
fit with physical evidence, and her story to Otis Wahlburger
is completely different from her previous story. She claimed
not to remember when or where she married Vernie (even
though she has total recall on so many other details from
those years), the story she told me about how she met
Ronald does not square with other things she told me
about her research and her stepdaughter, and what it all
meant when I lined up the dates. Still, I don't have as
much evidence here as some others. **I give her a 1.**

4. *Cunning/manipulation.* One of the letters from the psychiatrist listed how she manipulated her family members,
and her parents were not shy about giving other examples. Also, her brother told me Suzanne got great plea-
sure when she outsmarted others. Psychologist Paul
Ekman has termed this "duping delight," the thrill some
people get from fooling—and therefore controlling—another person. Excitement, contempt, and amusement are
all contained in duping delight. I am repeating here the

statement from Suzanne's brother about his reaction when he found out she had gotten the insanity plea. "I realized she had conned the system," he said. "She's always been smart and tries to fool people. This time it worked." On this item of the scale, **she gets a 2.**

5. *Lack of remorse or guilt.* This goes without saying. All I heard was Vernie's cruelty and how kids mistreated Danny after the murder, or how people thought less of her. Even when Louisa wanted to give me Vern's police badge and wallet, because I was his family, Suzanne replied, "I'm his family, too," and said she'd keep it. On the probate documents when she was applying to get all of Vern's assets, they asked her relationship to the deceased. "Widow," she wrote everywhere. And I'm thinking, well, who made you a widow? **I give her a 2.**

6. *Emotionally shallow, sometimes called shallow affect.* Though I knew Suzanne for years back in the 1960s and '70s, I was sufficiently young that I don't feel comfortable making an assessment on this item from back in that time. But I spent fourteen hours talking to her in the past couple of years. It was impossible to engage her in any conversation that had any degree of emotional depth. She talked about things that happened, about how smart she is, how boring husbands are, and so on, but if I tried to get her to talk about what she might have felt for Vernie (or anyone else for that matter), she was stumped. She couldn't remember if she loved him. Then later, "I must have been attracted to him," but she couldn't ever say how, even though I'd given her lots of prompts. When she talked about the murder, she had the same level of affect as when she was commenting on her dinner. And whenever a topic came up that she didn't want to talk about, she started a conversation with Holstein, her dog. **I give her a 2.**

7. *Callous/lack of empathy.* I never felt any emotion coming out of Suzanne during our fourteen hours together,
and I am pretty good at knowing what people are feeling,
partly due to growing up in an alcoholic home. The only
thing I sensed was that she was burrowing into my
emotions, trying to figure me out. I saw it in her eyes.
When I'd bring up subjects of my family, my uncle, his
daughter, Shannon, or even her children and issues in
their lives, never did I feel the least trace of empathy.
The situation of the police badge: Rather than Suzanne
thinking how thoughtful it would be for me, Vern's
niece, to have something of his, she immediately claimed
sovereignty. During the last meeting, when we discussed
my writing a book with Suzanne as a main character, she
got so angry, so defensive, that the callousness was
scary. I mean really scary. **I give her a 2.**
8. *Irresponsibility.* From various reports she didn't seem to
give her children much attention, and after Vernie was
murdered, it seemed she essentially abandoned Danny.
Her parents reported that she took no responsibility toward anyone in the family other than herself. Yet I am
without complete information; **I give her a 1.**
9. *Inability to accept responsibility for own actions.* She
murdered my uncle, or was somehow involved in a
cover-up. Did she want to pay for her crime? No, she got
off on insanity, cashed in his life insurance, took all his
assets, and made sure his daughter, Shannon, got nothing. And she blamed it all on Vernie's cruelty. Did she
ever think of divorcing him? She was surprised at the
question the first time I asked. During the next visit,
when I asked it again, she was more prepared. She probably did think about divorcing him, but she didn't
because counselors confused her. **I give her a 2.**
10. *Need for stimulation and gets easily bored.* She told me
during that first visit, probably three or four times, how

quickly she got bored with her husbands. And how the work she did was not satisfying. So when she had enough assets accumulated from the four different husbands, she no longer worked and went to school full-time. Interestingly, she never seemed to work full-time after that. She taught as an adjunct at the College of St. Catherine and had some kind of a law practice, but I don't think it was very successful, from what I've been able to determine. Or maybe it was just too boring to meet one client after another. Did I mention she ran for the state legislature and got her real state license, and also became an insurance broker? **In this category, she gets a 2.**

11. *Parasitic lifestyle.* She did work a couple of years before she murdered Vernie, though her brother claims she never really worked, but got rich from all of her ex-husbands. After one of her alleged attempts at suicide, she stopped working, but I'm not sure how long. It was during this time that she and Vernie bought the 35 acres, plus cabin, in northern Wisconsin. And she also told me her second husband had an affair, but she waited a couple of years to divorce him, until he had a decent level of assets. She fought for the inheritance from her third father-in-law, even though she was already having an affair with Vernie, and she got divorced as quickly afterward as possible. **I give her a 2.**

12. *Lack of realistic, long-term goals.* The fact that she had three divorces and three children from three different fathers when she moved in with Vernie indicates someone who's not thinking ahead. She did go to school and get a lot of degrees in a short time, but that did not seem to lead to any fulfilling or remunerative career. It seemed mostly so people would admire her. She didn't think through, or didn't care about, the effect the murder would have on her children. **I give her a 2.**

13. *Impulsivity.* I saw this on a number of occasions during her connection to Vernie, when she'd go off in one of her rages because someone didn't talk to her enough, or Jenylle's name was mentioned. Plus, as mentioned above, marrying and divorcing so quickly, back in the 1950s and '60s, was very impulsive. **I give her a 2.**

14. *Poor behavioral controls.* See above and her rages, and also how she would announce to anyone in the room how Vernie was not going to get any sex unless he did what she wanted. **I give her a 2.**

15. *Early behavioral problems.* Her parents went on and on with the detective about her jealousy, her tantrums, the chaos she'd created in the family. **I give her a 2.**

16. *Revocation of conditional release.* She didn't seem to have any problems here that I could see. **She gets a 0.**

17. *Juvenile delinquency.* No evidence here. **She gets a 0.**

18. *Criminal versatility.* I don't know enough about her life outside the murder and its aftermath. Why did she have so many jobs way back then, and nothing substantive later on? It's probably related to her problems, but I don't have enough information. **She gets a 0.**

19. *Many short-term marital relationships.* Do four husbands by the time she is thirty-four years old count? **I give her a 2.**

20. *Promiscuous sexual behavior.* The fact of her multiple marriages and the affair she had with Vernie, while both were still married, and her showing up in Boscobel, Wisconsin, with a boyfriend a few months before the murder, all of this points to someone who uses sex to gain power. **I give her a 2.**

The cutoff for psychopath is between 26 and 30 depending on which expert you read. **My assessment of Suzanne's score is 30.**

Another aspect of psychopathy has to do with emotions, but taken from a different angle from what I've already discussed. Psychopaths are better than average in gauging fear in others, which makes them more facile in finding palatable victims. It was scary to consider how many times I might have been around someone who was checking out *my* fears to see at what level I could be manipulated.

One of the documentaries I watched featured a psychopath who explained how he looks for his next victim. He screens for vulnerable women by sending out an "empathy bomb," which means he'll say something like, "My parents didn't love me much," or "I've never told anyone these things," or "I really need someone to understand all my troubles." Then if the woman doesn't respond in a caring and empathetic way, he moves on, because, "What's the point?"

Suzanne evidently used a sort of empathy bomb with people. A number of old family friends and associates told me how much sympathy they had for her. One couple, Bertram and Linda Kresnick, stood up at Suzanne's marriage to John Briggs in 1952. After I dialed, Linda picked up the phone and Bertram got on another line. When I explained who I was and what I was doing, Linda almost yelled out, without any hesitation, "Oh, Suzi, I remember her well! She was my boss in the mimeograph department, back when we used to duplicate exams for professors, using that awful purple ink, and we were in the Commerce Building in Sterling Hall. She married John, who was a TA and doctoral student in the Commerce School. John's father taught in a small college in Maryville, Tennessee."

I was pleasantly surprised by the level of detail Linda had after more than fifty years. She went on about her friend: "Suzi had a messy life. A sad background. She told me about it, but I know it was a difficult life. I felt sorry for her." Linda repeated this three times: "I felt sorry for her." Was this Suzanne's MO even back then, to seem like the victim?

After having talked for about thirty minutes, Linda got more reflective. "Suzi was unusual, now that I think about it. Even a bit unhinged, with all her personal problems. At one time she had told me how her mother had given birth to a stillborn girl, and I felt so bad for Suzi. Then she mailed me a picture with a baby in a coffin. Dead as a doornail. It really scared me. We had a strange relationship. But she was a smart girl."

When I asked her about Suzi's dating, Linda said, "Oh, yes, she was really out there. She wasn't unattractive, she didn't dress very sexy, but she had some 'come hither' look that men were drawn to."

I asked if she remembered an Egyptian guy, as Suzanne had told me she had been engaged to someone from Egypt, and my research had uncovered her being the secretary of the Islamic Cultural Association in 1952. Linda said she had some recollection of the Egyptian guy, but she couldn't remember the details and said it wasn't long after that Suzi married Briggs. Interesting that an Egyptian man named Abbas Assam was also an officer in the Islamic Cultural Association, and then became an usher at the Briggs/Chappington wedding in 1952. Turns out Abbas Assam already had a wife back in Egypt, but perhaps Suzi didn't know that, or perhaps it was someone else.

Writings on psychopaths indicate they "mimic" others, because they have no empathy and don't feel emotions the way the other 99 percent of the population does. As Suzanne had told me, she was smart in the brain, but she "never factored in emotions" enough when dealing with other people. People with average empathy would probably not say such a thing, because we don't have to go through some incredibly complicated mental gymnastics to understand someone else's emotional reaction. Psychopaths, however, have to learn, as a pigeon does, that one kind of behavior leads to a certain outcome. For example, if you criticize and complain, you'll get defensiveness and anger.

I've learned that psychopaths must manufacture their understanding of the world and relationships in an *intentional* manner—unlike more normal people who learn about human dynamics as they continue to mature without perhaps even noticing much of the learning until later.

Based on my new awareness, I found it fascinating that Suzanne did her doctoral research and dissertation about how a person learns, by observing other people and relationships. In other words: how to mimic and then become accepted as a member of society. Though the topic of her dissertation is parental kidnapping, she explains early on that the theoretical foundation comes from "Symbolic Interactionism," a sociological framework that basically says we are shaped by our socializations.

However, when Suzanne expounds on this theory in her work (Brandon, 1987), which she does for about fifty pages, it sounds more like a manual for a psychopath to learn how to be considered a normal human being. One of my professors in graduate school said we all go into our fields of study to fill our unmet needs. In my career as a full-time professor, I saw, over and over, how the psychology departments had the wackiest faculty, political science had the least "political" members, management departments (my usual academic home) had little ability to manage their own affairs, and so on. Therefore it was no surprise that Suzanne would be drawn to a topic that spoke to her lack of ability to naturally understand human dynamics. She described human beings as biological individuals who learn to relate to others by developing an intricate set of values and meaning. She went on:

> The individual gradually becomes able to respond to
> gestures, objects, and other stimuli as meaningful to

him/her in the same way they are meaningful to others . . .
Relationships . . . are duplicated in many different people . . . Identity is "situated" . . . Not only is this situated
identity essential as a BASIS for initiating interaction, it is
crucial for guiding and anticipating the course of that interaction . . . focused on the negotiation which occurs in the
diagnosis which is the outcome of a psychiatric interview.
NEGOTIATION of reality takes place. (pp. 66 & 68)

Suzanne should be an expert regarding negotiation of reality,
considering her meetings with the psychiatrists and the police.
Even though her story never quite made sense, it was ultimately
her narrative that carried the day, leading to her insanity plea,
eleven months in the hospital, and being declared completely
cured not long after. Interesting to note, that in the hearing to determine her final sanity, she waived the right to have two psychiatrists examine her and chose to just have one. Who was chosen?
Dr. Glover, who had already signed off on her insanity plea in late
1970. And Dr. Glover had originally been brought in at the request of Suzanne.

Another shocking revelation was the sloppiness of her final
dissertation, done at the highly regarded University of Minnesota.
It was filled with grammatical errors and typos and a citation
style I've never seen before, and I've been on many doctoral and
master's committees. I wondered how this got past the university
librarian, who is charged with making sure every single dissertation is without even one tiny mistake. After I wrote my own dissertation, passed the final oral examination, and then had to turn in the
revised manuscript to the graduate school, I had near-anxiety attacks
for weeks. So many stories circulated about how one misspelled
word would force the entire document back and you'd have to
delay graduation. Those were the days before word processors,

when any stray or incorrect mark meant retyping the entire page. Until I got the actual doctoral diploma in the mail, I was sure they were going to find too many spaces between words on, say, page 136. And that would be it. No doctorate.

So how did Suzanne manage to work the system? I looked up her committee. Her advisor was dead, and one member I was able to reach didn't remember much about her. But Suzanne did go on at length about her advisor in her acknowledgments. He—oh, did I forget to say it was an older man? According to Suzanne in her acknowledgments, he seemed to have spent an inordinate amount of time helping her complete the dissertation.

CHAPTER TWENTY-EIGHT
Final Thoughts on Cigarette Burns and Marriage Licenses

That one cigarette burn on Suzanne's back multiplied: from one blister, on March 1, 1970, to as many as five sores, on April 21, seven weeks later. Here's what Dr. Washburn wrote after he examined Suzanne a few hours after the murder:

> Examination of Mrs. Stordock at this time revealed a
> ½ cm (5mm) circular burn over her right scapular area
> judged to be between a first and second-degree burn in
> severity. It was not blistered or weeping. She indicated
> that prior to the shooting while trying to embrace her
> husband that he had purposely burned her back with a
> lighted cigarette.

At the preliminary hearing in April, Sheriff Leslie testified that he saw one cigarette burn on Suzanne's back, after her attorney had pointed it out to him. Under cross-examination, Leslie was asked if there was more than one burn. Leslie answered there could have been, but he only saw one. How is it possible, I wondered, if she did have more than one burn, her attorney Kenneth Orchard did not make sure Sheriff Leslie (and Dr. Washburn) saw *all of them* that night in the City-County Building, around the time she was arrested? But wait, in the less redacted police reports I got later on, Orchard did just that—showed him, I mean. And the sheriff still testified he saw only one burn.

Cigarette burns make up about 10 percent of all abuse, but they are most common in children. Intentional cigarette burns generally have a 7mm to 10mm diameter, distinct outlines, and a center crater. This assumes the victim is a child who has been held down and is not able to move. If accidental, the burns would be oval and more superficial, because the child would move quickly. Therefore, if an adult is burned, unless the person is forcibly held, the burn would not be round, but rather oval. And most often perpetrators leave more than one sore.

Suzanne told me several times that Vernie burned her while dancing and she thought he was putting an ice cube on her back. After hearing this numerous times from her, I tried it on myself and held an ice cube up to my neck and my back. I can say definitively it did not feel like a hot burn of any kind, inflicted by a cigarette or a hot pan. Anyone with reasonable intelligence could immediately tell the difference.

But let's just assume she thought it was an ice cube, but it wasn't. If that happened in the bar, surely someone would have noticed if she had been burned because she would have very likely screamed out in pain. If they were dancing at home, then it had to be in the ten minutes between 1:20 A.M. when the Oregon friends, Mr. and Mrs. Ace, left and David got home. David testified that they were arguing about a cigarette burn while he was going upstairs.

This means during that ten minutes between when the neighbors left and David got home, Vernie would have had to put on some music and secretly get some ice in his hand. The police reports say that the Aces declined a drink and that Vernie had a beer, so no ice would have been out. Automatic ice-making units came later in the 1970s, so Vernie would have had to take out a metal ice-cube tray, pull the handle back, and wrestle the ice out, which back then was a noisy process.

Then he would have had to leave the kitchen (if she had been there, she would have seen him retrieve the ice) and would have swept her away to the music. This, by the way, was not characteristic of my uncle, and surely not at 1:22 A.M. after they'd both been drinking, on a night that several people noted he was more quiet than usual. And on a night that he wanted to get to sleep because he was going to see his daughter the next day.

Then after he gets her swaying in his arms, he has to pull up her sweater without her realizing (while they are moving) and burns her on the top right of her back. If they were dancing and he needed access to her back, wouldn't his hands have been closer to the bottom of her back, and also easier for him to reach under the bottom of the sweater?

You might wonder why I keep saying "sweater." Couldn't she just as easily have been wearing a dress? Remember they started the evening bowling with their league. Nobody wore dresses to go bowling. She would have either had a sweater or a front-buttoned blouse, which went all the way up to her neck. That was bowling attire in Wisconsin in the late '60s and early '70s.

And if Vernie and Suzanne were dancing, or even just standing there while she tried to hug him, he'd have had to reach under her sweater or blouse, with a lighted cigarette in his hand. And wouldn't the blouse/sweater have been shown in evidence because it would likely have also gotten burned? In order to completely miss burning her clothing, he would have had to have her turn with her back toward him, lift up her top, and apply the lighted cigarette.

Let's go back to her earlier story of the hugging (or even the dancing). When he put his hands (one of them with the cigarette) inside her clothes, did she think he was feeling her up and that's why she just stood there? And once she felt the pain, wouldn't she have jumped back, if only from her reflexes? Dr. Washburn said the burn was round, suggesting the person remained still while the burn was penetrating the skin. However, it didn't seem to be deep enough for a crater, which suggests to me someone burning him- or herself just enough for it to show, but not enough to inflict too much pain.

The cigarette burn, which months later became plural, became Suzanne's only defense for her actions, for her psychotic break. And to this day, people in Oregon, some of David's old friends, and David's ex-wife all say that those burns were the cause of the shooting that night. That either Suzanne was pushed to the limit because of the abuse, or that David was protecting her from the abuse. And where did they hear this? Likely from the recounting of the preliminary trial in the two Madison newspapers on April 21 and 22, 1970.

As for any previous abuses by Vernie or reporting of abuse, I have found no other examples, from searching through court and police documents, newspaper accounts, interviews of friends and family and Oregon residents, or the pointed discussions I had with Suzanne and her two living children, who reported no previous abuse.

Vernie's past had a quiet and friction-free marriage. Suzanne's past was filled with multiple divorces, temper tantrums, dish smashing, broken-bottle attacks, crying jags, and suicide attempts. And when I've listened to people tell me that Vernie was shot because he had abused Suzanne, I cringe inside, and I hurt, knowing the injustice of opinion based on unsubstantiated information. That's one of the problems when there is a murder, as the victim isn't around to defend himself. I am comforted by the fact that forensic science can dispel some of the untruths. And I am grateful to the Wisconsin judicial and police systems for keeping these records for so long and for allowing me access.

As to the matter of the marriage license, I had searched for more than two years, sending letters to vital records offices of a number of states, searching myself through Dane County marriage records, checking online with other states, and accessing four different genealogical sites, most of which offer services to hunt down marriage licenses. I even checked via phone with Minnesota and vital records in some counties in Iowa (close to Boscobel, where Suzanne's parents lived), and I have a certificate from Illinois that they did *not* get married there. In my research, I did find marriage licenses for Vernie and Jenylle, for Suzanne's other four marriages, and dissolution registration for Vernie and Jenylle's divorce, as well as the three divorces Suzanne got. Nothing anywhere on a marriage license for Vernie and Suzanne. I came to believe what Franklin said: They just told people they were married.

Here's what I think happened. Suzanne moved her kids to the Oregon, Wisconsin, house around January 1964. Soon after, Danny found Vernie and Suzanne naked in bed, but they told him it was all right, because they were already married. However, Vernie was not even divorced yet. That legal milestone didn't go through until June 10, 1964, and under Wisconsin law back then, you had to wait one year before remarrying. So Vernie would not have been free for another wedding until June 1965. Suzanne, likewise, had gotten her divorce from Irving Gast in November 1963, so she wasn't free to marry yet, either.

After the naked-in-bed incident, we can assume Vernie moved into the house, because the kids all thought they were married. I spent two years trying to figure out if they actually did get married and was having no success.

This brings us to probate. It took me months to make sense of the probate documents, partly because some of the pages were fuzzy, but mostly because, like the sheriff's report, they weren't designed for easy reading. It was just endless claims, receipts, reports, letters from the bank in charge of probate, appraisals, stipulations, and so on for ninety-three brain-numbing pages. I did see that Suzanne kept requesting money, over and over again, during the course of several years. Just four months after the murder, in a show of extreme remorse, I imagine, she put in a claim on the estate of more than $41,496. She claimed she'd loaned Vernie thousands of dollars since 1964 and that she, herself, had spent $30,000 on the mortgage and repairs of their joint house in Oregon. The house wasn't even worth that much. She'd purchased it for $13,000 in March 1964 and sold it in 1973 for $26,000. But every time she put in a claim for some of Vernie's assets, she'd have to list her relationship, and she always put "widow." What if she had instead written down "confessed murderer"? In the end she got the life insurance (Shannon sued the company and lost) plus $23,279, which included Vern's half of the house. However, the increase in value of the property all went to Suzanne. So that was another $13,000. This means her take was $52,279 ($315,979 in 2018 dollars), plus other assets, with more detail in the following chapter, where you'll see I discovered her windfall was much more.

A prosecutor friend of mine suggested contacting the law firms of Suzanne's attorneys, Kenneth Orchard and Jack van Metre (both of whom died decades ago), as there might be some interesting materials lying around in a storage room or someone's garage, and so Madison paralegal Adam Premo (who had been recommended to me by attorney David Walsh, one of Danny Stordock's Guardians ad Litem) and I did some investigating. He was told that Van Metre's files had been destroyed many years ago, and after weeks with both of us searching for Orchard's children, his daughter finally told us she had shredded his files five years ago. She commented, "I remember my dad having to leave the house during the middle of the night because one of the clients had shot her husband in the head. . . . It sounded like such a gruesome case at that time that these few details stuck in my head."

Another piece of information that has gone missing is any background on Suzanne Stordock. As I mentioned, I've accessed four genealogical services, plus one newspaper archive. In the old newspapers I can find Suzanne Stordock (almost exclusively related to the murder), and she also had a thesis published. But anywhere else that I have looked, even one of the services that specializes in arrest records, she has evaporated as an entity (except for one esoteric search I did in the Minnesota court records. Seems Suzanne Brandon married Ronald Aaronson August 26, 1983 and must have forgotten she hadn't legally changed her name. So on September 25 of that same year, she petitioned the court to change her name from Suzanne Stordock to Suzanne Brandon). We know Suzanne Stordock was arrested for first-degree murder in March 1970, but neither that name nor that arrest is anywhere to be found, other than old newspapers. I can find information on Elmira Brandon, Suzi Chappington, Suzi Briggs, Suzanne Gast, and Suzanne Brandon, but there is nothing on Suzanne Stordock. It's like that identity *never existed.* Or as if someone had records destroyed. My research associate, Gregory Smith, who knows Wisconsin state records better than the freckles on his own hands, found too many records related to Suzanne and this case missing. "The Sheriff probably had them destroyed," he told me several times.

CHAPTER TWENTY-NINE
Careers and Money

Consider an ambitious woman back in 1960s Wisconsin before affirmative action, before women's rights had taken hold. What if she was smart, driven, and prevented from attaining the kinds of positions she felt such a genius should attain?

Even after going to school for so many years and getting her bachelor's, master's, doctorate, and law degrees at two prestigious institutions (University of Wisconsin and University of Minnesota), she didn't have full-time employment. Anyone with that background could have certainly gotten some academic position *somewhere*, and probably a decent faculty job in Minneapolis–St. Paul, which boasts ninety-three institutions of higher learning in the greater metropolitan area.

So what did she end up with? A position as adjunct professor teaching sociology and women's studies at the tiny College of St. Catherine (now University of St. Catherine), which you've likely never heard of. I have, because it was not far from my house in St. Paul during the years I taught at Metropolitan State University. It occurred to me that I easily could have walked close to her at a Barnes & Noble or some restaurant and not even realized who she was.

As someone who's spent most of my academic career hiring lots of adjuncts—and then in recent years teaching as an adjunct—I can

confidently say those part-time positions are the bottom of the
heap. Anybody who is smart and enterprising, who can do research and get along with others reasonably well (and that last
one doesn't even matter many times), can get some academic job,
certainly back in the late 1980s and early '90s. There had to be
something wrong in the way she presented herself or her record,
or she could have gotten something, somewhere.

Maybe she never got a full-time position because of her lack of
any research beyond her thesis, which was, by the way, a replication of her stepdaughter's work. Perhaps she was not able to do
any research that was more than mimicking. Such a track record
is okay for an adjunct, but not a full-time professor. Or maybe she
never needed to work again, after all the money she got from her
marriages. And perhaps, if you believe her brother, she never really
wanted to work. She did make some effort to set up a law practice,
but it appeared to have been run out of her and Ronald's condo,
with the same phone number as her home, so I doubt she had
many clients. Her specialties fit her background, though, and they
were family law (five marriages, three divorces, so a lot of experiences), wills (she came to benefit from Vernie's and Ronald's),
and probate (I got all ninety-three pages of Vernie's probate documents, which detailed how she got everything, always listing
herself as "widow").

Before her degrees, she was someone whom the world did not
seem to appreciate for her gifts. Her various jobs were all secre-
tarial, certainly not earning enough to live in the style to which
she wanted to be accustomed. She started with nothing, coming
from a farming family in southwestern Wisconsin. Her wealth
seems to have come from the various marriage endings. I have no
data on the first divorce, but some information from the second
union on.

Her attorney had told her not to divorce Briggs yet, because
he'd just finished his degree in 1954 and had been hired as a bro-
kerage supervisor for New York Life Insurance. Wait until he's

got some assets, the lawyer said. So she went with him to New York City and waited until 1958 to divorce him. I am assuming she did quite well in the divorce; otherwise why would she bring up the whole issue of his assets some sixty years later? I am estimating $20,000 as her take. Plus I found out, almost by accident, that when he died—mysteriously—in 1974, she was left with "a lot of money" from some life insurance policies. My estimate is $30,000 (or $154,000 in 2018 dollars). There had to be a wad of money, because Suzanne's brother said she was a multimillionaire from her divorces, even before she met Vernie. My estimate of her take from her first two marriages equal $329,314 in 2018.

By the third divorce I started to get actual numbers. Between Irving Gast's inheritance that she got (split with his first wife, where each got $15,000) and the house, which she sold for $16,500 in 1964, her proceeds were $31,500, which is $260,098 in 2018 dollars.

Moving on to her fourth presumed marriage, with my uncle, after she (or David) murdered him, she got $13,000 in life insurance, plus $23,279.59 from the estate (including his half of the house and the cabin/acreage in northern Wisconsin), then also the increase in value of the house (she sold it in 1974 for $26,000, double what she'd paid in 1964), plus the increase in value of the Boscobel properties, totaling $6,000 or $37,370 contemporaneously. So her total from that marriage was $68,279.

Then, if you consider in 1973, after she got out of the hospital and off parole, she took the proceeds from the Oregon house and bought a house in Madison for almost exactly the same price, we might think of this as continued use of Vernie's estate money. When she sold that house in 1978, she got a $32,100 profit, or $117,078.84 in today's dollars.

But wait! After poring over fuzzy probate documents for the seventh time, I noticed some words tucked away in the life insurance information and blurry enough to have been passed over by me in the previous readings: *double indemnity.* She got $26,000, not $13,000. How did she ever convince Minnesota Life Insurance Company that it was an accident when she shot Vernie, hitting him square in the temple? After I did some digging, I found out insurance companies will sometimes pay double indemnity for murder, but only if the beneficiary was not the murderer or a conspirer. And she was, after all, *not guilty* by reason of insanity. So I had to add another $79,956.03 contemporaneously to her gain. And this means revising my previous estimate of her gain from the marriage to my uncle.

That means her total take for her fourth marriage was $100,379, or $606,700 in 2018 dollars.

Right now I imagine many readers might be confused by all of

(Elmira) Suzanne Brandon Chappington Briggs Gast Stordock Aaronson's Marriages with Financial Gains

Suzanne's marriage to	Dates of marriage	Children born	Date of divorce or death
L. Harry Chappington	March 29, 1947	Louisa Chappington, October 20, 1948	Divorced February 7, 1951
John M. Briggs	April 16, 1952	David John Briggs, January 11, 1953	July 29, 1958, in Mexico
Irving B. Gast	June 27, 1959	Danny Stuart Gast, September 16, 1960	November 5, 1963
LaVerne G. Stordock	No Wisconsin marriage record (see p.332)	Adopted Daniel Stuart, date uncertain due to sealed adoption records	March 1, 1970, homicide
Ronald Aaronson	August 29, 1983	None. Ronald had 2 grown children from first of his three marriages	October 2, 2010, natural death

the husbands and the timing of the various marriages and divorces. In order to help them gain clarity, here's another marriage spreadsheet, this time with the financial information (see table on p. 276).

Suzanne profited from the two marriages that were between June 27, 1959, to November 5, 1963 (four years and four months), and then from late 1965 (some question about the marriage itself) to March 1, 1970 (four years and perhaps six months), or eight years and ten months with the sum of $131,879, which in 2018 is $866,798, or a yearly "salary" of $96,856. Not bad for a secretary from Boscobel, Wisconsin, with less than one year of college. (See table below.)

We can surmise from her real estate dealings that she was a

Divorce granted to	When (ex-)husband died and where	Proceeds, if known, in 2018 dollars
Suzanne Chappington	1995, Fairbanks	N/A
Suzanne Briggs	1974, Maryville TN, mysteriously	$329,314
Suzanne Gast	1977, San Francisco, suicide, overdose	$260,098
N/A	1970, Oregon, WI	$606,700
N/A	2010, Minneapolis, MN	Estimated $600,000; bulk of his estate left for Suzanne to live on, then reverting to his 2 children

Summary of Marital Financial Gains, 1959–70

Which marriage	Proceeds in contempora-neous dollars	Proceeds in 2018 dollars	Yearly "salary" from proceeds
Marriage #2, to Briggs (1952–1958)	$50,000	$329,314	$52,690
Marriage #3, to Gast (1959–1963)	$31,500	$260,098	$58,890
Marriage #4, to Stordock (late 1965?–March 1, 1970)	$100,379	$606,700	$134,822
TOTALS & AVERAGE from 2, 3 and 4	**$181,379**	**$1,196,112**	**$82,134 (average)**
TOTALS & AVERAGE from 3 and 4	**$125,879**	**$866,798**	**$96,856 (average)**

shrewd businesswoman. Was the discarding of husbands a strategy to build her wealth? If money and prestige were her goals, then accumulating and perhaps even confiscating husbands' assets were far more successful than any kind of job she would have been qualified for with her diploma from Boscobel High School. You can see from the numbers here that crime does, indeed, pay. With the cash empire that she amassed from Vernie, she was able to get those higher-education degrees, which would surely give her the regard from others she had been denied for way too long. She presumably took that knowledge and experience into her fledgling law practice, that perhaps was more for show than actual career-building, but she did present herself as being an expert in probate and wills. *Indeed.*

She made the most off Vernie, because she didn't have to share it with the castaway spouse. You might ask why she didn't divorce or eliminate her fifth husband. Maybe because her sexual allure had waned. She was, after all, fifty-five when she married Ronald. And I imagine hooking up with a husband killer would be a serious deterrent for many potential mates. Perhaps she told her boyfriends and potential husbands the story she told Otis Wahlburger, the one about how Vernie beat her all the time, and then that night he ran down to the basement to kill himself, with her running down after him and struggling with the gun, which went off and killed Vern. It made her look so much more sympathetic than her taking a rifle, aiming at his temple from a few feet away, and then shooting. And who's going to bother to look through court transcripts or go to the library and look up old copies of the *Madison Capital Times* on microfiche? When she finally did remarry, it was to Ronald. And Ronald being a doctor meant she had someone with a serious income, and research shows that as narcissists and psychopaths age, the urge to murder decreases. She must have told me about seven or eight times that she married Ronald for his money, but she was still looking for it. Then she'd look at me with what was to her a winning smile and wait for me to laugh. Why would that be funny, unless it was somehow in the realm of possibilities? I've known many, many women in my lifetime and I can't recall anyone else joking like that about a dead husband.

CHAPTER THIRTY

Danny, the Other Heir

I remember Danny as a thin, sensitive, socially awkward kid who was Suzanne's third child, a product of her third marriage, to Irving Gast, but who was later adopted by my uncle. Various reports of family members talked about how neglected he was, the "kick-around child," how he was really raised by the "kindly Mrs. Freeman" after the murder. He'd never known his two half brothers from his birth father, because they hadn't seen him since he was a one-year-old.

I learned more about Danny during a second discussion with Jocelyn's son, Marvyn, who told me Danny had lived with them for a while in West Madison, when Danny was a teenager. This fits with what the Gast brothers had told me. When Suzanne moved to Madison to her new home, probably without Danny in tow, Danny would have been fourteen and Marvyn three years old. Likely, Danny stayed with Jocelyn until he graduated from high school. It was sometime not long after high school that Danny tried to go and live with his half brother Mike, who resided in St. Louis.

Danny evidently was in the army for a short while and lived in California briefly, most likely when David was working in Silicon Valley, but he spent most of his life around Madison, Wisconsin, and worked as a nursing assistant until he died of apparent suicide in 1992. Louisa's story was that Danny didn't really mean to kill himself; his boyfriend had just broken off the relationship, and Danny was despondent. He tried to do a fake suicide to scare the boyfriend, but he mistakenly took too many drugs and actually died. This pretend self-destruction attempt gone wrong has believability, because Suzanne's psychiatrist said she used the threat of suicide to control family members. And don't we all learn good and bad behaviors from our parents?

I had many questions. Why was Danny so poor when he'd been awarded half of Vernie's insurance money and state retirement fund? Everyone else in that family bought houses when they got inheritances, so why wouldn't he have done the same? There was no record of any real estate purchases in Wisconsin by Daniel Stordock. And why was he showing up at his half brother's home, nearly destitute, at age twenty? Danny was supposed to get the money at age eighteen. It is possible he blew it all in two years, but I have found no evidence anywhere that he actually received even some of his inheritance. According to the guardian ad litem (GAL) appointed on Danny's behalf during the probate process, there should have been court filings every year on behalf of Danny's interest in the estate and on the disposition of the assets. Even after repeated searches in the court records by one of the competent clerks, nothing was found.

In October 2015 I managed to get a copy of the coroner's report on Danny and the related police files. Danny's best friend, Callen Harty, had called the police on April 14, 1992, when Danny wouldn't answer his door for days. Danny had threatened to kill himself a couple of days before, but no one believed him, no doubt because he'd made such threats before and had even landed in the hospital after attempts, a type of behavior he no doubt learned from his mother. Upon entering Danny's apartment, they found him lying faceup on the bed, with his hands resting on his chest, clothed in white tennis shoes, white socks, washed jeans, and a red-and-white long-sleeved shirt.

Another of Danny's friends, Roger Waugh, said he had given him some opium recently, which turned out to be one of the four drugs that killed him. The other three were morphine, codeine, and diphenhydramine (which many people have used as either an antihistamine or a sleep aid). Though Louisa told me Danny never meant to kill himself, the coroner's report does not support such a conclusion. Danny ingested fifty times the fatal dose for morphine, ten times the fatal dose for codeine, and double a fatal dose for the diphenhydramine. Since Danny was reported to be an experienced drug user, as well as a nurse's aide, surely he would have had some idea of fatal doses of medications.

I wanted some connection to Danny, since he was so amorphous in my mind, and I had no sense of him as a grown-up. So I tried to find the two friends listed in the coroner's report. Roger had died, but Callen Harty was alive and well, doing work as a sexual-abuse counselor, and had written books about emotional healing. So I called him. We had an instant rapport.

Callen told me Danny had been his best friend since 1982, and they had been on-and-off roommates. Turns out that Roger was the boyfriend who had just broken up with Danny. Callen said Danny had a severe manic-depressive disorder, and when he would meet someone, he'd fall in love immediately and get very clingy, which would doom the relationship, sending Danny into an emotional abyss. Danny was loving and giving, but had led a life filled with pain, all the way back to his childhood.

He also told me Danny had a love-hate relationship with his mother, Suzanne, and only loved her out of obligation, and that she would often drive him crazy. Callen didn't know Suzanne well and had evidently only met her at the funeral, but he did know Danny had a "very complex family tree." One thing Danny and Callen had in common was that they both had been sexually abused as children, but Callen never found out any of the details from Danny. Danny talked a lot about Vernie, about what a good father he was and how much he missed him.

Callen is a beautiful writer and I want to share what he wrote in 2012 about Danny, because it gives insight into Danny and the family:

Last week marked the 20th anniversary of the death of my friend, Dan. I've been wanting to write about it, but it is very difficult. He was one of the first people I met when I moved to Madison in 1982. That means I only knew him for ten years and four of those years I lived in Denver. But we were very close, like long-lost brothers, like a couple without the romance, even when I was a thousand miles away. When I moved back to Madison in 1991 I moved into the same building as him and our friendship resumed where it left off in 1987.

Dan more or less introduced me to the gay community of Madison. Through him I met many, many people and settled comfortably into queer life in the big city after coming out in a small town in southwestern Wisconsin. He was the first person I ever knew to be a drag queen and while he was always a little nervous on stage he loved dressing up. He would select odd little numbers (songs and clothes) and have fun with the performances—he never took himself too seriously. In his drag world, at least.

He was also very troubled in some ways. Early in our friendship Dan told me about the loss of his father, a man he clearly admired and who had been murdered in a small town in Wisconsin, a case that to my knowledge is still unsolved. He had a lot of suffering in his background and he shared that with me. Every time he fell in love, which was often, I was the one he talked to about it. He desperately wanted love and would start talking of marriage and life-long relationships after one or two dates, sometimes even before the first date. I think he often scared people off who could have loved him because he was so desperate for things to work.

As I read what Callen so eloquently wrote about Danny, I felt empathy. Danny most certainly had an attachment disorder, which caused these overwhelming feelings of neediness in relationships. Callen goes on:

Dan was also the first person I knew to be manic-depressive, something I have encountered in many others since then. He explained what it meant and how it felt in ways that helped me to understand what he was going through. When he was manic he was perhaps the most fun person in the world to be around—very funny, sharp-witted and sharp-tongued, hilarious really, and he drank in life in all its fullness. I had some of the best laugh-ing jags of my life with him. On the contrary, when he was depressive he could be very difficult to be around because he dwelled in his depression in all its fullness, too. He could bring *others* down with him because the gloom was so deep. Dan felt everything fully, whether he was in a happy or depressed state. He took medication for his condition, but didn't always stay on the regimen the way he should.

Dan was always honest about his illness. He was always honest about everything. He would confess the most intimate things to people, sometimes too open too quickly. I think ultimately it was because he wanted most of all to be loved and accepted and he didn't feel that in his life, so he opened himself up at the first indi-cation that someone would care enough to listen. We balanced each other nicely that way, as I am a natural empath, and I could take on his pain sometimes, even when I was depressed myself.

At least two times while I was in Denver Dan ended up in the hospital after suicide attempts. I felt guilty for not being there for him. When he died at the young age of 32 it was from an overdose. I don't know if the coroner ruled it a suicide, but I knew that it was. At the time I was in a new and wonderful relationship that is still going strong more than 20 years later. Dan was struggling to salvage one that had degenerated into fights and jealousy. I think he felt that it was his last chance at love and that if it didn't work out he would never have anyone. He needed to be with someone to feel fulfilled.

At the time both Dan and I were spending a lot of time with our boyfriends. One day Brian and I were at Brian's apartment where he was cooking a nice dinner for us when we got a phone call from Dan's workplace asking if we had seen him, as he hadn't been into work for a couple days. My heart sank. The one thing that had been going right at that time was his job, which he really liked. I realized we hadn't heard from him in a couple days either. I hung up and tried calling and got an answering machine. Something told me that he hadn't collected his messages. There was something about the machine that if there were a lot of messages you could tell by how long it took before it beeped to allow a new recording. I knew. At that moment I knew. I told Brian we had to go downtown to my apartment building right away.

When we got there we raced up to the fourth floor to Dan's apartment. There was something on the door handle that had clearly been there for a while, so we knew he hadn't been in or out. We made a phone call and within a short time the apartment manager and police were there to open the door and check on him, but of course they found him unresponsive. It had been a couple days. One of the policemen asked if I wanted to see him and I said no, then broke down sobbing in Brian's arms. It was one of the hardest moments of my life.

Brian and I went to my apartment and started to call some friends. Soon an ambulance pulled into the parking lot. We stood at the window watching. When the front door opened and an EMT started to come out of the building in front of a stretcher a bird suddenly flew right up at my apartment window directly in front of us. Brian turned and fell to the couch and I turned to him. By the time we got back to the window the EMTs were closing the door of the ambulance. It was an incredibly powerful and symbolic moment that neither of us will ever forget.

I have often heard people say that suicide is selfish. I think I disagree with that. It may be thoughtless, but Dan was not a selfish person. He was one of the most generous people I have ever known. He and I were roommates a couple times and always shared what little we had—and we always had little at that time—with those who had less. Our apartment was known as the Hotel for Wayward Homosexuals because we let so many people live with us at various times—friends who lost apartments, runaways, friends who were kicked out by their partners, strangers we met at the bar, and on and on. We should have had a revolving door on the apartment.

The thing is when a person is suicidal, when they are in that much pain and despair, they are not thinking about the effects of their actions on others. I have been there myself and yes, in a way suicide can seem selfish because a person gets so wrapped up in his or her own pain. But the thing is the feelings of sadness and despair are so strong that you cannot see through the haze to even think about anyone else. It is not because you don't care about others; it's that you forget about others because the pain is so strong that is all you can focus on or feel.

So I don't blame Dan for leaving. He did what he had to do for himself in that moment. I am confident that if he had known that people would be grieving him twenty years later he would not have left. He would have understood that in fact he was loved and accepted, and that really was all he ever wanted.

Callen mentioned Suzanne's reaction to Danny's death almost offhandedly. It took the police a few hours to locate Suzanne and give her the bad news. Soon after, she called Callen. One of her first reactions to him was "This had to have been a murder. We have to make sure the police investigate." Though she evidently contacted law enforcement, they were quite convinced it was a suicide and did no further investigation.

I wondered if this was a common response to a suicide, to believe it had been a murder. But as I was to learn, there were other mysterious deaths around Suzanne. Was the reason she suspected murder that she was projecting from her own experiences?

CHAPTER THIRTY-ONE

Munchausen or Serial Killer?

Many have heard of "Munchausen syndrome by proxy," in which a parent, usually a mother, instigates illness in her child in order to gain attention. I always wondered why the name of this disorder had to be so complicated, until I learned about "Munchausen syndrome," where a person acts *as if* she were sick in order to be the center of attention. The more modern name is malingering. Munchausen is primarily a female disorder involving someone with an immature personality, fragile ego, narcissistic inclinations, low self-esteem, and overwhelming desire to have attention focused on her.

Many of these characteristics were listed in the letters about Suzanne from the psychiatrists. And then think of Suzanne, who became an invalid with no medical reason. After her fifth husband died, she moved to Alaska to be with Louisa, who had a full life and many responsibilities. It is not unreasonable to think that Suzanne, who had neither job nor husband, would be on the periphery of action in Louisa's busy Alaskan household. After some months Suzanne started to use a cane and had trouble walking, all of which required Louisa to spend an increasing amount of time on her mother.

When they moved to Tennessee, Suzanne was a complete invalid (though I saw her stand up and walk, when she thought I wasn't looking) and the center of the universe. When Suzanne was hungry, everyone prepared food. If she had to pee, all other actions ceased. And remember the letter of one of the psychiatrists, who said she used suicide threats to control the family. As he wrote, *She has tended to dominate members of her family . . . tying together the family by means of crises.*

But let's get back to the Munchausen syndrome by proxy, because two of Suzanne's three children were so ill in their childhoods that they were in the hospital often and reportedly on the verge of death more than once. I doubt if such numbers are statistically possible. This syndrome most affects mothers, and they will even poison their own children to get the attention they desperately crave.

Consider Suzanne and her three children: a total of four people. Three of the four—two children and one mother—had severe illnesses that caused other people to reorganize their lives. David and Danny had serious heart problems and were often hospitalized and barely clinging to life. It seems highly improbable to me that a mother and two of her three of her children would all be so ill.

Literature suggests that Munchausen women use means that have little chance of forensic discovery, such as holding their hands over the mouth and nose, to restrict breathing, or otherwise smothering the victims. Could that have been what happened to the very wealthy father-in-law number three, with whom Suzanne was alone in his hospital room the night he died? An important element here is the timing. The father-in-law "conveniently" died, so she was able to gain her share of the inheritance and then quickly divorce husband number three to be with my uncle. And how strange that a son (1992) and son-in-law (Jocelyn's second husband) both died in the same year, and both deaths freed Suzanne either financially or emotionally, which I'll explain later.

During my research I came across several other mysterious deaths, most of which had some financial or other payoff for

Suzanne. Could she have been involved? Or was this my imagination running amok? *Could* she be a serial killer? Aren't those usually guys who find naïve young women or men to rape and kill? Not if she's among the number of female serial killers, who tend to only murder for some benefit (usually money), who stick to family members and often favor less violent (and subtler) methods, such as poison. Because she will sometimes wait for years for the need to destroy someone else, people don't often see the *pattern* of killing. According to the world-renowned expert on female serial killers, Penn State professor Marissa Harrison, most of the women she's studied are middle- to upper-middle class, are serial monogamists, are white and Christian, are above average in attractiveness, two-thirds are related to their victims, with one-third murdering their husbands and almost half murdering their own children.

Harrison has argued that evolutionary psychologists theorize that men are motivated to leave their sperm in as many women as possible, and are therefore more motivated toward sexual characteristics when choosing a mate; while women look for someone with resources, which was necessary in ancient up to not-so-distant times, so she would have someone to protect her and her young children. In a similar vein male serial killers are often motivated by sex, and women serial killers by financial gain.

I stumbled on this line of thinking from Harrison just a few days after discovering the double indemnity payments to Suzanne, and more specifically when I got a long-awaited death certificate in the mail. It was for Suzanne's second husband, John Briggs, who was also the father of David.

David had told me briefly that his father had died and left him an inheritance he'd lived on for years, but he was vague about when his father died. After several pointed questions he finally told me it was after Vernie passed, maybe a couple of years. Even at that time I wondered how could someone not know when his own parent had died? But that wasn't much of a concern back then, because it was before I'd seen a cluster of deaths around Suzanne in the 1970s and then the 1990s. Some months later, when I'd interviewed David's high school friends, they wondered, quite emotionally, where in the world he had gotten money to buy such an expensive house in Madison in 1974. So I looked for documents and discovered that his father had died on July 14, 1974, and I figured David must have gotten some life insurance (considering his father was an executive in a life insurance company) that would have paid up within a few months, so he could buy that house. Getting money through insurance can take just a few months, while probate usually takes much, much longer, often years. David signed a contract for the house on September 30, 1974, just two and a half months after his father's death. Presuming most people spend a month or two looking for a house, that would mean he started his home hunt very shortly after the funeral. The first payment for the house was not due until November 1, as he must have been told when the insurance policy would pay out.

Other questions I asked David about his father were always answered very vaguely. I got the impression he might have died from some heart problems, but it was all very fuzzy, and only after repeated questions did I get even the thinnest of answers. David told me his father had no other children, though I discovered later he had remarried and was only forty-four when he died. It is possible David's father might have had another child and ultimate heir *if* his life had not been cut off so prematurely.

I also found that after John had remarried, he remained in New York City, but he died where he had grown up, in Maryville, a small city in East Tennessee, in an area that was antislavery in the nineteenth century and was pro-Union during the Civil War. I wondered if John had gotten into an accident or something, recalling David being very vague when I asked questions about his father's death. Wanting to know more, I sent away for the death certificate of David's father, John M. Briggs. Several weeks later the response came.

The envelope said Tennessee Department of Health and I ripped it open. It did not say which day John Briggs died, and the cause of death was redacted, because I was not next of kin. But it did say the body was found by David Briggs on July 15, 1974. So David, who had confessed to my aunt that he had murdered Vern, and whose mother had proven that "crime pays," found his dead father and soon after got a windfall inheritance.

I needed more information and called John's now seventy-nine-year-old brother, Joseph, who I discovered was away on a swimming marathon off the coast of Greece. His wife told me no one knew exactly why John had died, and her husband did not like to talk about it. I tried calling officials in Blount County to get a coroner's report, or police report, which are public record, but it turns out this tiny, rural Tennessee county doesn't pay much attention to its records. Each coroner takes the records with him, and the police reports have also been lost into the ether.

David surely would have told me something more about his father's death, would have answered the questions churning in my head. What was John doing in Maryville? How did he die? Was there a police investigation? But I couldn't ask David, because he was dead. And forget about Suzanne. Even if I hadn't been *literally* scared to see her again, she would never give me any satisfactory information. Most times I asked a substantive question, she had a convenient memory lapse.

What about David's former wife? During one of my conversations with her, I asked her if David had ever talked about his father's death. Though I suspected he hadn't gone into much detail with her, I was shocked when she told me, "He never talked about his father at all." How could you be married to someone for eight years and never talk about a parent? David was young when his parents got divorced, but he'd kept in contact with his father and grandparents, and he even lived with his father's brother for a while.

I had one other option: to ask Suzanne's brother, who by now seemed like an old-time buddy, and someone I felt totally comfortable with. He seemed like a real good guy.

"Do you know anything about the death of David's father?" I asked, hoping for some random fact that might help me figure out the riddle.

"No, I don't really," he said in his usual silken and deep voice, and my heart dropped in disappointment. "But I do know my sister got a huge amount of money after he died." I was speechless. Here was another wallop I did not see coming. I was sitting at my desk in my New York apartment, staring out my office window at a large air shaft and brown and reddish bricks with flickers of sunlight glinting off them in the late-day light.

"But they had been divorced for quite a while," I said, so much in a stupor that I wondered if he'd think I was on drugs.

"I know, and she still got a ton of money from some life insurance policies. There was a point, back in the seventies, when she was a multimillionaire, just from all the money she got from her husbands. I don't think she worked a day in her life, but she knew how to invest her money. She's a smart cookie. She bought some properties in Boscobel and kept my dad busy with repairs the last years of his life. I gotta hand it to her on that."

The idea that Suzanne had also profited from the death of her second husband caught me off guard. I just sat in my office chair for twenty minutes, trying to process this, and averting my eyes from the pile of papers needing care. I knew I had to check this insurance payment out. Her second husband, John Briggs, had been living in New York City, in Greenwich Village, and working as a manager for New York Life Insurance Company at the time. He'd climbed his way up the ladder and was publishing academic articles in journals, as well as traveling around the country, giving talks on how people are motivated regarding insurance. In fact, two articles came out in the 1990s that referenced his work in the '70s. The publications and lectures stopped abruptly when he died in July 1974. It made me sad to see this man of great potential, who had been remarried for twelve years, cut down at age forty-four. I could see from studying his history that his best days were still ahead. Amazingly, that was the exact age at which my uncle was murdered.

The next morning I went down to New York Surrogates Court and looked up probate cases, hoping I'd find information about the disposition of his estate. Nothing was there under his name. The clerk told me that back then, people were not bound by law to go through probate. So I called up Blount County, where he'd grown up and died so suddenly. Maybe that's where the probate was. But I found another blind alley and was told again there was no legal requirement in Tennessee for probate. Just for luck, I checked in Wisconsin, where he had lived for some years. Nothing there, either.

Would I ever find the details of her inheritance from the ex-husband who died so suspiciously? Months later I thought perhaps what I needed was some professional help, so I hired a private investigator to see if he could find anything regarding John Briggs and his will or probate. He had no luck, either.

Those weeks until the brother, Joseph, got back from his swimming event in Greece seemed endless as I waited to be able to call him and try to find out something, *any*thing, about John's death. He came to the phone and I remembered the warmth in his voice, and it made sense to me that he had been a minister for years, because you could just feel how loving he must have been with members of his congregation. I told him I had collected all the publications and newspaper articles about his brother. Would he want me to send those? Yes, of course. And I told him how sorry I was for his loss, as I had lost one brother when I was just thirteen and another when I was older. Same as he had lost two brothers, one in World War II. I told him how impressed I was with his brother's career, and I hope I communicated that adequately, because in the moment I was feeling pain for what was perhaps an unnecessary death. Could he tell me about it?

"John was visiting Maryville, staying in his favorite hotel, the Holiday Inn on Alcoa Highway, but no one knew he was there."

What? Why would he have come all the way down from New York City to Maryville, Tennessee, where his parents and brother lived, and not tell anyone?

"David found him, but he'd been dead for a while. There wasn't any sign of foul play with him being attacked or committing suicide. And I'll tell you, I've read that autopsy many times and it is confusing and basically inconclusive. Maybe his heart just stopped. That's what we all thought."

I asked him whether Suzanne had gotten some money.

"Yes, that's correct," he said matter-of-factly, and I wondered if he'd even considered before that such information might be a clue to the death. Even though they were divorced, he confirmed what I had assumed: Suzanne was the beneficiary on at least one life insurance policy, for a great deal of money.

Not only was the death suspicious, but now there were two people who benefited greatly from the death, both David and his mother, the duo I think responsible for my uncle's murder four years earlier. And what was David doing there? He was, by all accounts, knocking around the country at that time, though it seems he had his base in Madison for another eighteen months. Was Suzanne in Mayberry, I mean Maryville, too? Had she lured John down for some tryst? Why otherwise would he go incognito? And if you want to get rid of someone, was there a way to do it secretly?

I asked a pathologist friend if you could kill someone without being detected. *"Oh, heck yes,"* he said, "by using sodium cyanide, arsenic, or methanol, which is the base ingredient in antifreeze. Fifteen percent of poisonings go undetected. Methanol itself has a taste indistinguishable from alcohol, so it would be easy to put it in someone's drink, and unless there is a very complicated third-level toxicological screening, no one would be the wiser. Methanol poisoning brings drowsiness, confusion, lack of coordination and eventually cardio and pulmonary collapse and death, all within one to seventy-two hours from ingestion. Methanol poisoning has symptoms that are similar to heart attacks."

That made me think that if you wanted to eliminate someone, perhaps using poison or some similarly subtle method, better not pick New York City, with its top-notch detectives and scientific equipment, or certainly not Madison, where Suzanne still lived, because a death of another husband might not be treated with such pity for her, the victim. How much smarter to do it all in rural Tennessee, in a county with the barest of law enforcement and where people would not likely assume the worst.

All of this brings me to the next case. About a month after the revelations about the death of David's father, I got the death certificate of Anthony Freeman, Jocelyn's first husband. Through newspaper articles and phone calls with his son, I had learned Anthony died in a car crash, but when I saw the cause of death on the certificate, it wasn't until the fourth cause that I found "fractured spleen, fractured left clavicle and ribs," which were the sorts of things you'd expect from an automobile accident. The first two causes were cardiopulmonary collapse (heart and lung failure) and lactic acidosis, which can also be caused by ingestion of methanol. Either he had some spontaneous heart attack, which caused the crash (there were no other vehicles involved), or perhaps he was given some methanol, which caused drowsiness and confusion, and he lost control of his car. Was Suzanne and/or David visiting them at the time? I will never know.

And then I started to wonder if there were other mysterious deaths of people who were conveniently disposed of? So I looked at all the people around Suzanne who died before or after my uncle. Besides the homicide of my uncle, most of the other deaths were either suicides or heart failure. I wondered if that was normal.

When I explained all of this to my physician brother-in-law and mentioned about her third husband's suicide, he said, "How do you know it was suicide? Unless there was a note, or the police and coroner did a deep investigation, chances are it was not suicide." As a result of that conversation, I contacted the San Francisco police and coroner, but there hadn't been an autopsy and the police had not investigated.

And then it occurred to me that David had lived out in Silicon Valley, perhaps around that time. But, try as I did with police and coroner, I could find nothing else about that death. Even her third husband's grown son told me he learned about the death years later, when he Googled his father.

Another interesting coincidence I discovered was that both of Jocelyn's husbands died of heart failure, and both at times that Suzanne might have needed some support from Jocelyn. Certainly in the years after Vernie's murder, Jocelyn took over the raising of Danny until he was eighteen in 1978. William Freeman died in March 1974, just after Suzanne had moved to Madison and when she was finishing up her undergraduate degree and working on her thesis. We already know Suzanne was jealous and lost control when things didn't go her way. Did she want more from Jocelyn than she could give and thought she'd eliminate one of Jocelyn's distractions? It's a theory I can't prove.

Then Jocelyn's second husband, Roger Afterton, died of heart failure just a few months after Danny died, a time when Suzanne was reportedly more vulnerable than usual. And why did Jocelyn forbid there being an autopsy for either death of her beloved husbands? Isn't that just a little strange, unless some influential person whose love she was desperate for encouraged her to push science aside? (see table on the following two pages).

All the Deaths Surrounding Aunt Suzanne

Name	Relationship to Suzanne	Age at death	Date of death
Abraham Gast	Wealthy father-in-law	78	November 18, 1962
Vernie Stordock	Husband?	44	March 1, 1970
Sophie Gast	Former sister-in-law	56	July 4, 1971
Esther Briggs	Former mother-in-law	73	July 4, 1971
Anthony Freeman	Son-in-law	42	March 12, 1974
John M. Briggs	Ex-husband	46	July 14, 1974
Irving Gast	Ex-husband	52	November 20, 1977
Danny Stordock	Son	32	April 8, 1992
Roger Afterton	Son-in-law	44	June 13, 1992
L. Harry Chappington	Ex-husband	71	October 25, 1995
Jocelyn Rhoades Freeman	Illegitimate and later adopted daughter	64	April 27, 2009
Ronald Aaronson	Husband	86	October 2, 2010
David Briggs	Son	61	December 18, 2014

Cause of death	Notes
Heart failure	She inherited a lot of money; she was alone with him the night he died.
Homicide	Forensic files do not agree with court verdict.
Heart failure	She babysat son Danny the night of Vernie's murder.
?	
Car accident, but main causes cardio-pulmonary collapse (heart/lung failure) and lactic acidosis, consistent with methanol poisoning	Jocelyn's 1st husband. She forbade an autopsy.
Mysterious; heart failure?	Suzanne got lots of money on life insurance.
Suicide, overdose	
Suicide, overdose	Was supposed to receive half of Vernie's estate.
Heart failure	Jocelyn's 2nd husband. She forbade an autopsy.
Lung cancer	
Heart failure	Three days after I pressed him for info on the murder.

CHAPTER THIRTY-TWO
Was She an Abused Wife?

I was ready for the encounter. At 8:30 P.M. on a Monday in September 2015, the only place to get together in Oregon, Wisconsin, was McDonald's, which was situated on a large lot in an elongated strip mall with a liquor store, H&R Block, and U.S. Cellular. Right across the road was Holy Mother of Consolation Catholic Church Cemetery, which seemed oddly appropriate, as I was to meet a couple who had some connection to the location where my uncle was murdered.

As I pulled my rental Ford into McDonald's blacktop driveway, I looked at the well-kept grave sites, with tall green trees and carefully tended flower beds, and hoped I could get some "consolation" on this additional trip to Oregon. Sitting in the back of the restaurant, in an orange-and-brown-plastic booth, were Alice and Michael Seeliger, who had lived in the Mansion from 1977 through 2001. Though I had talked to Alice a couple of times on the phone, this was our first physical meeting. Maybe because they'd moved into that big and expensive house back in 1977, I assumed they were older than I am, but as I looked across the table and listened to them, I realized we were all about the same age. When they got the house, they were a young couple with small children. As with everyone else who had owned the home, it was more than they bargained for in work and cost.

"I can't think of a weekend where we did not work on that house," said Michael, straightening out the trucker's hat he wore over his brown hair. He was dressed in jeans, T-shirt, and a light brown jacket. "There was the roof in total disrepair and all of the woodwork needed refinishing. And then windows, gutter, carpet, updating the kitchen, you name it. When we got someone to paint the gable on the south side, I had to give them specific instructions on how to take the wood apart, because it was heated and formed in a circle, and if you just painted it, the wood would swell and you might get mold."

Alice smiled and I saw the light in her eyes as her husband talked. She had on blue slacks and white blouse and had short, attractive gray hair in a style that was between a pixie cut and a bob. She spoke next. "After twenty-four years we finally didn't have the energy to keep doing it, and our kids were grown. They weren't happy when we sold it, but it was just too much." Then she got serious and looked at me.

"Everyone in Oregon believes that David killed your uncle," she said, "that he was defending his mother against some serious abuse. And I guess to repay David for that protection, Suzanne confessed. But because Vernie was a cop, the police didn't want his abuse to become public, so they let her take the rap."

The problem with that story is there is no history of any domestic violence: no calls, no reports. Well, you say, she was afraid to call the police because Vernie was one of *them*. But even all the people who were interviewed said they never saw any examples or symptoms of abuse. I even checked recently with Detective Tim Blanke, at the Dane County Sheriff's Office, who said he also found no indication to believe there was any abuse by Vernie. When they were searching for the police reports on the murder, they made a thorough sweep for anything with the name Stordock and nothing else came up. And we know Suzanne's mother had reported to the police on her daughter's violent temper and threats to kill Vernie. Even Suzanne's own children could not come up with examples of Vernie's alleged abuse.

My uncle was no saint. He drank too much after living with Suzanne for a while, and he could get into fierce arguments with her. But I never, ever saw him behave in a way that would suggest physical abuse. This fits in line with my mother's side of the family. Although alcohol was a constant companion, Stordock family drunks tended to be the happy docile kind, with perhaps a few words yelled just now and then. My mother, the alcoholic, was never mean or violent. My father brought violence into our family and he didn't even drink, but he was from a different family system.

After poring through legal documents and interviewing more than sixty people, I found no evidence of Vernie's abuse. I tried to keep my mind open, because what if Vernie had actually hurt her? But I couldn't get Suzanne or anyone else to give me even one instance of his abuse.

He was a man she had trouble controlling, as he was ready to leave her for his first wife. Yet ultimately she was able, at last, to control him by ending his existence. Still, I wanted more details from her, so I asked how she was able to put up with his purported cruelty. Her reply, "Well, you might say I did not."

Yeah, Suzanne, and let's now talk about your psychotic break.

CHAPTER THIRTY-THREE
Forensic Experts

During the summer of 2015 I hired two forensic experts. The first one, Dr. Jason Kolowski of Forensic Insight Consulting LLC, who spent much time with me and always had an air of über-proficiency in his voice, helped me to re-create the crime scene in 3-D, using the forensic data. Kolowski referred me to former law professor Christine Funk, who agreed to go over all the court transcripts and police reports to give me her reactions and opinions. I wanted to know whether I was delusional in the questions I was asking and whether the conclusions I was coming to were sound.

After reviewing whatever court and police documents I had at the time, Professor Funk called me. "I can't believe no law faculty member has written up this case yet. It's got an unbelievable amount of legal gymnastics."

I could tell from listening to her that she didn't take any poppy-cock from anyone, because she sounded supremely confident and competent. She asked if I could find more documents, because she was not able to make some evaluations with what I had given her. I promised to visit Madison again. Then she sent me a report that analyzed the legal arguments in the case, where she commented upon how quickly the prosecutors seemed to accept the insanity plea, and how the prosecution had changed the charge from first-degree murder to first-degree manslaughter for no apparent reason.

Rather than asking Professor Funk to interpret the rest of her report, I decided to wait to see if I could get more information, because she told me then she'd be able to give me a more complete assessment. She had told me to call up the District Attorney's office, because the case was open record and they would surely have what the Clerk of Courts was missing. Unfortunately, the Dane County DA's office only keeps records since 1979, so I struck out there. Later on, Gregory Smith told me all the old DA files were sent to the State Historical Society and he spent many days searching diligently, even having the librarians pull files from archives in another location. Gregory found nothing, which fits with his theory that the sheriff had records destroyed.

In one of my many talks with Kolowski, who was creating the 3-D crime scene, I mentioned to him what Detective Blanke had said about how the police were surprised at how the case turned out, and how Funk's analysis, so far, seemed to be more on the legal documents.

"What I am seeing," I told him, "is how a lot of the evidence got ignored by the district attorney's office, so it was more than the legal arguments, because those legal arguments were based on incomplete or faulty evidence. But maybe I'm seeing it that way because it was my uncle and I am biased."

His reply was swift. "You won't find any investigator who is *not* biased. A detective gets a theory in his mind, and then he looks for the evidence to support it, ignoring whatever disagrees with his theory. We call that 'tunnel vision.' Not paying attention to evidence is rampant in law enforcement. And many times the forensic data is right there for them to see, but they don't. I've watched so many cases where the science is swept aside in favor of some guy's interpretation of the case."

Kolowski seemed to be talking about Suzanne's case. Once the DA decided to go with the insanity plea, nobody bothered to follow up on the forensic evidence, which seemed pretty clear to me—and to Officer Pledger—that Suzanne could not have been the shooter. Kolowski went on without me prompting him.

"From all the forensic evidence and court documents I've seen, Dorothy," he said as I waited expectantly for the rest, "your uncle's murder warrants more investigation and reexamination of the scientific data."

A couple of months later he completed a thorough analysis of the forensic data and had built a number of 3-D images of the crime scene, both using Suzanne's "story" in one scenario, and then using the forensic evidence in another. The last thing he said to me as we tied up our business together: "After examining all the evidence, there's no way Suzanne was the shooter."

Little did I know I would soon get some more affirmation from law enforcement.

CHAPTER THIRTY-FOUR
If She Did Have a Psychotic Break

After piecing together all the police and court reports, plus in-terviews with over sixty people, I've tried to consider that maybe, just maybe, Suzanne did have a psychotic break. If so, then this is how the events would have had to go down:

Suzanne and Vernie went out and had fun at the bowling alley on Saturday night, February 28, 1970. She was loving him and enjoying herself. Then he wanted to leave, which she didn't ap-preciate, but she didn't make a scene, until he said he was going to see his daughter, Shannon, the next day. Then she blurted out loudly, "Is there something I should know about?" He left, and she stared off into space. Then she thought it was time to go, but she was afraid to drive their brand-new car, so a married couple they knew slightly—Donald and Arlene Ace—offered to drive her home in her car, since they had come with someone else. She agreed. On the way they saw Vernie walking back downtown, ev-idently to pick up the car, so Suzanne wouldn't have to try and drive it home.

Vernie and Suzanne invited the couple inside. The husband had a beer in the kitchen with Vern, while Suzanne showed off her an-tiques and the downstairs renovations to the wife. The couple left. Then Suzanne ripped into Vernie about visiting Shannon and he yelled back and told her to lay off. Then she tried to calm him down and went to hug him. He teased her for being so jealous. She felt something on her back like an ice cube and pulled back and saw a cigarette in his hand, which he had stuck underneath her sweater to burn her.

Suzanne yelled at him and he yelled back. David came home and Vernie let him in. David went upstairs to his room, got into bed, called his girlfriend, and fell asleep.

Meanwhile, Suzanne yelled at Vernie some more about the burn, and he told her she deserved it, and how much nicer Jenylle was. Then he went upstairs, took his clothes off, and got into bed, turning on the electric blanket on her side to make the bed warm for her. It was a cold night. He was looking out for her—just like he walked back to get the car so she wouldn't have to drive it.

Suzanne was so overwhelmed with anger and fear that she lost touch with reality. Perhaps she thought she had been abducted by aliens that were directing her behavior. Or maybe she thought the neighbor's dog was giving her signals of what to do. She went to the den and looked at all of the guns, not knowing anything about them. Two were in the corner on the floor, but the one on top of the gun rack—six feet seven inches off the floor—looked the most interesting.

The aliens told her to take that one. So she pulled a chair from the dining room and climbed on it to get the heavy gun down. Then she put the chair very carefully back in the dining room, which was on the other side of the house, because the aliens told her not to leave any evidence. Since both the police and Franklin reported no sign of any furniture being moved, she must have returned it exactly, within half an inch, to its position at the table.

Then she rustled around, looking for ammunition in two different places. It's confusing, because Vernie had bullets for at least ten different weapons and she didn't know an 8mm from a .357. So she tried different kinds until she found one that fit in the barrel. Problem is, there was no evidence of anyone foraging through the ammunition drawers. It must have been the aliens telling her which bullet to select. Or, perhaps, after she'd messed up the drawer, she straightened out all the ammunition so it would look as if no one had been searching there, which is not something that sounds very psychotic.

She stormed upstairs, at the behest of the extraterrestrials, and stood in the hallway, with the gun behind her, and called out to Vernie, who looked at her. She said, "Vern, there's something funny about that corner, have you ever noticed?" Vernie sat up, looked toward the corner. Just at that moment Suzanne picked up the gun, held it hip high, and aimed it toward Vernie's head and pulled the trigger. *POW!* His head exploded and he slumped over onto the floor. Somehow Suzanne ended up with blood splatters on her body and brain tissue in her hair, even though his head exploded on the wall opposite from where she was standing.

Suzanne dropped the gun and ran to David's room, saying "Vernie, Vernie" and went downstairs. David followed. Suzanne said she shot Vernie, so David went back upstairs and saw the body and the rifle, which he picked up to see if it was still loaded. He cocked it and the spent shell came out, at which point David threw the rifle down and went back downstairs.

Second option of *something like* a psychotic break, or not:

The couple that brought Suzanne home left the house around 1:20 A.M., after which Vernie and Suzanne started arguing. What's this about Shannon, Suzanne demanded. Finally Vernie blurted out, "I can't live like this anymore. I'm going back to Jenylle." Suzanne started screaming at him that she'd never, ever give him a divorce, so Vernie said, "Well, then shoot me."

He went downstairs, got the most powerful (and complicated) gun off the highest rack, loaded it, took it upstairs, and tried to give Suzanne a short lesson in firearms. He told her to go back and stand past the doorway and he'd look away, because he didn't want to face down the gun barrel. She backed up, held the gun at hip height, pulled the trigger, and blew off half of Vernie's head.

His instructions must have been really effective, as this was the first time she had ever held a gun, much less pulled a trigger, and the one bullet hit the target perfectly.

Even with this scenario we still have one big problem: The blood and brain tissue ended up all over Suzanne. Laws of physics, as well as the police reports, indicate that the blood and brain were hurled in the direction *away* from the shooter.

CHAPTER THIRTY-FIVE

Why'd She Do It?

If it wasn't a psychotic break, why would she kill (or arrange to kill) Vernie and face a possible sentence of life imprisonment? Was she so certain that someone high up in the government would protect her (in a *Godfather* kind of way) that she didn't have to consider a worst-case scenario? This was a woman, three-times divorced, who certainly knew how to end a marriage nonviolently. The difference here, I think, is that Vernie is the one who wanted to move on; whereas in Suzanne's previous relationships she was the one who installed the EXIT sign.

Let's consider for a moment, though, the possible rationales for her brutal act.

1. Vernie wanted to leave her and she was not about to put up with such behavior. I'd seen her fly into jealous rages enough times to know she was capable of completely losing her composure and striking out with violent intent. A lawyer in the Washington State Attorney General's Office told me that every death found in a domestic violence case in their state had one thing in common: The victim was trying to leave the perpetrator, trying to get out of the relationship.
2. She wanted to be seen as a savior. Perhaps Suzanne was

a sociopath or psychopath, as my psych-nurse cousin says. My research indicates one of the only ways a psychopath can feel happy is to feel esteemed in the eyes of others. Consequently, they spend a great deal of energy trying to look good, to gain other people's admiration. During my fourteen hours of interviews with Suzanne, I found her saying lots of things to make herself look good, which, sure, we all do. But there's a boundary beyond which a normal, non-narcissistic personality doesn't go. For example, saying multiple times about how intelligent she was. Going on and on about her degrees, her theses, her ability to be such a wonderful mother and stepmother, her endless repetitions of how cruel my uncle was, which I surmised to be an excuse for killing him. And how many people admired her, or even were in love with her, such as her father-in-law Abraham Gast. What better way for people to think highly of a woman than to say, "She protected her son from a murder rap and pleaded guilty herself"? Thoughts similar to this are what I've been hearing for the past thirty-six months as I did this research. Who was offering such an explanation? Members of Suzanne's family, as well as friends of David from his high school days. Those who echoed this sentiment always had this longing emotion in their voice, as if they were thinking, *I wish someone would sacrifice that much for me, too.*

3. Suzanne had always put a lot of energy into getting her name in the newspaper and she reveled in that attention. One of the first things she did after Vernie was shot was to get on the phone and start calling lots of people, announcing, "I just shot Vern." And then guess whose name and picture popped up in many Wisconsin papers for the next three years? Mrs. Suzanne Stordock. One of her prime motivations might have been to become the center of attention. What better way to gain notoriety

than to admit to murdering your husband, who was a
high-ranking state official? Later in life, she maintained
being a central figure at home by becoming an invalid.
The whole house revolved around her schedule, her need
to eat and pee, and her aches and pains.

Also consider that Suzanne's own aging parents, James and
Annabelle Brandon, drove thirty miles on icy country roads to
visit the DA in Grant County and reported Suzanne had previously threatened to shoot her husband. They later denied the allegation (after no doubt being chided by one of their children), but
I find it hard to understand why they would go to all that trouble
to get to the DA's office otherwise.

CHAPTER THIRTY-SIX

One Possible Scenario

Having spent almost three years reading and rereading court transcripts, police forensic files, and newspaper accounts, visiting the crime scene, spending hundreds of hours finding witnesses pertinent to related people and incidents, as well as studying police diagrams of the crime scene, I find that what actually happened that night has come into clearer focus for me. After David died, I knew the chances of me ever knowing the real truth had dissipated, but I think I have come close. I could not prove these conclusions in a court of law, but then I mostly never expected to get any legal redress.

Suzanne had gone through three divorces already, but in each case, she was the one leaving. No husband had yet dumped her. If she had nuclear reactions when her mother-in-law talked to the former wife, what can we expect if Vernie was going to go back to that same former wife? Not only would she have been humiliated, but she would lose control of her husband and the family as it was then structured. And she would lose some of their joint assets.

So in late February 1970, however, Suzanne had a problem. Her man wanted to leave and she could never allow it. Threats of suicide and withholding sex hadn't worked, so what's next? Her house had many guns, but she didn't know how to load or shoot. And she wouldn't even know which one to pick and maybe not even where the ammunition was. We already know from the psychiatric report that she had a habit of pitting one family member against another and that she had neurotic attachments, and she used threats to get her way. This is a woman who was skilled in manipulation—and that's what her children were formed with. And she knew it. She knew how to control them.

Suzanne sent Danny away for the night. Letting him stay with a babysitter in Oregon wouldn't do, because what if he got homesick and showed up back home? So she took him to stay overnight with "loony" Aunt Sophie, the sister of her third husband, who lost his parental rights (or perhaps gave them up). This was the same Aunt Sophie of whom Suzanne spoke with derision.

Suzanne went out with Vernie to the bowling alley and acted like nothing was wrong. She laughed; she sat on his lap. But when he wanted to leave, her cool started to evaporate and she told him "no." He said he wanted to go see his daughter the next day. Such information would not have been welcomed by Suzanne, who managed to get Shannon taken out of Vernie's will, as well as his life. I feel fairly confident that Suzanne liked the fact that Vernie and Shannon hadn't seen each other for a while. When she heard him say he was going to see her, it must have whetted her ferocious jealousy.

Suzanne had some friends drive her home, because she was afraid of damaging the new car that she and Vernie had just bought the day before. However, my psych-nurse cousin swore Suzanne is not the kind to lose control through alcohol, but would want others to think she had, especially on that night. Then she and Vernie were alone in the house. It was 1:30 A.M., exactly the time David got home, but evidently after the bar friends had gone home. Hearing David enter, Suzanne could have easily started an argument with Vernie. David went upstairs and heard them argue some more. David told the police that his parents were arguing about a cigarette burn, but that would mean the burn would have had to have been inflicted at the bowling alley, because Vernie and Suzanne had been at home with friends until just a few minutes before David arrived.

Suzanne yelled and Vernie went upstairs in exasperation. That's when I think Suzanne took out a cigarette, lighted it, then took off her sweater. Remember, this was a frigid Wisconsin night and people dressed warmly. Even though she told me that he burned her while they were dancing, that might have been more believable if it was mid-July, when a woman might wear a backless dress. But we're talking about March 1, in one of the coldest states in the country. So she got the sweater off, took the cigarette, pulled one arm so that the elbow was up nearly to the shoulder, and she burned herself, being careful not to scream out from what must have hurt mightily. After she put her sweater back on, she went upstairs and slipped into the master bedroom and got a bottle of pills from Vernie's attaché case, which was likely on one of the chest of drawers to the side of the bed Vernie slept on. This was something she'd done before, so Vernie didn't pay attention. She walked to the closet and she quickly took off her skirt and sweater, putting on her pajamas and robe. As she slipped out the door, she noticed Vernie had taken off his clothes and was lying down to sleep.

Suzanne went to David's bedroom. He'd only been home a few minutes and was on the phone, sitting on the edge of the bed. Suzanne looked grim, so David hung up. (David and the girlfriend both said they talked until 2:00 A.M., but after David's friends disavowed any knowledge of said girlfriend, I am doubting what she said.) Suzanne came and knelt before him, crying, saying, "How could he do it? How could he do it?" She kept her voice low enough so that Vernie wouldn't hear anything and come down the hallway to see what the problem was. David kept asking what had happened and she finally turned around, dropped her robe, pulled down the top of her nightgown in the back and moved so close to him the burn was inches away. He grimaced and started to get angry, but she covered his mouth. *"Shhh,"* she whispered, adding, "Vernie said this is just the beginning. He's going to kill me. First thing in the morning when he's completely sober, he's going to go and get one of his guns and shoot me in the head."

David argued with her. Vernie would never do such a thing. He'd never kill anyone. But she told him, "He's fed up with having to support my three kids and háving to pay for this expensive house. He's cruel, David, cruel, cruel, and the only way he knows how to solve problems is with guns. He's going to kill me, I tell you. And he told me he'll kill you next, because you would be a witness."

"Let's go to the police," David suggested, but she told him no one would believe that such a heralded cop and state investigator was capable of murder. They always take the side of cops. And due to all her suicide attempts, they'd just say she was crazy. David told her they could run away, go to her brother Bob's house, and then fly to Franklin's in Las Vegas.

"He'll find me. He'll find us. How do you think he was able to get so many convictions for those mob guys and bust that prostitution ring? Because he's relentless. He'll never let me go. *Never.* He blames me for breaking up his marriage and he has to punish me. Only you can save me, I mean *us,* David!"

By this time she was clawing at him, grasping for patches of his T-shirt as she gasped for air, nearly hyperventilating, but all in hushed tones. "You've got to help me, David. Please, please." This went on for a while as a slightly inebriated David didn't want to make the situation worse. Try as he might, he couldn't calm his mother. She got more and more hysterical and finally declared, with just enough pity and desperation in her voice, "I can't stand it, waiting for someone to gun me down like an animal."

She showed him a bottle of pills that she had taken out of Vern's attaché case. David had likely seen her handle lots of bottles of pills, so this was nothing new. She rattled the contents in his face. "It's better if I just take this whole bottle now and end it. There'll be no mess to clean up." She opened the bottle, poured a pile of pills out onto her hand, and made a movement to put them in her mouth.

A deep fear came over David, because he'd lived through several of her suicide attempts and believed it was only good fortune that saved his mother in previous attempts. "No, Mom, no!" He helped her guide the pills back inside the bottle.

"Then help me, please, David. Help me find a gun that will do the trick on the first try. You know there can't be a second shot after a missed one, because he'll strangle me right then and there."

David sat there, stunned. Remember that psychiatrist Roberts said that Suzanne "tended to dominate members of her family, has had neurotic attachments and alliances with family members bidding one against the other, tying together the family by means of crises, and at times, threats of suicide."

"Help me get one of the guns down." When he looked alarmed, she said, changing her intent to suit his mood, "I just want to scare him, to let him know he can't threaten me like that anymore." (If David and girlfriend did talk until 2:00 A.M., then this whole scene would have gone faster.)

As they left David's room, she poked her head into the master bedroom and saw Vernie had fallen asleep, nude, on his side of the bed. She quietly closed the bedroom door, and she joined David walking down the front stairway, carefully, so Vernie wouldn't hear them, for the back stairway was solid wood and the front is carpeted. They were in the den, looking at four guns on a high rack and two leaning on the wall in the room's corner.

"What about one of those?" She pointed toward the corner, thinking this would be faster. "Vernie knows which one is the deadliest. If you want to scare him, the Mauser will be best," he said as he reached up as high as he could. It was almost seven feet off the floor, so it took some balancing, which was not easy after having those beers, even if the whole situation was sobering him up. He got the rifle down. Suzanne then asked where the ammunition was for this particular weapon, because Vernie kept shells locked in two different places. "You don't need to load it, if you're just going to scare him!" David said.

But Sue convinced him that Vernie can tell when it's not loaded and he would just laugh at her and burn her with another cigarette. After the gun was loaded, Sue asked him how to shoot it, and he attempted to show her, but he realized she was never going to hold it convincingly, and he tried to talk her out of the whole gun-scare tactic. Her resolution was firm. "Do you want your mother dead tomorrow?" Being so close to him, she almost spat in his face with the raw emotion. "Protect me, David!"

Finally her goal was achieved. David was riled up, and she clumsily lifted the gun. Though it looked like a fumble, she'd been rehearsing her motions on the nearby rifles for days. If she didn't fumble horribly while holding the gun, he wouldn't get how incompetent she'd be. He had to believe she'd never be able to scare Vern.

"Oh, Mom, this will never work," he said as he tried to take the gun from her, but she clung to her strategy.

"Okay, then I'll just take the pills and you won't have to protect me ever again."

David started crying and grabbed the gun, agreeing to scare Vern. They both walked up the stairs. She asked him how to set the gun up in the hallway. "Let me go in and just point the gun at him," David whispered.

"You can't," she said, "because he'll grab it from you and then shoot me. Figure out someplace out here in the hallway to set it up."

David dropped down on his left knee with the gun resting on his right leg and showed Suzanne how he could aim it right toward the side of the bed where Vernie slept. "We'll scare him good, Mom."

She started crying and hugged him, then said desperately, "No one can threaten Vernie, David. You know it won't work." She paused and took a deep breath. "It's him or me."

David just stared, but his mother showed him the cigarette burn again. Then she said if he didn't help her, then when Vernie murdered her, it would be David's fault and he'd remember that the rest of his life. David nodded.

Sue kissed him on the cheek and told him the code words, the ones to pull the trigger on: "Do you hear me?"

Turning around, she opened the master bedroom door, leaving it wide open. She had the bottle of pills in her hand, and she went over and shook Vernie, waking him up. She was careful to stand on the other side of the room, so that he wouldn't look toward the door.

Vernie was by now sitting up in bed, looking toward Sue in the corner away from the door, and she said, calmly and slowly, "Vernie, we have to talk. You said you want to leave me and go back to Jenylle." She raised the bottle of pills and shook it, and went on. "You know I can't live without you, so I just took half this bottle of Seconals. It won't take long."

By this time Vernie was completely awake and started pleading with her, but realized he had to act fast. He leaned forward toward the phone on the floor, intending to call an ambulance so they could come and pump her stomach. She smiled at his gullibility and taunted him, "If you leave me, it's going to be on *my* terms, honey."

While he was going for the phone, Vernie gave her that *"not again"* stare, indicating he'd reached his tolerance level on her self-harming threats. She knew that look and realized she never, ever was going to be patronized by this man again and shouted, "Do you hear me? *Do you hear me?*"

David was nervous, but he heard the code words and took aim at Vern's head, making sure his mother was out of range. Then his index finger pulled the trigger. *Bang!* The right side of Vern's head was blown away and splattered all over the headboard and the wall above, as well as the edge of the adjacent wall and onto Sue, who was standing right where the two walls intersect. Suzanne looked behind her on the dresser and realized the drug-filled attaché case would not look good in that location, so she moved it to the other side of the room. She must have been in a hurry, because she probably did not notice on top of the case was pieces of bone and flesh from Vern's head. Such tissue on the top would not be possible in the new location, as it was very far from the body.

I've given this a great deal of thought in the past three years, and I think it had to have happened that way. According to forensic reports, the gun was shot from several feet away, coming from the direction of the hallway and the door of the opposite bedroom. Vernie was sitting on the side of the bed, right in front of the telephone on the floor, and leaning over slightly when he was shot. This was evident from the height at which the bullet went through the headboard and wall. The headboard gunshot hole was three feet seven inches from the floor.

If Vernie had been looking at the shooter, he would have gotten shot straight in the face. But the angle of the shot was directly into the left temple and straight out the right temple—what was remaining, anyway, after the shot. This means Vernie had to be looking at the corner of the bedroom, but with his head slightly down. The only items in that corner were two dressers, at right angles to one another.

As far as I can imagine, there aren't many reasons for Vernie to be looking right at the intersection of the dressers around 2:00 A.M. and not be distracted by the sights and sounds of David setting up the gun and cocking it. Perhaps someone had closed the bedroom door, but if the shooter opened it, Vernie would have looked toward the door. If he hadn't been distracted, he would have looked over toward the shooter. Someone had to come in the room and walk to the other side, away from the shooter, and get Vernie to look toward the corner. And remember this was a career law enforcement officer, who had worked for years undercover and would be highly trained to notice any small signs of danger. What this means to me is that someone was definitely diverting him, in that very corner, and there were only two people in the house. Suzanne had to be doing something compelling, which could have been about him leaving her. Then *bang!*

Vernie slumped over onto the floor and his brains splattered all over the walls and into laundry baskets, and even one piece in Suzanne's hair, which one of the officers noticed and removed later at the police station. The bullet entered the left side and exited the right, causing the right side of Vernie's head to explode. Most of the blood and brains went onto the bed and the wall around the bed, because those were to the right side of Vernie.

It's not physically possible for the blood to splatter and brains to fly *toward* the shooter, because the left side of the head, which faced the shooter, was not damaged except for a small entrance wound of the bullet. To me, this is the most compelling reason Suzanne could not have pulled the trigger. Unless this case defied the laws of physics, the blood and the brain tissue were hurled in the same direction as the bullet, which was away from the shooter. In order for Suzanne's version to be true—that she hoisted up this heavy gun and pulled the trigger—it would have to be true that the blood and brain tissue exploded out of the right side of Vernie's head, but circled back in midair toward the shooter.

I also have to take into account Vernie looking at the corner, with his head slightly down, when he was shot. This was a trained marksman, a lifelong law enforcement official who was trained to survive in hostile conditions, to notice acts of violent aggression. How could he *not notice* someone aiming a gun at his head, unless he was distracted to look away? The bullet entered the left temple and exited in the same place on the other side, which means the angle of his head is determined. From my reading of the coroner and police reports, this means there had to be two people involved, because I can't think of any other reason why Vernie would be looking toward the corner at this time.

After the shot was fired, I believe, David woke up from his manipulated stupor and panicked. It's attempted murder, we'll get arrested, he shouted. Calm as a whipped meringue after the beater comes out, Suzanne quietly told him she was going to take the insanity plea. He didn't have to worry, as long as he did what she told him to do. And if for some reason the insanity plea did not work—which she doubted would happen—David could then confess, and because he was a juvenile, he'd go to reform school for a short time and be done with it. She told him how grateful she was that he saved his mother's life. Just stick to the story, David, and we'll both be fine. You protected me, now it's my turn to protect you from the police.

I've had a great deal of time to consider why Suzanne took the rap. At first, one would think, she's a mother and she'd want to protect her son. But what kind of mother manipulates her son to kill his stepfather? For me the whole protection idea does not fit in with her behaviors in the rest of her life. So what is the reason, then?

If it's true that Suzanne wanted Vernie dead, and chose somehow to use a gun (of which there were many in the house), she very likely had already thought her strategy through. I believe from all the research I've done, she *had to* know someone in the judicial system had her back, that she would be able to get an insanity plea, which, as we know, was not that easy to obtain in Wisconsin back then. But even so, she could have let David, who was a juvenile at 17, go to jail and prison and avoided her eleven months in the hospital. What would she have lost in that scenario? Firstly, her picture would not have appeared repeatedly on the front page of as many newspapers, as merely the wife of the murder victim, rather than the confessed murderer.

But perhaps more important, if David had been arrested, he would have been interrogated more intensely and, because I knew David quite well, I think it nearly impossible he would not have told some officer or cellmate that his mother had put him up to it.

As the shooter Suzanne could claim diminished capacity and loss of touch with reality. But if she was instead the instigator, she could have been arrested for conspiracy to murder. How would it be possible to claim loss of touch with reality when the person in question is masterminding a rather complicated murder? And, as Suzanne surely had researched, "aiding and abetting" a murder carried stiff incarceration penalties in Wisconsin's judicial system. We're talking years in a prison, not a hospital.

I think all of this was in her mind as Suzanne led David downstairs. Going to the kitchen phone, she quickly dialed the sheriff at home to say she shot Vern, and then she tried to calm down David, who went back upstairs for a moment, then came downstairs again. Maybe Vernie's still alive, he screamed. Get the ambulance here. David was very upset, because it hadn't yet registered that Vernie was dead, so he was full of anxiety about whether his stepdad was alive or not. Suzanne made more phone calls.

The police came and noted the difference between David's and Suzanne's demeanor. He was wildly emotional and she was without affect, but the officers reported she seemed polite, cooperative, and sane. ADA Mussallem later used her lack of affect as proof of insanity, but it could just as easily have been a symptom of being a sociopath or a psychopath.

Suzanne and David were taken to the sheriff's office. They threatened to arrest David on first-degree murder. But Suzanne wouldn't say anything until her attorney arrived. After he did, Suzanne confessed, saying she would do so with the understanding she'd take the insanity defense. What psychotic person is so in charge of reality a few moments after her "break" that she can understand the legal system and the value of an insanity defense?

I remember Franklin telling me that she conned the system. He said she was always trying to fool people, to show how much smarter she was than anyone else. And I guess this time, she was.

CHAPTER THIRTY-SEVEN

Hindsight of the Sheriff, et al.

Detective Tim Blanke, of the Dane County Sheriff's Office, had been thoughtful, sensitive, and a good listener on the phone, even telling me how his office was dumbfounded about how Suzanne's case had proceeded back in 1970. But was he just placating me? Lots of books and articles have been written on verbal aikido, manipulative sympathy, how people seem to agree with you, only in order to get you to stop disagreeing or asking questions. The sheriff's staff knew I was digging around and maybe it was just easier for them to concur with my skepticism on how the evidence was ignored during the prosecution of the case.

I needed another batch of information from the county clerk and the records offices and thought it was just quicker to go there myself. And as long as I was in Madison, maybe I could meet with Detective Blanke. "Come on over," he said, and we scheduled a time for Tuesday, September 15, at 10:00 A.M. I spent Monday researching records at the county clerk's and then drove out to Oregon to meet some former residents of the Mansion, getting back to my hotel really late. I set my alarm, and when I woke up, I realized I wouldn't have time for breakfast if I wanted to look decent. So I just made a cup of coffee in the room and got ready. But what to wear? Nothing too fancy, as this was the sheriff's office, not with stockbrokers. I chose a business-casual blue plaid dress with a black duster jacket.

Fearing I'd get lost or not find any parking, I ended up arriving fifteen minutes early. It was a beautiful, clear day in the high seventies, and I wondered how many days like this Vernie had experienced working in this neighborhood of state office buildings, many of which were bright off-white brick with gleaming glass windows. When I got to the "Safety" building, there were a few people, wearing threadbare clothing, with barely washed hair, smoking cigarettes just outside the entrance. The receptionist for the sheriff's office was behind some bulletproof glass and had poofy hair and long lime-green nails. She shoved a pressed-woodchip clipboard with some paperwork through the opening. My reward for answering all the questions correctly was a temporary ID badge. Coming to greet me was Detective Blanke, who had a football player's physique, at five feet ten inches, with brown hair and a well-trimmed goatee. He wore a dress shirt and tie and had the warm kind of smile that could melt a Wisconsin snowdrift in the middle of January.

He walked me to a small meeting room, which had stuffed furniture, including a couch. I sat on a fabric chair and Blanke sat opposite. A minute later we were joined by tall and shaved-headed Detective Scott Lehman and by Lieutenant Alicia Rauch, who was the ranking officer and the person I had talked to several times on the phone while trying to get the forensic files. In her forties, with bob-length, slightly curled hair and a navy suit befitting a lieutenant, she shook my hand with warm emotion.

"This is where we often meet with families of the accused or the victims," Blanke said, pointing to some toys tucked neatly in a large plastic container in the corner. I wondered why all three of them were there. Had I done something wrong and they were going to counsel me to take another course of action? Was it necessary to subdue me with a *trio* of law enforcement officials? We made small talk and I thanked them for sending me the forensic files, a resource I had come to appreciate as the most vital information source I had on the murder. Without those documents, I said, it would have all been conjecture and groundless accusations.

Lieutenant Rauch smiled as she spoke. "After you contacted us, we didn't even know if we had records back that far, but I had Linda [a pseudonym] search through some dusty boxes of microfiche in storage. They weren't labeled very carefully, so she had to go through one film after another, sliding each page through the reader. Three weeks later she still hadn't found anything and we were about to give up the search, when we heard her yell across the office at the top of her lungs, 'I found it!' Everyone ran over to the screen and we saw that first page of the report from March 1, 1970. A lot of us read it and we couldn't really believe how the case progressed."

As I listened to her, I remembered how distant and remote I had thought she was when we talked months ago, before I ever knew whether I'd get the reports. But on that day in the sheriff's office, I found out how wrong I had been when Detective Blanke turned to me and said in a measured voice, "If David were still alive, we'd reopen the case." I don't remember what they said immediately afterward, because I was overcome with emotion. Tears streamed down my cheeks. Good thing they had a box of tissues on the table next to me. For the next few days I alternated between elation at being vindicated in my search and castigating myself for not investigating Vernie's murder earlier, even a few years previously would have made so much difference. I thought about how David had died just when my questions started getting more intense, and how convenient his death was to Suzanne, which even back then I had noticed. With the only other person in the house that night dead, any digging I did on the case would be legally fruitless.

Bringing me back to the moment in the sheriff's office, Lieutenant Rauch spoke. "We saw too many red flags in the report," she said.

"What were they?" I asked.

Blanke answered quickly, which made me realize he'd thought a great deal about this case. "Those first two phone calls were very telling," he said. "Suzanne's first call was to the sheriff in his home and she said, 'This is Mrs. Stordock and I shot my husband,' while the second call was to the dispatcher, where her words were 'My husband's been shot.'" I sat there dumbfounded and told him I had missed that one about the difference in the two calls.

"I didn't pick up on it, either," said Lieutenant Rauch. I asked Blanke to explain more.

"Those two sentences give a completely different message. One names the perpetrator and the other is more passive. It doesn't really solve the crime, but it's a reason to ask more questions."

It was my turn to speak. "They interviewed all their friends and people in the bars that night. In fact, they talked to many of them twice, with one of the questions being what kind of relationship Vernie and Suzanne had. During this time they spoke to some of Suzanne's family, but why no one in *my* family. We would have had a *lot* to tell them about their relationship."

"We noticed that, too," said Blanke. "And how David was never really interviewed."

Then Rauch offered her warning signs: "The whole psychotic break and handling a complicated weapon by someone who everyone says has no knowledge of guns. We know that in a psychotic incident, your motor skills would decline, which makes it impossible for an unskilled person to manipulate that difficult rifle. When I finished the report, it was like I had read a book that ended at chapter eight and you're wondering how it turned out. A lot of things were never resolved."

It took me a while to absorb these insights, because I previously thought no one in law enforcement would want to admit such errors. My mind went to that first conversation with Lieutenant Rauch in early 2015 and she was asking me if David and Suzanne were still alive. Suddenly, sitting across from them in Madison, Wisconsin, I realized she had been trying to find out if they *could* reopen the case. Just from reading the 1970 reports, they saw the problems. I had no awareness of their suspicions and how thorough they were, and how they cared, even back to old, sort-of-cold cases from before most of them were born. My heart sank when I realized they could not reopen the case. Couldn't they go for conspiracy to murder? I asked desperately. Of course, they could not. Not with David dead.

That's when I realized I had been fooling myself. Though I had believed the previous two years that I was seeking answers, not legal justice, as I sat across from those three members of the Dane County Sheriff's Office, I now knew the truth. I did want someone to pay, to get convicted and go to prison. But it was too late.

Blanke then asked me, "You told us David had confessed to your aunt. Did she ever tell anyone?" I was taken aback, because I realized I had never asked her. Probably because I was too shocked by the revelation, but also because if she had told anyone, surely I would have heard about it before forty-five years had elapsed. So I called Aunt Maxine soon after and asked her.

"Yes," she said quickly, as I realized how sharp her memory was for a ninety-one-year-old. "I told your mother, your grandma, and some others, but none of us believed him. We all thought he was covering up for his mother. And, anyway, she got off with practically nothing and what would they have done with him, a juvenile? We couldn't bring Vernie back, no matter what," she said with resignation. "And it would only add to your grandma's pain to have to live through all the horrific details once again."

Some people may find this hard to believe. Here we had a confession to the murder and my family basically did nothing. What I have come to know, though, is that is how my working-class family and others in our neighborhoods behaved. We respected people in authority and expected them to do the right thing. And we never felt we had any right to complain. Only after working as a waitress in college did I realize I could send food back if it wasn't what I had ordered. Imagine generations of decent, down-to-earth blue-collar folks giving in and giving up time and again. After many years, resentments would develop towards those in authority.

Back in the sheriff's office I told them I really wanted to find an 8mm Mauser rifle, as it was important in my research, and how in New York City the gun shops are only listed with phone numbers, no addresses, and you can't even make an appointment unless you have a gun permit. Lehman said they might have one in their evidence room, but it turned out they didn't. Call a gun shop in Sun Prairie, they said, giving me the name as we parted and I thanked them again.

Could they ever know how much they'd helped me, Shannon, and the rest of our family? I'll never see police officers the same way again. As Blanke walked me out, he apologized to me that the case could not be reopened. I could feel his palpable regret.

When I got to my car, I called up the gun shop they recommended, but had no luck. I then called every weapons store in the region and finally talked to a shop owner who said, yes, he had a Mauser. And it was in the most unexpected location: Oregon, Wisconsin. Could this have been the very same weapon? Maybe not, but at least I could see a real Mauser and hold it.

I drove thirty minutes to the south end of town and found a small beige building, with a huge parking lot in front. The owners ran both an outdoor recreation store and the gun shop. Entering the front door, I came into the recreation area and couldn't find where the guns were sold. After I asked, I was pointed to a door tucked away, almost hidden. I walked into a long room with rifles all along the left side and the back, and with a waist-high glass counter on the right. A tall, thin man in loose jeans, in his late thirties with some tattoos on his arms, greeted me and spoke with an accent that sounded more Tennessee than Wisconsin. His name was Johnnie. Rather than pretending I was actually looking to buy a weapon, I told him the story. He'd never heard about the murder, but he must have felt enough empathy, because I sensed an outsized willingness to help as he handed me the long Mauser rifle. It was much heavier than I had imagined. I held the butt in my right hand and the chamber and barrel in my left. It didn't take long for my hand to get tired. Looking down at the chamber and the bolt and the trigger, I realized just how perplexing it would be to manage this firearm.

"This is a very complicated weapon," Johnnie said with the seriousness of someone who knows the carnage that is possible. "The way that bolt action works, there is no way an unskilled person can pick up a rifle like this and work it. Even if they handed the weapon to someone and gave her the correct bullet, she ain't gonna know how to load it, release the safety, and know what to do with the bolt. And she ain't even got the strength for holding that heavy war rifle up and aimin' it."

I thanked Johnnie and drove an hour to meet Shannon and another cousin, to go over some old family photos.

After we got settled in, I told Shannon I'd been to the Dane County Sheriff's Office and they'd told me they would have reopened the case. She and I looked at each other and then cried together for the next half hour.

"I always knew it was a cold-blooded and calculated murder of my father," she said as she wiped tears away. Though we never said so, I knew we were both lamenting the fact that our quest had started so late. If only we'd found Suzanne and David more than a couple of years ago.

While engaging in self-criticism about the loss of precious time, I also thought I was near the end of my research. I had talked to around sixty people by this time and had pored through all the police and court documents so many times I had parts memorized and could list off the names of the lawyers and many of the officers working the murder back in 1970.

One area missing was talking to someone involved in the probate process. In the documents I noticed one name that kept appearing and that was Gordon Neil, who was the attorney for the probate bank, First Wisconsin National Bank.

Mr. Neil and I had a pleasant discussion. He had been a young attorney when he was asked to supervise the probate for the case.

As was common, he never actually met the parties involved, as he was making sure the paperwork and payouts were legal. He told me one person I should contact was P. Charles Jones, who was a public defender that visited Suzanne in jail the night of the murder. What? I said. She had her own attorney. Neil didn't know how Jones got there, but he *was* there.

"You need to call Jones," he said. "I'm sure he has some very interesting off-the-record information for you." As he talked, I realized that name was very, very familiar. Wasn't his name on quite a few of the Stordock probate documents?

"Yes," replied Neil. "Not long after that he got appointed as a probate judge." What I discovered as soon as I hung up was that Jones had died several years ago. His wife had passed away. But while I was on the call with Neil, I asked about marriage licenses and probate. He told me there was a "Proof of Heir" section, which might help. However, looking later on, the only document in that section was a statement Suzanne made and was notarized that everything she said was true. And the woman at the clerk of courts said she'd never seen a marriage license in any probate files.

Then I told Neil I'd been unable to verify a marriage between my uncle and Suzanne. "That would be fraud," he said. "But I don't know the statute of limitations on fraud in Wisconsin." I looked it up and it is six years. Another disappointment.

* * *

Talking to Neil got me enthused about digging more in related areas. During the probate process a guardian ad litem was appointed to represent the interests of the minor child, Danny Stordock. Then I discovered a second one had been appointed, but the reason for the change wasn't clear. I did manage to talk to the first GAL for about an hour, and he was extremely helpful, and he talked briefly about the other guardian ad litem, who was a well-respected attorney who had recently retired as a trustee of the University of Wisconsin. But because I felt overwhelmed by all of the writing I still had to complete, I reasonably concluded there was no need to talk to the second GAL.

Something inside me kept pulling, though, and I finally called and left a message in November 2015. Almost a month passed and I hadn't heard anything. And why would I? It must be very surprising and unsettling to find a message on your voice mail from some unknown woman who had a slight connection to a client you briefly represented forty-five years ago. Then the phone rang.

"Hi, this is David Walsh and I got your message."

My mind raced. I had called so many people, but then it clicked: the second GAL. There was something about his voice that let me know he was approachable, and I felt the complete decency behind the words. This was a good man.

Walsh said he had been hired because he had already made a name as a hardworking lawyer who would do anything (legal, that is), and they needed someone to find case law regarding the life insurance policy. Under Wisconsin Common Law, a person who was responsible for the injury or death of someone else cannot benefit. So he argued all of the insurance money should go to Danny and none to Suzanne. He found some case law to back it up.

Walsh suggested I talk to a number of people, most of whom I'd already been in touch with. "Oh, and call James Boll, the DA at the time. He'll have many insights to share with you," he said seriously. "I see Boll often and I can tell him you'll be contacting him."

I hesitated. What do I say now? Here's a friend of James Boll, the DA who originally prosecuted the case and turned it over to ADA Mussallem. James Boll was the man I called on March 8, 2015, and after I introduced myself and asked if he remembered the case, he said without even a half-second hesitation, "No, I don't remember anything about it."

Everyone else I had contacted had paused to think and then often asked me a clarifying question before they started to respond, whether they had any memory of the event or not. But at that moment on the phone with the smart, successful, well-connected and cordial attorney, who was a friend of Boll's, I decided to be completely honest, knowing anything I might say would likely get back to Boll.

"Boll told me he didn't remember anything about the case," I said, slowly at first, hoping I wasn't offending Walsh. "Even though Boll spent the next forty minutes telling me stories with vivid details about being district attorney during all the demonstrations in the late sixties, and also about the other three capital-murder cases active during that time period."

Now it was time for Walsh to hesitate. "I can't believe he doesn't remember," he said. "I don't believe it." He told me he might have a file on Danny and would look for it. Because I was going to visit my sister near Milwaukee the following week, we made an appointment.

When I got to his office in Madison, the well-suited seventyish man with dark hair ushered me into the conference room, with a long, oval, hand-carved, wooden meeting table and a panoramic view of Lake Mendota. I thought I was in heaven.

Walsh proudly pointed to a cluster of buildings across part of the lake. "That's the new Health Sciences campus," he noted proudly, telling me how that had come about during his tenure as a UW trustee.

Then he changed the subject to the Stordock materials. All those long-ago files had been destroyed, he said, but we chatted about details of the case. He told me how after he had come up with case law determining Danny should get all the life insurance, Suzanne's attorney quickly came back with a settlement, giving Danny one-half. It was plain they understood Suzanne had no legal basis to claim *any* of the money. Walsh wasn't clear on why that deal was made, but Suzanne ended up with half of the insurance money, though my research indicates Danny likely did not get his share.

I told him about my suspicions that Suzanne and Vernie had never been married. He got serious and said, "That would have been major fraud." Yes, I replied, but the statute of limitations is six years. Then he said something that made me silently sing, *Hallelujah that God made lawyers, and I am sitting right across from one, and a really good one at that.* He said, "It might be six years from the time you discover the fraud."

I think I stopped breathing at that point. And I asked him if he could help me. He referred me to paralegal Adam Premo, who could possibly help me solve the marriage puzzle. And thus Premo began his task.

After six months, which was two and a half years since I'd started searching, Premo e-mailed me one day and said he had searched the entire country and found nothing. He was only waiting on Iowa to get back, but it looked like there never had been a wedding, and I'd already checked several counties in that state that were close to Wisconsin, so likely Premo was correct. I called Shannon. We were excited to get some answers.

Premo e-mailed me again, thirty minutes later. Iowa had just contacted him. There was not only one marriage license, but two were found in two different cities in Iowa. One was June 10, 1965, and the other one was April 28, 1967. At first, Premo thought there was a divorce in between, but he found no evidence. The only thing he and I could figure out was that Vernie's divorce was June

10, 1964, and Wisconsin had a one-year waiting period. It could easily be assumed that getting married June 10, the following year, would be legal, but perhaps the period of waiting actually started June 11, which was the first full day after the divorce. Once they realized the mistake, they went back to a different town in Iowa and had another ceremony.

Why Iowa? They must have known that Iowa didn't care much about Wisconsin politics or crimes and that's where they went. Vernie was well-known in Wisconsin, Michigan, and Minnesota, and they likely worried the wedding would be reported in a newspaper read by people who knew him, and that it would then be picked up in Madison papers. They wouldn't have wanted anyone to know they had been "living in sin" since early 1964. After 1967, however, Suzanne was his legal wife and she did inherit most of his assets.

But back to that day in Walsh's Madison office, before I worked with Premo, I got up to leave and he just looked at me with his wise, kindly face and softly said, "There is no way that Boll doesn't remember this case. I specifically remember talking with him about the case a few years after he resigned as DA and went into private practice." (That was early 1971.) "He told me he had doubts about who the shooter was. So I know he remembers the Stordock case."

I was dumbfounded and stood there wondering if I should try for the eighth time to call Boll again and see if he would pick up or return my calls. But what would be the advantage for him to tell me that he did remember the case? He had a long and illustrious career and didn't need any questions, at the final stage of his life, about cases he prosecuted. Even if I did talk to him, I doubted he could answer as to what really happened, because he admitted to Walsh in the mid-1970s he wasn't sure who the shooter was. What was he going to say?

I imagined: *Look, when I had the case, Suzanne was charged with first-degree murder. Then Mussallem took it over, and I tried not to interfere too much in the assistant DA's cases. It seemed unfair to other murder suspects to reduce her charge from first-degree murder to first-degree manslaughter, but, hey, that was his call.*

All of that made sense, so I wondered if it was even worth dialing his phone number again.

CHAPTER THIRTY-EIGHT
Good-bye, Jenylle

As I was nearing the end of writing the first draft of this book, I got a call at 1:00 A.M. on a Sunday in June 2015 from Shannon, who was sobbing.

"Mother's gone," she said in between heaves of air intakes. This was a call I had expected and dreaded, because my beloved Aunt Jenylle had been in and out of the hospital since March. Shannon had, in fact, left her home in Eugene, Oregon, on March 1 and hadn't returned since, in order to be at her mother's side during several illnesses. Shannon and Jenylle had always been very close.

There was to be no funeral. Nevertheless, I wanted to jump on a plane to be with Shannon. Unfortunately, I had pneumonia at that time so that I could barely stand up for even a few minutes. My doctor had ordered strict bed rest and no travel for a while.

Jenylle had passed on. Jenylle, who'd loved Vernie fiercely but quietly, who had seemingly waited almost seven years for him to find his way back to her, and was never interested in anyone else until after he died. We all thought the reconciliation was inevitable, and Vernie had even confided so to some friends in Beloit.

Looking back on all the evidence and all the interviews with so many people, I now believe he was on the verge of making this change, and that is why David said he had changed the last two weeks of his life and why people commented on how quiet he was that evening. That same evening he mentioned to Suzanne (and was overheard by others) he was going to see his daughter the next day. Did he buy the new car two days before to make the trip down to Carbondale, Illinois? Did he hope that was a first step in getting back with his one, true love, Jenylle? Did he yearn to have back the loving, quiet life that he'd so carelessly thrown away in the torment he thought was passion and maybe even love?

At last they are together again. RIP, Vernie and Jenylle.

CHAPTER THIRTY-NINE
Suzanne's Last Curtain Call

On Thursday night, March 23, 2017, Louisa texted, **Mom passed away this afternoon.** Suzanne had been gravely ill for months and had been given days to live in early March by hospice professionals, so this was no surprise.

The past few weeks had been a flurry of activities, including workshops I gave, United Nations meetings, and a trip to Montana for my grandson's third birthday. *No matter what,* I told myself, *I am going to the funeral.* Didn't matter that it would have been complicated to cancel the UN sessions, to work around the birthday party, or to reschedule the workshop, which ironically was about "Achieving Happiness."

Two close friends tried to talk me out of going to the funeral, thinking I'd be in danger, but I knew nothing would keep me away. I arrived home exhausted from Missoula and Big Sky Montana, late on March 22, hoping for some days of much-needed rest. Twenty-four hours later I got word of the death. Messages of condolence and thanks went back and forth between Louisa and me. Then I called my sister and, finally, Shannon, to let her know.

"I have such mixed feelings," she said more softly than her usual upbeat conversational style, and I knew her emotions were pulling her in different directions. "I feel sorry for Louisa and her family, for their loss. But I so wanted the book to come out before Suzanne died, so she could read that we know what happened." We talked about where the funeral might be.

"Won't it be in Tennessee?" she asked, because that's where Suzanne had lived and where she died. "Isn't that where David is buried?" Not until she said that did I realize the services would not be near Chattanooga. "David is buried near his paternal grandparents and his father, you know, the second husband. She wouldn't want that."

Finally Shannon's energy came back and she exclaimed, "But she had so many husbands, and all buried in different places! How could one choose?"

That's when I remembered that only days after his funeral Suzanne had requested to be buried next to Vernie. My grandmother refused, and I assumed Suzanne had long given up that hope. "I am pretty sure Minneapolis," I said, more certain than I had reason to be.

Late Friday night Louisa sent me the long and detailed obituary (cost: $700, as Louisa reported), which had the funeral location: Minneapolis. I made a flight reservation and diddled around trying to find the cheapest car and finally just gave in and booked with my normal National, because I did not have the stamina for price comparisons.

Then I called a friend for a place to stay, all the while trying not to focus on some of the words in the obituary, which had been written by Louisa. "Devoted wife." Well, one could argue with five husbands, you almost had to be devoted to the idea of being a wife. But what if you had confessed to murdering one? How does one then redefine "devoted"? And all of the obstacles she overcame in search of her achievements. You mean like beating a murder rap? It listed her various children, grandchildren, her degrees, but no mention of previous husbands, or of her murder confession. But then, why would Louisa include all of that? Wasn't it her job to shed the best possible light on her mother's life? Still, two of the people at the service asked me afterwards why there were so many different last names among her children.

And speaking of children and grandchildren, I thought about her grandson, Jocelyn's son, Marvyn Rhoades, who lived near Madison, Wisconsin. Marvyn and I had spoken in friendly conversation two times about eighteen moths ago, and he had told me neither he nor his sister knew how to contact Suzanne. That was a hint that Suzanne's claims of being close to them were exaggerated. Thinking perhaps he did not know of her death, I phoned Marvyn, but the number was disconnected. A Google search turned up his obituary from July 2016. Reading this made me profoundly sad. He was only forty-five years old, just one year older than my uncle was when he died. Way too young to die, even from cancer as Marvyn did.

Then I looked again in Suzanne's obituary. Not only did Suzanne's obituary have him listed as a survivor, but his name was spelled incorrectly. He was Marvyn Rhoades, but the obituary said "Marvin." And in his obituary there was no mention of Suzanne or family.

The day of the funeral I got up at 3:40 A.M. to catch a 6:00 A.M. flight, hoping there would be no delays so I could make the ten-in-the-morning service. I turned the steering wheel of my square-shaped Kia rental car and pulled into the small and well-kept Jewish cemetery, with carefully trimmed hedges and sumptuous flowers placed just-so on many graves. Because I was running a few minutes late, I had texted Louisa and hoped they'd wait for me, but I had not wanted the large group of people I expected to end up being inconvenienced by my tardiness.

As I got out of the car, I looked for the crowd. Only Louisa and her son were there, plus the rabbi, who led the three of us through some prayers and the placement, with upside-down shovels, of dirt on the plain, ivory-colored casket, which had already been lowered into the newly dug grave. A multitude of torn roots could be seen in the clumps of dirt on the edges of the hole, and it reminded me of how living things can get cut off without warning.

Later at the memorial service the rabbi gave a moving eulogy, based on information from Louisa (which ultimately came from Suzanne), about how Suzanne had always said she was the most fortunate person alive, having been able to do *everything* she wanted. Did that include the unusual act of murder? And the rabbi recited that Suzanne and Ronald had told each other everything and decided they would never look to the past, only the future. How I ached inside, wanting to get up and shout at the eleven other people who were in the chapel, *If only my family had ever had the option to look to the future with my uncle. Why were we robbed of that luxury?* Isn't it always people who do wrong who are pleading to forget the past?

We were also told, as Louisa had recounted at lunch, that Suzanne was the valedictorian of her one-room schoolhouse in Wisconsin. I know she did not mean her high school, because the valedictorian of that class of 1946 was one Reva Riley, and it was not a one-room high school. So she must have meant grade school. What would it mean to have a valedictorian in a class that was in a one-room schoolhouse with all eight grades? I had imagined there might be five kids per grade, but Suzanne's brother told me when he was a student there, it had only thirteen students in all the grades.

Suzanne was four years older, so perhaps there were a few more when she graduated, but the most it could have been was three people in one grade. Does it mean anything to be the smartest kid of three? And, anyway, having grown up in rural Wisconsin and attending a three-room school, I can say for certain I never, ever heard of any one-room (or even three-room) schoolhouse having a graduation with a valedictorian. Even if it was true, why would someone who had gotten a master's, a doctorate, *and* a law degree even care about how she did in grade school?

After the graveside service, Louisa, her son, and I went to lunch at an organic restaurant close to the synagogue, biding time until the memorial service at 2:00 P.M. We were seated in a corner booth, which provided some comfort and a measure of privacy. Louisa ordered salmon and fried greens, reminding us how they grew all their own vegetables at home and were used to healthy food.

At the grave and at lunch Louisa had to cling to her son and me. Her eyes were overcome with a universe full of grief and sorrow, more than any one person should have to bear. I had to get up periodically and walk to the wait station to keep getting more brown-pulp paper napkins to catch the ocean of teardrops coming out of Louisa's bleary eyes. Where did all that fluid come from, when she had been barely eating or drinking for days? The son kept coaxing Louisa to ingest some greens, just as I'm sure Louisa had done with him as a child. "Please, Mom. You need to eat." She would just stare ahead and ask for more napkins and then take a sip of her red Pinot Grigio wine in the tall, clear goblet. "At least eat the salmon, Mom. Please."

Louisa could not contain her anguish, which was intensified by the fact her husband had suffered a stroke almost the same day Suzanne had been given days to live by the hospice nurses. At the memorial I could feel Louisa's pain encompass the entire chamber.

My emotions were all over the place. I had to use every last particle of my energy to let only my empathetic side come out, and to keep the painful, sarcastic bits to myself. I could see Louisa in agony, her body barely sitting upright, holding back a tsunami of tribulation. Deep inside me was the pain of loss, mixed with the happiness of memories of my uncle. Such a complex feeling is something like the Portuguese word *saudade*, which signifies the suffering of separation from a loved one at the same time you remember the wonderful times. *Saudade* is felt most deeply if you know they will never come back. What I wanted to say to her, but did not, because I knew she needed time to process the deep well of pain in her soul, was this:

Louisa, Louisa, I know the agony you are feeling, the pain so intense that you wonder if you can take the next breath, and imagine you won't wake up tomorrow. And if you do, you won't be able to get out of bed or place one foot beside the other. And how would you accomplish even taking two steps when your chest is so heavy you think a giant is sitting on you and will never get off? You look in the mirror and see eyes so red they are as burned flesh, stinging with sorrow and all puffed, as if in an anaphylactic allergic reaction. You can't eat for days and then you will stuff yourself with unhealthy food, trying to fill the empty void in your heart, an abyss you discover will never, ever be healed over. You will look at everyone who is your mother's age and wonder, why couldn't she have lived longer, too? You will read obituaries for years and notice all the people who were born in your mother's year. You will meet women who remind you of your mother, and you will have a hard time standing up, remembering the wounds inside you since she died. And as you see someone her age in a few years, you will wonder what she would have looked like, had she survived. You will wake up every morning and notice the sky a little less blue, the robins singing slightly off-key, the grass not quite so green. Years later, you will start to feel as if the world might look good again, and you can finally smile sincerely. Then something will trigger you, perhaps you will find a picture of your mother or someone will mention her name, and you will break down in uncontrollable sobs, wondering if you can ever halt the staccato breathing-in that comes when you try to stop crying.

Louisa, all of this is what my family has suffered for over forty years, since my uncle died. We have never gotten over it. In fact, I am certain it is what hastened the early deaths of my mother and her brother, the last son of my grandmother, who outlived her children by fifteen years and often cursed heaven to be in such a condition. It stole Shannon's father from her, a relationship that can never be replaced. She was still a kid, and became a girl without a father. Your mother died at eighty-eight, a time when family can at least say, 'She lived a long life.' When someone is killed at forty-four, such words cannot form around anyone's lips. We never had even minutes to prepare for his death, no medical diagnosis, no hospice. Only a calamitous shock. Can you now understand what the murder did to us? That is asking a great deal, I know, but it would bring me much comfort. Please understand.

CHAPTER FORTY

The Police Badge

Perhaps you are wondering what became of Vernie's police badge, the one Louisa had found in their house, the one Suzanne would not relinquish, the one Louise promised me after her mother died. I never got it.

Three weeks after Suzanne's funeral, I sent Louisa a message offering the services of Shannon and myself to come and help her go through any boxes in her house, or organize stuff in closets. Whatever she would need. Louisa responded, asking if she had ever met Shannon, commenting that she must be a lovely young woman. Louisa apologized for all the suffering that had been buried over the years, which was the first time anyone in her family had shown remorse. She promised to send any of our family things she found, which was a relief, because Shannon and I were keen to get any of the old Stordock photos.

I told Louisa she and Shannon met once, ages ago in Oregon (I didn't elucidate that it had been a total surprise to Shannon to discover her father had a girlfriend), and then I asked about the situation with the badge. No response for almost a month. What to do? I didn't think it was ethical or moral for me to suggest I would write about this lack of cooperation in the book, as a kind of threat.

I decided to lay both Shannon's and my soul bare. I explained

how Shannon had been left with nothing, not even one photo-
graph, after her father died, and how it would mean the world to
her (and to me), if she got the badge and any pictures. That very
same day, Louisa responded and said of course, Shannon should
get her father's badge and photos. I was not prepared for the rest
of her response. What are Shannon's feelings about her mom and
Vernie's tragic marriage, she wondered. And also, what was the
nature of what I was writing about what happened? Even though
Louisa knew the book that included Vernie and the murder, she'd
never asked before about the tone. She'd been completely supportive of my research and the book until this message.

I understood her concern. Suzanne's family had been able to
move forward with their lives and their new names and could
somehow act as if the murder had never happened. My family, on
the other hand, had no such luxury, as one of our loved ones had
been brutally taken from us, leaving a gaping hole and emotional
wounds that would never ever heal. Still, Louisa wanted me to
know how grateful she was that we had reunited.

I felt the same. Whatever Suzanne had done, Louisa had been
an innocent bystander who had been nonetheless caught in the
decades-long undertow that no one could truly escape. The more
research I've done, the more sympathy I've felt for Louisa and
her brothers, who were taken on a roller-coaster ride through life
that they surely would not have chosen had they been given any
agency.

When I read her message inquiring about Shannon's feelings, I
thought, well, what do you expect her to feel about the woman
who confessed to murdering her father? Then I called Shannon
and asked her.

"You mean about the woman who broke up my parents' marriage, resulting in my mother and I living at a lower standard of
living and me having to go to a community college and never realizing my dream of being a veterinarian?" she said with an unusual
ferocity. "You mean about the woman who said she murdered my

father, who got all his assets, including his life insurance?" Silence on the phone as I heard Shannon breathing and then she shouted, "I hope she burns in hell."

Now it was my turn to breathe deeply. I had never, ever heard Shannon talk like this, and I realized once again how deep her agony has been all these years. My own awareness of her searing pain was underscored when I went through the hundreds of photos in my research and found several, at different ages, of her and Vernie hugging with an intense, all-encompassing love. You could see the tight bond between the two, I mean you could *feel* it. Shannon continued, "I'll call her and tell her." No, I said. Better not to. "Then I'll post in on her Facebook page," Shannon declared. I begged her, don't escalate it now, please.

I tried to think of a way to communicate with Louisa that would not rupture our relationship, as I have come to love and respect her. So, my response was to tell her I was confused. Was Shannon to get the badge and photos only if she felt positive feelings towards Suzanne, and if I was writing what was acceptable to her? She must have realized what Shannon was going through, because she noted that Shannon would feel what she would feel. But, please she asked, what is in the book? She said she did not want the tragedy of her mother's and Vernie's relationships made public any more than her mom had wanted it.

For weeks, months, I could not figure out what to say to Louisa, that poor soul who was caught in a vortex beyond her control. Thoughts went through my mind of pulling the book. I knew the information in the book would be difficult for Louisa and her family, but then I thought of what my family has been through the past forty years. I remembered my uncle Vernie's brain tissue splattered all over the walls, the bed, and the floor in the Oregon mansion. And the legal injustices that followed. I realized I had to tell this story.

Louisa, I am sorry for what this book will do to you. If there were a way to spare you the pain, I would do it. I did change your name in hopes of mitigating the sorrow you'll feel. My biggest regret with this project is that it will add to your suffering. Maybe someday you can understand my motivations to somehow right the wrongs that were perpetrated so many years ago, to vindicate my uncle, to answer questions lingering on the hearts of all my family members for forty-plus years.

I agree, Louisa, that it was tragic. Unbelievably sad. But for me to keep the truth hidden would not bring my uncle back, nor would it unbreak my grandmother's heart, nor heal Shannon's soul, and it would not give me back the man who had been my surrogate father.

CHAPTER FORTY-ONE
Thoughts on Complicity and Redemption

After I excitedly explained some of the recently uncovered details to a friend who had followed this case with me, he looked at me and said, "But that's just your version. So much is one person's interpretation of the truth over another." I stared back and replied, "The truth is, someone blew off half my uncle's head."

And yet . . . he had a point. Objective truth is still subjective. As I've spent hundreds of hours picking through minute details in police, psychiatric, and coroner reports, I realize many of the details that seem important to me were either ignored or disregarded completely by officials. Was there just too much scattered information for the district attorneys to go through? But isn't that their job? If someone confesses, does that preclude any further studying of evidence, especially when that evidence contradicts the confession?

Having just watched the documentary *Happy Valley* about Jerry Sandusky, Joe Paterno, and the aftermath in State College, Pennsylvania, I was struck by how the attorney for nine victims talked about the complicity of the community, of everyone's willingness to *not* dig deeper and to look the other way. What does that say about my uncle's murder?

Shannon sent me an e-mail not long after *Making a Murderer* appeared on Netflix, captivating the entire nation. She asked, "Was this a Wisconsin thing?" And she wondered, "Is the justice system in Wisconsin, small-town Wisconsin, so flawed? Has it been going on for years?"

I had, in fact, been wondering the same thing and responded to her: Maybe we just all assumed everyone was more-or-less honest, that no one looked beneath the surface of clean appearances and polite, even deferential behaviors.

The gradual realization that Wisconsin had its fair share of corruption created a kind of identity crisis in me. When I used to tell people where I was from, the images in their minds and mine were cheese, cows, and happy farmers, who maybe drank a little too much beer on weekends. But now people say, "Oh, *Wisconsin,*" and start talking about the hypocritical officers of the law who have corrupted the judicial system. I now know the truth lies somewhere in between.

And there we were decades back, living in what became our own familial hell after the murder. How was it that I saw Vernie and Suzanne argue, that Louisa reported it being worse the last couple of months, and not one—I mean *not one*—of the friends and neighbors who were interviewed by the police ever offered even the slightest indication of any trouble between Vernie and Suzanne?

Vernie certainly had friends, even if people reported that Suzanne did not. They went out every week to the bowling alley and the other bar, and Vernie took guys on hunting trips. David had a circle of close friends. Did they really not see *any* indications of problems? Were they like the people in State College, who just didn't want to see it? Oregon, Wisconsin, is a small, quiet, friendly town, and maybe having a volatile couple just didn't fit the profile. I've seen studies where they ask people to listen to someone talking about a topic and then test them on what they heard. People did not even hear things that disagreed with their worldview.

After Vernie's murder case was turned over to ADA Mussallem, he had the detectives go back six months after the incident and interview the very same people, who said the very same things. Why didn't he interview family members, on either side, who knew more intimately about the problems between the two? Suzanne's mother and father had been interviewed during the first round, where she was the only person to talk about Suzanne's chaotic, jealous, and violent side. But the DA interviewed the mother not on his own volition, but because of something *she* initiated.

Ten days after the murder she and her husband (Suzanne's father) drove thirty miles to the office of the DA in Grant County, where they lived, in southwestern Wisconsin. They reported that Suzanne had threatened to shoot her husband, which had precipitated a visit by a detective to the parents.

And detectives also interviewed Suzanne's brother Bob, but not her other brother, Franklin, nor any of us from Vernie's family. And not David. Why would you go back—again—to the various townspeople who had already told you they barely saw Vernie and Suzanne and didn't really know much about them? Was it busywork, to pretend you were actually doing something?

So I ask myself: Were people in my family complicit somehow? We all knew they were fighting, and it was getting worse. We knew Vernie wanted to go back to Jenylle, that Suzanne had an explosive and jealous personality, and we knew there were guns in the house. Shouldn't one of us have pulled Vernie aside and told him to get out of there *fast,* and take his guns with him? Or maybe staged what we now call an "intervention" with Vernie? No one would have believed back then, nor do I now, that talking to Suzanne would have helped. On the contrary it could have only made things worse, though I can't tell you how. Maybe she would have done it one of the weekends I was visiting them. I don't know.

But just like the people in State College, we never considered the possibility that such a horrific crime would be committed. It was too unthinkable.

And yet, my uncle *was* murdered, and everyone in my family has lived (or died) in the shadow of that horrific act so long ago. I didn't even realize the heaviness of the homicidal vapor we were encased in all these years until I started doing my research and began talking deeply with everyone in my family. And why was the pain of Vernie's death so deep for me, his niece? I understand why his daughter, Shannon, has overwhelming grief, but what was it for me? Then I understood how Vernie had been a father figure to me, had taken care of me, watched over me until he was brutally eliminated. Spending years reading through all the court transcripts, forensic and coroner's reports, interviewing more than sixty people related to the case, helped me work through the pain, and I can now see through to the other side.

And when I was close to finishing the book, I started worrying that the story here would only add to what has become a conspiracy-theory obsession in our culture. But how could I deny what happened and all the facts I've uncovered that suggest something was not right in how the case was handled in court? I feel compelled to tell the story.

When I started this project, I had hoped to find answers. One thing I've learned, though, is I will never know exactly what happened that night, nor will I ever know exactly why Suzanne had so many mysterious deaths around her. And I have considered the possibility that the murder was a mob hit, that my uncle had uncovered some inconvenient truths, and maybe Suzanne was paid off, and maybe the call she made to the sheriff was to let him know that the problem was "taken care of." Perhaps it had been orchestrated by some doctor who lost his license, one Vernie had investigated, or some other angry target of Vernie's skilled police work. All of this is speculative. But what I do know, unequivocally, is that what transpired the night of my uncle's murder was not the story Suzanne told, and it was not how it got played out in the court hearings.

Just because the perpetrator and her lawyers—and even an ADA—said something happened one way, it ain't necessarily so. As a researcher I know the discipline required to discern the truth and know you cannot make a chocolate cake if you start out with beef, potatoes, and carrots. The culmination for me, then, after considering all the information in the police and coroner's reports, was when I realized no matter how I arranged my thinking, I would not end up with the conclusion that Suzanne had a psychotic breakdown and pulled the trigger, killing my uncle. I believe in science and the scientific method, and, in this case, the forensics spoke loud and clear.

SOURCES

BOOKS

Atwood, M. (2002). *Negotiating with the Dead: A Writer on Writing*. New York: Anchor Books.

Babiak, P. & Hare, R. D. (2006). *Snakes in Suits: When Psychopaths Go to Work*. New York: HarperCollins.

Bonn, S. (2014). *Why We Love Serial Killers: The Curious Appeal of the World's Most Savage Murderers*. New York: Skyhorse Publishing.

Brown, S. (2009). *Women Who Love Psychopaths: Inside the Relationships of Inevitable Harm with Psychopaths, Sociopaths, & Narcissists*. Minneapolis: Book Printing Revolution.

Capote, T. (1965/2007). *In Cold Blood*. New York: Modern Library.

Cleckley, H. (1950/2015). *The Mask of Sanity*. Mansfield Centre, CT: Martino Publishing.

Collins, J. (2001). *Good to Great*. New York: HarperBusiness.

Ebrahim, Z. & Giles, J. (2014). *The Terrorist's Son: A Story of Choice*. New York: TED Books.

Ekman, P. (2007) *Emotions Revealed* (2nd ed.). New York: Holt Paperbacks

Finkel, M. (2006). *True Story: Murder, Memoir, Mea Culpa.* New York: Harper Perennial.

Fried, R. M. (1990). *Nightmare in Red: The McCarthy Era in Perspective.* New York: Oxford University Press.

Fuller Torrey, E. (2008/2012). *The Insanity Offense: How America's Failure to Treat the Seriously Mentally Ill Endangers Its Citizens.* New York: W. W. Norton & Company.

Gage, N. (1983). *Eleni.* New York: Ballantine Books.

Gilligan, J. (2001). *Preventing Violence.* New York: Thames & Hudson.

Hare, R. D. (1993). *Without Conscience: The Disturbing World of the Psychopaths Among Us.* New York: The Guilford Press.

Hazelwood, R. & Micaud, S. G. (2001). *Dark Dreams.* New York: St. Martin's Press.

Larson, E. (2003). *The Devil in the White City: Murder, Magic, and Madness at the Fair that Changed America.* New York: Vintage Books.

Millon, T., Simonsen, E., Birket-Smith, M., & Davis, R. D. (Eds.). (1998/2003). *Psychopathy: Antisocial, Criminal, and Violent Behavior.* New York: The Guilford Press.

Mumford, L. (1956/1978). *Transformation of Man.* Gloucester, MA: Peter Smith.

Munro, R. (2002/2012). *Iron.* London: Nick Hern Books.

Philips, Michael. (2008/2012). *The Undercover Philosopher: A Guide to Detecting Shams, Lies, and Delusions.* Oxford: Oneworld Publications.

Pollock, J. (2014). *Ethical Dilemmas and Decisions in Criminal Justice, Eighth Edition.* Belmont, CA: Wadsworth.

Raine, A. (2013). *The Anatomy of Violence: The Biological Roots of Crime.* New York: Vintage Books.

Reik, T. (1959). *The Compulsion to Confess: On the*

Psychoanalysis of Crime and Punishment. New York: Farrar, Straus, and Cudahy.

Roethlisberger, F. J. (1977). *The Elusive Phenomena*. Boston: Harvard University Press.

Ronson, J. (2011). *The Psychopath Test: A Journey Through the Madness Industry*. New York: Riverhead Books.

Rule, A. (2008). *The Stranger Beside Me*. New York: Pocket Books.

Stout, M. (2005). *The Sociopath Next Door: The Ruthless Versus the Rest of Us*. New York: Harmony Books.

Stone, M. H. (2009). *The Anatomy of Evil*. Amherst, NY: Prometheus Books.

Walker, R. (1995). *To Be Real: Telling the Truth and Changing the Face of Feminism*. New York: Anchor Books.

Williams, C. M. & Tidwell, J. E. (2013). *My Dear Boy: Carrie Hughes's Letters to Langston Hughes, 1926–1938*. Athens, GA: University of Georgia Press.

Zayn, C. & Dibble, K. (2007). *Narcissistic Lovers: How to Cope, Recover, and Move On*. Far Hills, NJ: New Horizon Press.

ARTICLES

Anthes, Emily. (2015, May 9). "Lady killers." *The New Yorker*. May 9.

Black, D. (1995, December 12). "Scientists probe psychopaths' dark hearts." *Edmonton Journal*, p. B8.

Boddy, C. (2010). "Corporate psychopaths and productivity." *Management Services, 54*(1), 26-30.

———— (2006). "The dark side of management decisions: Organizational psychopaths." *Management Decision, 44*(10), 1461–75.

———— (2011). "Corporate psychopaths, bullying and unfair supervision in the workplace." *Journal of Business Ethics, 100*(3), 367–79.

————, Ladyshewsky, R., & Galvin, P. (2010). "The influence of corporate psychopaths on corporate social responsibility and organizational commitment to employees." *Journal of Business Ethics, 97*(1), 1–19.

Boomer, R. (2002, May 6). "Studying psychopaths 'not for the squeamish': Dalhousie Univ grad student's research leads to new findings." *Dalhousie University Daily News*, p. 5.

Clairmont, S. (1999, October 7). "'Incurable' psychopaths could fill health centres." *The Spectator* (Hamilton, Ontario), p. A1.

Finlay, S. (2011). "The selves and the shoemaker: Psychopaths, moral judgment, and responsibility." *The Southern Journal of Philosophy, 49*, 125–133.

Goldberg, C. (2003, July 20). "Data accumulating on psychopaths: New insights on identifying people without feelings. Therapy rarely effective for those who fake emotion." *Toronto Star*, p. A14.

Goldberg, C. (2003, July 27). "Inside the minds of psychopaths: Scientists come closer to finding out what makes them tick." *Victoria Times-Colonist*, p. D5.

Gregory, A. (2017, September 18). "The Sorrow and the Shame of the Accidental Killer." (Annals of Psychology). *The New Yorker*, pp. 28–32.

Haji, I. (2003). "The emotional depravity of psychopaths and culpability." *Legal Theory, 9*, 63–82.

Harris, G., Rice, M., & Barbaree, H. (2006). "What treatment should psychopaths receive?" *CrossCurrents, 9*(3), 19–20.

Harrison, M., Murphy, E., Ho, L., Bowers, T., & Flaherty, C. (2015). "Female serial killers in the United States: means, motives, and makings." *The Journal of Forensic Psychiatry & Psychology, 26*(3), 383–406.

Hathaway, W. (2005, December 18). "Contours of evil: Inside psychopaths' brains: Researchers study how the mind works when there's no remorse." *Hartford Courant*, p. A1.

Howard, R. & McCullagh, P. (2007). "Neuroaffective processing in criminal psychopaths: Brain event-related potential task-specific anomalies." *Journal of Personality Disorders, 21*(3), 322–339.

Marshall, L. & Cooke, D. (1999). "The childhood experiences of psychopaths: a retrospective study of familial and societal factors." *Journal of Personality Disorders,* 13(3), 211–225.

McKeen, S. (1994, December 12). "Without remorse: Searching for the psychopaths among us: Psychopathy test." *Edmonton Journal,* December 12, p. B8.

Munro, M. (1991, December 30). "Psychopaths leave wide trail of traits." *Calgary Herald,* December 30, p. B3.

Nichols, S. & Vargas, M. (2007). "How to be fair to psychopaths." *Philosophy, Psychiatry, & Psychology: PPP, 14*(2), 153–155.

Oner, E. (2015). "The case of factitious bleeding Munchausen Syndrome." *Journal of Evolution of Medical and Dental Sciences, 4*(48), 8416–8419.

Palmgren, G. (2012). "Scientists decode psychopaths' brains." *Science Illustrated, 5*(3), 50–55.

Pham, T. & Philppot, P. (2010). "Decoding of facial expression of emotion in criminal psychopaths." *Journal of Personality Disorders, 24*(4), 445–459.

Porter, S. & Woodworth, M. (2007). "'I'm sorry I did it . . . but he started it.': A comparison of the official and self-reported homicide descriptions of psychopaths and non-psychopaths." *Law and Human Behavior, 31*(1), 91–107.

Shapiro, T. (2012, November 11). "The Wisdom of Psychopaths: What Saints, Spies, and Serial Killers Teach Us About Success, by Kevin Dutton." (book review). *The Washington Post,* p. B7.

Sifferd, K. & Hirstein, W. (2013). "On the criminal culpability of successful and unsuccessful psychopaths." *Neuroethics, 6*(1), 129–140.

Spears, T. (2009). "Psychopaths use charm, lies to fool parole officials: researcher." *CanWest News*, February 4.

Vargas, M. & Nichols, S. (2007). "Psychopaths and moral knowledge." *Philosophy, Psychiatry, & Psychology: PPP*, *14*(2), 157–162.

MOVIES

Ai Weiwei: Never Sorry (2012). Weiwei Ai, Dan Ai, Lao Ai. Dir. Alison Klayman.

All Good Things (2010). Ryan Gosling, Kirsten Dunst, Frank Langella. Dir. Andrew Jarecki.

Basic Instinct (1992). Michael Douglas, Sharon Stone. Dir. Paul Verhoeven.

Bliss (1997). Craig Sheffer, Terence Stamp, Sheryl Lee. Dir. Lance Young.

Body Heat (1981). William Hurt, Kathleen Turner. Dir. Lawrence Kasdan.

Cake (2005). Heather Graham, David Sutcliffe, Taye Diggs. Dir. Nisha Ganatra.

Chinatown (1974). Jack Nicholson, Faye Dunaway, John Huston. Dir. Roman Polanski.

The City That Never Sleeps (1924). Louise Dresser, Ricardo Cortez, Kathlyn Williams. Dir. James Cruze.

The Conversation (1974). Gene Hackman, John Cazale, Allen Garfield. Dir. Francis Ford Coppola.

Criss Cross (1949). Burt Lancaster, Yvonne De Carlo, Dan Duryea. Dir. Robert Siodmak.

D.O.A. (1950). Edmond O'Brien, Pamela Britton, Luther Adler. Dir. Rudolph Maté.

Dear Murderer (1947). Eric Portman, Greta Gynt, Dennis Price. Dir. Arthur Crabtree.

Deathtrap (1982). Michael Caine, Christopher Reeve, Dyan Cannon. Dir. Sidney Lumet.

Dolores Claiborne (1995). Kathy Bates, Jennifer Jason Leigh, Christopher Plummer. Dir. Taylor Hackford.

The Departed (2006). Leonardo DiCaprio, Matt Damon, Jack Nicholson. Dir. Martin Scorsese.

Donnie Brasco (1997). Al Pacino, Johnny Depp, Michael Madsen. Dir. Mike Newell.

Double Indemnity (1944). Fred MacMurray, Barbara Stanwyck. Dir. Billy Wilder.

Dracula (1931). Bela Lugosi, Helen Chandler, David Manners. Dir. Tod Browning.

Election (1999). Matthew Broderick, Reese Witherspoon. Dir. Alexander Payne

Enron: The Smartest Guys in the Room (2005). John Beard, Tim Belden. Dir. Alex Gibney.

Evidence of Blood (1998). David Strathairn, Mary McDonnell, Sean McCann. Dir. Andrew Mondshein.

Fatal Attraction (1987). Michael Douglas, Glenn Close. Dir. Adrian Lyne.

Gaslight (1944). Charles Boyer, Ingrid Bergman, Joseph Cotten. Dir. George Cukor.

Get Shorty (1995). Gene Hackman, Rene Russo, Danny DeVito. Dir. Barry Sonnenfeld.

Gilda (1946). Rita Hayworth, Glenn Ford, George Macready. Dir. Charles Vidor.

The Goebbels Experiment (2005). Udo Samel, Kenneth Branagh. Dir. Lutz Hachmeister.

The Grifters (1990). Anjelica Huston, John Cusack, Annette Bening. Dir. Stephen Frears.

Happy Valley (2014). Dir. Amir Bar-Lev.

Hollywoodland (2006). Adrien Brody, Ben Affleck, Diane Lane. Dir. Allen Coulter.

An Honest Liar (2014). James Randi, Deyvi Peña, Penn Jillette. Dir. Tyler Measom, Justin Weinstein.

Hostile Witness (1968). Ray Milland, Sylvia Syms, Felix Aylmer. Dir. Ray Milland.
House of Games (1987). Lindsay Crouse, Joe Mantegna, Mike Nussbaum. Dir. David Mamet.
The House on Telegraph Hill (1951). Richard Basehart, Valentina Cortese. Dir. Robert Wise.
Identity (2003). John Cusack, Ray Liotta, Amanda Peet. Dir. James Mangold.
In a Lonely Place (1950). Humphrey Bogart, Gloria Grahame. Dir. Nicholas Ray.
Infamous (2006). Toby Jones, Daniel Craig, Sandra Bullock. Dir. Douglas McGrath.
Insomnia (1997). Stellan Skarsgard, Maria Mathiesen, Sverre Anker Ousdal. Dir. Erik Skjoldbjaerg.
Jagged Edge (1985). Jeff Bridges, Glenn Close, Peter Coyote. Dir. Richard Marquand.
The Killing (1956). Sterling Hayden, Coleen Gray, Vince Edwards. Dir. Stanley Kubrick.
Kiss Me Deadly (1955). Ralph Meeker, Albert Dekker, Paul Stewart. Dir. Robert Aldrich.
Klute (1971). Jane Fonda, Donald Sutherland, Charles Cioffi. Dir. Alan J. Pakula.
Kumaré (2011). Vikram Gandhi. Dir. Vikram Gandhi.
L.A. Confidential (1997). Kevin Spacey, Russell Crowe, Guy Pearce. Dir. Curtis Hanson.
The Lady from Shanghai (1947). Rita Hayworth, Orson Welles, Everett Sloane. Dir. Orson Welles.
Laura (1944). Gene Tierney, Dana Andrews, Clifton Webb. Dir. Otto Preminger.
The Letter (1940). Bette Davis, Herbert Marshall, James Stephenson. Dir. William Wyler.
Little White Lie (2014). Dir. Lacey Schwartz, James Adolphus.
Matchstick Men (2003). Nicolas Cage, Alison Lohman, Sam Rockwell. Dir. Ridley Scott.

Malice (1993). Alec Baldwin, Nicole Kidman, Bill Pullman. Dir. Harold Becker.

Mildred Pierce (1945). Joan Crawford, Jack Carson, Zachary Scott. Dir. Michael Curtiz.

The Morning After (1986). Jane Fonda, Jeff Bridges, Raúl Juliá. Dir. Sidney Lumet.

Murder, My Sweet (1944). Dick Powell, Claire Trevor, Anne Shirley. Dir. Edward Dmytryk.

Murder One (1988). Henry Thomas, James Wilder, Stephen Shellen. Dir. Graeme Campbell.

The Naked City (1948). Barry Fitzgerald, Howard Duff, Dorothy Hart. Dir. Jules Dassin.

Night and the City (1950). Richard Widmark, Gene Tierney, Googie Withers. Dir. Jules Dassin.

The Night of the Hunter (1955). Robert Mitchum, Shelley Winters, Lillian Gish. Dir. Charles Laughton.

Night Train to Lisbon (2013). Jeremy Irons, Mélanie Laurent, Jack Huston. Dir. Bille August.

Nightmare Alley (1947). Tyrone Power, Joan Blondell, Coleen Gray. Dir. Edmund Goulding.

Notes on a Scandal (2006). Cate Blanchett, Judi Dench, Andrew Simpson. Dir. Richard Eyre.

Notorious (1946). Cary Grant, Ingrid Bergman, Claude Rains. Dir. Alfred Hitchcock.

Out of the Past (1947). Robert Mitchum, Jane Greer, Kirk Douglas. Dir. Jacques Tourneur.

The Postman Always Rings Twice (1946). Lana Turner, John Garfield. Dir. Tay Garnett.

Presumed Innocent (1990). Harrison Ford, Raúl Juliá, Greta Scacchi. Dir. Alan J. Pakula.

Psycho (1960). Anthony Perkins, Janet Leigh, Vera Miles. Dir. Alfred Hitchcock.

The Quiet American (2002). Michael Caine, Brendan Fraser, Do Thi Hai Yen. Dir. Phillip Noyce.

Secrets & Lies (1996) Brenda Blethyn, Marianne Jean-Baptiste. Direc. Mike Leigh.

The Secret in Their Eyes (2009). Ricardo Darín, Soledad Villamil, Pablo Rago. Dir. Juan José Campanella.

Serpico (1973). Al Pacino, John Randolph, Jack Kehoe. Dir. Sidney Lumet.

Shadow of a Doubt (1943). Teresa Wright, Joseph Cotten, Macdonald Carey. Dir. Alfred Hitchcock.

Shutter Island (2010). Leonardo DiCaprio, Emily Mortimer, Mark Ruffalo. Dir. Martin Scorsese.

Side Effects (2013). Rooney Mara, Channing Tatum, Jude Law. Dir. Steven Soderbergh.

The Spanish Prisoner (1997). Steve Martin, Ben Gazzara, Campbell Scott. Dir. David Mamet.

Stories We Tell (2012). Michael Polley, John Buchan, Mark Polley. Dir. Sarah Polley.

The Strange Love of Martha Ivers (1946). Barbara Stanwyck, Van Heflin, Lizabeth Scott. Dir. Lewis Milestone.

The Stranger (2014). Lorenza Izzo, Cristobal Tapia Montt. Dir. Guillermo Amoedo.

Strangers on a Train (1951). Farley Granger, Robert Walker, Ruth Roman. Dir. Alfred Hitchcock.

Sunset Blvd. (1950). William Holden, Gloria Swanson, Erich von Stroheim. Dir. Billy Wilder.

Sweet Smell of Success (1957). Burt Lancaster, Tony Curtis, Susan Harrison. Dir. Alexander Mackendrick.

The Talented Mr. Ripley (1999). Matt Damon, Gwyneth Paltrow, Jude Law. Dir. Anthony Minghella.

Tell No One (2006). François Cluzet, Marie-Josée Croze. Dir. Guillaume Canet.

The Third Man (1949). Orson Welles, Joseph Cotten, Alida Valli. Dir. Carol Reed.

Three Days of the Condor (1975). Robert Redford, Faye Dunaway. Dir. Sydney Pollack.

Tomorrow Is Another Day (1951). Ruth Roman, Steve Cochran, Lurene Tuttle. Dir. Felix E. Feist.

Touch of Evil (1958). Charlton Heston, Orson Welles, Janet Leigh. Dir. Orson Welles.

The Two Faces of January (2014). Viggo Mortensen, Kirsten Dunst. Dir. Hossein Amini.

Under Suspicion (2000). Morgan Freeman, Gene Hackman, Thomas Jane. Dir. Stephen Hopkins.

The Usual Suspects (1995). Kevin Spacey, Gabriel Byrne. Dir. Bryan Singer.

The Verdict (1982). Paul Newman, Charlotte Rampling, Jack Warden. Dir. Sidney Lumet.

What Lies Beneath (2000). Harrison Ford, Michelle Pfeiffer. Dir. Robert Zemeckis.

White Heat (1949). James Cagney, Virginia Mayo, Edmond O'Brien. Dir. Raoul Walsh.

White Oleander (2002). Michelle Pfeiffer, Renée Zellweger, Robin Wright. Dir. Peter Kosminsky.

TELEVISION

American Greed (2007–15) (Seasons 1–9). Creator: Kurtis Productions.

American Justice (1992–2005) (Season 1–12). Creator: Towers Productions.

City Confidential (1998–2006) (Seasons 1–11). Creators: A&E Television & Jupiter Entertainment.

Cold Case (2003–10) (Seasons 1–7). Creator: Meredith Stiehm.

CSI: Crime Scene Investigation (2000–2015) (Seasons 1–15). Creator: Anthony E. Zuiker.

Dateline NBC (1992–2015) (Seasons 1–24). Creator: NBC News.

Empire (2015) (Season 1). Creators: Lee Daniels, Danny Strong.

Homicide: Life on the Street (1993–99) (Seasons 1–7). Creator: Paul Attanasio.

Law & Order (1990–2010) (Seasons 1–20). Creator: Dick Wolf.

Making a Murderer (2015). Miniseries. Directors: Moira Demos and Laura Ricciardi.

NYPD Blue (1993–2005) (Seasons 1–12). Creators: Steven Bochco, David Milch.

Prime Suspect (1991–93) (Seasons 1–3). Creator: Lynda La Plante.

"Revenge." *Alfred Hitchcock Presents* (1955) (Season One). Dir. Alfred Hitchcock.

Snapped (2004–15) (Seasons 1–14). Creator: Jupiter Entertainment.

True Detective (2014) (Season 1). Creator: Nic Pizzolatto.

48 Hours (1988–2015) (Season 1–28). Creator: Judy Tygard.

48 Hours on ID (2010–15) (Season 1–6). Creator: CBS News.

ACKNOWLEDGMENTS

We live and work in groups, supported by social networks often so deep and so extensive that we might, at times, not realize the tremendous influence with which they shape our lives. I am a human who draws inspiration and sustenance from my family and friends, and I am deeply grateful for their love and support. My work was further aided by the unexpected and abundant kindness of strangers or people I barely knew, who gave me invaluable information, with each nugget providing another piece of a giant, complicated puzzle that took three years to assemble.

Firstly, I have to thank Lieutenant Alicia Rauch and Detective Tim Blanke, of the Dane County Sheriff's Office, for providing me not only with the much-needed police reports, but also patience with my questions and the willingness to tell me the truth. And I want to thank "Linda" for spending months poring through dusty microfiche files to find the information. Next I have undying appreciation for Karen Meier, of the Dane County Clerk of Courts, who nearly became my personal research assistant for over one year, providing me with necessary court transcripts, probate documents, and other numerous types of records that she often had to search weeks to find, all with a cheerful and persistent attitude. Jeffrey Sholts, of the Dane County Medical Examiner's Office, provided me with several very important coroner reports, including that of my uncle. There were so many other county clerks in so many places across the country that were immensely helpful, and I am thinking of women in Iowa and in Minnesota, in Blount County, Tennessee, Beloit, Wisconsin, and Rock County, Illinois. But one stands out, and that is Rachel Thomason in Sawyer County, Wisconsin, who took extra time and energy to help me unravel some mysteries about my uncle's hunting cabin and the Fred Weir who bought it from Suzanne many years later. Speaking of Fred Weir, I talked to about twenty people in Spring Green, Wisconsin, before I found Brad Hass, who had worked with Fred for many years. He was forthright and helpful. One person whose phone conversation rocked my world was Kenneth Pledger, one of the first officers on the crime scene, and I marveled at his memory. Others who provided valuable insight were attorney James Sugar, who had supervised the Stordock probate, former Judge and District Attorney James Boll, who prosecuted the case for the first five months, the first guardian ad litem (lawyer for a minor child, in this case, Danny Stordock), and attorney David Walsh, the second guardian ad litem. Counselor Walsh is a recently retired University of Wisconsin trustee, whom I met with in December 2015 and took an instant liking to. He became such a source of assistance, I am filled with gratitude when I think of how much he continued to help me on this project, as did his associate Adam K. Premo.

In later stages of my research I was helped immensely by Dennis McCormick, who worked tirelessly with me to get the correct photos and front-page newspapers from the *Wisconsin State Journal* archives. Amy Sloper dug through old TV films to look for footage, while the amazing Gregory T. Smith found old records and images that I was told were long gone, and he managed to convince the sheriff's archivist to reduce redactions in the reports. Several people from the Beloit Police Department were helpful in securing photos of Uncle Vernie and were kind enough to speak on the phone with me and tell me stories. I am especially grateful to Howard Bjorklund, Captain Dan Risse, and Chief Roger Helser. David Zimdars, of the Beloit Historical Society, offered important assistance. Thanks to Sandy Day, who organized a photo being taken of my uncle's gravestone in the Veterans' section of Eastlawn Cemetery in Beloit. Special appreciation to Maggie Slingerhouse (who went above and beyond), editor of University of St. Catherine's newspaper, *The Wheel*, along with the faculty advisor Jill Jepson. And endless thanks to Stephanie Jones, Mark Lewis, and Brenda Wishau, of the *Racine* [WI] *Journal Times,* who really was there for me and helped me get clearance for a picture that was perfect for the photo spread in this book.

Current and former residents of Oregon, Wisconsin, were so welcoming and contributed greatly to my final product. They include current and former owners of the Mansion: Jan Bonsett-Veal, Alice and Michael Seeliger, as well as people at the Oregon Area Historical Society and the Village of Oregon, who spent much time tracking down information. They are Melanie and Doug Woodworth, Gerald Neath, and Sue Poole.

My uncle Vernie's best friend in Oregon, Joe Roznos, and daughter Cynthia, lifted up my spirit after I tracked them down and spent a long time talking to both. There were family members of Suzanne, Suzanne's husbands, Jocelyn, as well as friends of David, who helped me tremendously, but I am reluctant to put their names here, for fear of reprisals, so just let me say: I am grateful for your openness and honesty. And the daughter of the other woman accused of murder also in 1970 in Dane County became so close, I consider her a friend. I feel sad when I consider the pain Bonnie Privett Mink has suffered in her life caused by her mother's crime, and wonder at the amazing life she has created. One of Danny Stordock's best friends allowed me to use his name. When I first met him, Callen Harty was one of those people I felt I had known my whole life, and he told me others often say the same thing. He gave me wonderful insights into Danny's life and even shared some writing, a few paragraphs of which are in this book.

It is necessary to recognize Suzanne, Louisa, David, and Bobby for allowing me into their home and allowing me to ask often quite intrusive questions. David was the most forthcoming, and Louisa was eternally loving. Thank you.

And then I must generously thank the two forensic experts who helped me gain deeper insights from the police reports and court transcripts. Former law professor Christine Funk agreed that it wasn't just me thinking the court documents had their loopy moments, and Jason Kolowski, who built 3-D images of the crime scene, showed that I wasn't delusional in my interpretation of the police records. I was also aided by two artists, Maggie Ivy and Maxim Zhelev, who skillfully reproduced the computer images. I need to thank the supremely intelligent David Hare, whose checklist on psychopaths I became certified in, and who gave a captivating workshop, well organized by Heidi Meeke and Kelly Anderson of Criminogenic Solutions, LLC. Psychiatrists and other mental health professionals who aided me were Laura d'Angelo, Rose Presser, and Donna Stordock. Pathologist Fazollah Loghmanee and internist Iskandar Hai, along with Faizi and Hengameh Hai, offered valuable medical insights into death, suicide, and murder.

I had bountiful help from my thesis advisor, Kaylie Jones, who gave such clear feedback that it helped enormously in the rewrites. Star Black, as the second reader (and early inspiration for writing a "Wisconsin Gothic" memoir), gave a poetic (she is a poet, after all) evaluation that I ought to memorize. Lori A. May, as third reader, was most helpful. In addition, Carla Caglioti, Julie Sheehan, Magdalene Brandeis, and Robert Reeves were there with program assistance. Kaylie suggested I get Laurie Lowenstein to give me editorial feedback on the book, which I found enormously helpful. And then here was my hardworking and well-connected agent, John Willig, who helped me get the manuscript ready to send out. In fact, he did such a good job, I got two publishing offers. We decided to go with Kensington Publishing, which has been a wonderful, amazing experience, largely due to my über-competent, resourceful, and engaging editor, Michaela Hamilton. Much gratitude to all.

During these three years my friends were a source of encouragement, as well as idea generators. It was JoAnn Tedesco who encouraged me to use the opportunity of the thesis to write about the murder, while Janice Maffei, Deb Victoroff, Deborah Savadge, Janet Conrad, Gillien Goll, Adrienne Corn, Steven Cherry, Robert Landy, all guided me along the long path to completion. Longtime friend Hillary Chapman was the source of many captivating YouTube clips about cultish delusions and murder, and he provided me with a late-night telephone partner to discuss all things gothic, psychological, and manipulative. Longtime friend and journalist Monte Hanson gave me invaluable assistance and insights as I moved forward in the research. He's the one who told me I would have made a great investigative reporter. Friend of decades Larry Miller gave thoughtful feedback and plenty of inspiration. Bill Franzblau, my Off-Broadway producing partner, was always there with ideas for the book, the blurb, the title, whatever, and our mutual colleague Bill Hofstetter gave endless encouragement. And my assistants Allison Greer O'Bryant, Josh Quinn, and Aja Nisenson provided valuable support. Friends who have cheered me along include: Wendi Momen, Bob and Debbie Rosenfeld, Victoria Marsick and Peter Neaman, Susan Schor, Marianna Houston, Kate Weisman, Homa Tavangar, Mina Sabet, Lana Bogan, Joy Schneer and Doug Hutt, Lishy Price, Ron Browning, Amy Bassin, Mark Blickley, Patricia McGraw, Amy Lynch, Janice Maurus, Kent Zimmerman, Kenneth Ferrone, Carolyn Stalcup, Andi Seals, Deb Hungate, Barbara Sanders, Mark Cannon, Jefferson Slinkard, Joe Seltzer, Peter Vaill, Emileena Pedigo, Nicholas Ritchie, Kathleen McEnerny, Kit Bigelow, Roscoe and Kimberley LaMarque Orman, Mary Watson, Maggie and Dick Wenz, Judi Mills, Deborah Kondis, Patrick Redmond, Kurt and Leslie Asplund, Katrin Hilbe, Cheri Chakiban, Eileen and Sharon Weiss, Bob Ost, Gary Hughes, Donald Streets, Blythe Weber, Lisi DeHaas, Evangelia Kinglsey, Bruce Hager, Carl Murrell, Karen and Nolan Streets-Anderson, Kim and Julian McQueen, Doug and Suzanne Henck, Gina Mendello, Warren Blank, Bani Dugal, Adrienne Ewing-Roush, Mehr Mansuri, Arthur Dahl, Janine Ray, David Newell, Danielle Legg, and writing teachers Karen Hartman, Matt Klam, and Francine Volpe. And my longtime friend and colleague, Randy Cohen, writer extraordinaire, who was ever encouraging, as were other writer friends, Bruce Hager and Fred Gardaphé.

Finally my family, which is where it all started. My sister, Janet Mittelsteadt (and her husband Richard), was there, at every moment, to give me encouragement and many enlightening stories. My cousins Richard and Bill filled in some details for me, while their sister Donna, who is a psych nurse, gave me such deep insights I still get chills when I think of them. Cousin Katherine was able to relay several stories from her mother about the murder. And my sweet cousins on my father's side, who knew nothing of the carnage, but just love me, as I them: Marilyn Nowak, Kathleen Vincent, and Michael Shoemaker. Then, of course, my daughters Solange, Roxanne, and Elizabeth (and their husbands) were supporters throughout, with Elizabeth doing a great deal of background research and also typing up the much-copied and often blurry police reports and court transcripts to make them both more readable and searchable. Aunt Jenylle was there most of the time during the research. I instinctively knew not to interview her, as I sensed the pain was still too searing. Yet she was a beacon of integrity and love, my True North, as I moved forward. Another shining light was my aunt Maxine, who, sadly, died as I was finishing up the manuscript. Her incredible memory gave me important information, and she shared her gratitude I did this while she was still alive.

And then, of course, there is my cousin Shannon, LaVerne's only natural child (with Jenylle), my fierce partner in crime solving, without whose inspiration and sustained assistance I might have never taken on this project, and I surely would not have gone so deep. We thankfully had many moments of laughter on our journey, often when I would discover a fact that was almost too incredible to believe. "You can't make up this sh*t" became our mantra.

I cannot forget the dignity of my grandmother in the face of endless loss, who gave me the courage to overcome even the most burdensome of difficulties as I sought to learn the truth. My mother's pain from the loss of her "baby brother" helped me understand the grief of my entire family. And I must thank my Uncle Vernie for the boundless love he showed me, without which I would not have had the stamina to complete this long, arduous, but ultimately satisfying pursuit.

Connect with 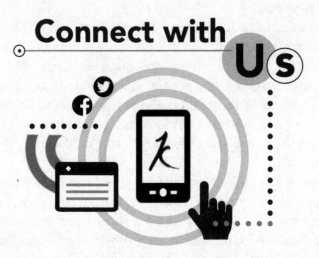 U s

Visit us online at
KensingtonBooks.com
to read more from your favorite authors, see books
by series, view reading group guides, and more.

Join us on social media

for sneak peeks, chances to win books and prize packs,
and to share your thoughts with other readers.

facebook.com/kensingtonpublishing
twitter.com/kensingtonbooks

Tell us what you think!

To share your thoughts, submit a review,
or sign up for our eNewsletters, please visit:
KensingtonBooks.com/TellUs.